CICS Concepts and Uses

Titles in the IBM McGraw-Hill Series

Details of these titles in the series are available from:

The Product Manager, Professional Books
McGraw-Hill Book Company Europe
Shoppenhangers Road, Maidenhead, Berkshire, SL6 2QL
Telephone: 0628 23432 Fax: 0628 770224

Jim Geraghty

CICS Concepts and Uses

A Management Guide

McGRAW-HILL BOOK COMPANY

London · New York · St Louis · San Francisco · Auckland
Bogotá · Caracas · Lisbon · Madrid · Mexico · Milan
Montreal · New Delhi · Panama · Paris · San Juan · São Paulo
Singapore · Sydney · Tokyo · Toronto

Published by
McGRAW-HILL Book Company Europe
Shoppenhangers Road, Maidenhead, Berkshire, SL6 2QL, England
Tel 0628 23432; Fax 0628 770224

British Library Cataloguing-in-Publication Data

Geraghty, Jim
  CICS Concepts and Uses: Management Guide.
  — (IBM McGraw-Hill Series)
  I. Title II. Series
  005.43

  ISBN 0-07-707751-2

Library of Congress Cataloging-in-Publication Data

Geraghty, Jim
    CICS concepts and uses: a management guide/Jim Geraghty.
      p.   cm.
    Includes bibliographical references (p.   ) and index.
    ISBN 0-07-707751-2
      1.   CICS (Computer system) I. Title.
    QA76.76.T45G47   1994
    005.4'3--dc20   93-28717
                                                                           CIP

12345 CUP 97654

Typeset by Paston Press Ltd, Loddon, Norfolk
and printed and bound in Great Britain at the University Press, Cambridge

To Margret and Sarah

Contents

Part II Application programming

Part III   Technical support

Part IV   Past, present and future

Foreword

The IBM McGraw-Hill Series

IBM UK and McGraw-Hill Europe have worked together to publish this series of books which provides an up-to-date and authoritative insight into the wide range of products and services available, and offers strategic business advice. Some of the books have a broader business bias, others are written with a more technical perspective. What they have in common is that their authors—some from IBM, some independent consultants—are experts in their field.

Apart from assisting where possible with the accuracy of the writing, IBM UK has not sought to inhibit the editorial freedom of the series, and therefore the views expressed in the books are those of the authors, and not necessarily those of IBM.

Where IBM has lent its expertise is in assisting McGraw-Hill to identify potential titles whose publication would help advance knowledge and increase awareness of computing topics. Hopefully these titles will also serve to widen the debate about the important information technology issues of today and of the future—such as open systems, networking and the use of technology to give companies a competitive edge in their market.

IBM UK is pleased to be associated with McGraw-Hill in this series.

Sir Anthony Cleaver
Chairman
IBM United Kingdom Limited

Preface

IBM's CICS is a giant of the computer world, but has remained largely anonymous for twenty-five years. Its importance to world industry and commerce is unquestionable, but little understood outside data-processing circles. This book seeks to explain CICS[1] to those who may have taken it for granted for years. The book addresses the question 'Why CICS?' as well as 'What is CICS?' It does so by examining the place of IBM's CICS systems in the lives of different kinds of computer user. It reviews a little of the history of the program, and looks at how its future may unfold.

The book is written primarily for executive managers and other decision-makers in diverse fields: industry, commerce, government, travel and education, to name but a few. Such readers need not have a background in data processing, but will nowadays want to be able to assess transaction-processing proposals from a position of strength.

The book should also interest data-processing professionals. They ought already to know something of CICS, but may want to learn more as its use becomes more widespread. Such professionals will include data-processing managers, application analysts and systems analysts, and students of Information Technology.

I make no apology for my enthusiasm for CICS. For fifteen years I have been fortunate to work with the designers of CICS, and with staff from the tens of thousands of corporations that use it. My enthusiasm is a reflection of theirs. I hope I can pass a little on to you.

Notes

[1] CICS, an IBM trademark, stands for 'Customer Information Control System'.

Acknowledgements

In writing this book, I have been able to call on the support of friends and colleagues around the world. The reviewers include: Sue Malaika, from CICS Development, who has encouraged me since I started the book; Bob Yelavich, who has reviewed most of the words I have written about CICS in fifteen years, and has provided valuable input and excellent feedback; and Guy Smales, who provided comments on, and input to, my section on user-groups.

From the start I have been supported by a variety of colleagues within IBM. Roy Blundell, Mike Jeffery, Tony Cox and John Page helped me with information on user-groups. Others, both inside and outside IBM, helped me to build on it: Hans van Dongen Torman of SEAS provided details of that user-group's Database Project, which covers CICS topics within Europe; Geoff Hegarty of IBM Australia gave me a lot of material on Australasian and Far Eastern user-groups. His colleague in IBM Japan, Yoshiyuki Sakurai, provided information on Japan GUIDE/SHARE.

In the year of the 1992 Olympics, I was fortunate to find two fine colleagues in the IBM Olympic support teams, who provided facts from which I could construct two case studies. Tor Brekken of IBM Norway gave me his notes on the Winter Olympics, and Ricard Pons Pallares of IBM Spain sent me details of the networks and CICS systems used in the Summer Olympics. A colleague from the past, Bill Causier of IBM Canada (retired), helped me with some of the history of the Olympics systems.

In addition, I am grateful to all the enthusiasts and visionaries I have met during my fifteen years with CICS, especially IBM's customers, whose hospitality and openness has enabled me to learn about their work. I hope I have represented them correctly in what I have written.

Finally, I thank my wife, Margret, who encouraged me to start the book, and then supported me patiently while I tried to finish it. And I thank my daughter, Sarah; though she howled with laughter at my drawings, she compensated by making encouraging noises about the early text.

Jim Geraghty

Trademarks

This book makes frequent use of words and phrases that are trademarks. The following is a list of the trademarks and the organizations to which they belong.

Trademarks of IBM Corporation

ACF/VTAM
AD/Cycle
AIX
AIX/ESA
AIX/6000
AS/400
BookManager
BookMaster
CallPath
CallPath CICS/MVS
CallPath CICS/VSE
CallPath SwitchServer/2
CICS
CICS OS/2
CICS/ESA
CICS/MVS
CICS/VM
CICS/VSE
CICS/400
CUA
DATABASE 2

DB2
Enterprise Systems
    Architecture/370
Enterprise Systems
    Architecture/390
ES/3090
ESA/370
ESA/390
IBM
IMS/ESA
MVS/DFP
MVS/ESA
MVS/SP
MVS/XA
NetView
OfficeVision
Operating System/2
Operating System/400
OS/2
OS/400
PCradio

Person to Person/2
Personal System/2
PR/SM
PS/2
S/390
SQL/DS
Storyboard
SwitchServer
SwitchServer/2
System/360
System/370
System/390
System Application
    Architecture
VM/ESA
VM/XA
VSE/ESA
VTAM
XT
3090
/400

Non-IBM trademarks

Microsoft (Microsoft Corporation)
Microsoft Windows (Microsoft Corporation)
Teletype (American Telephone and Telegraph Company)
Touch-tone (American Telephone and Telegraph Company)
Touchscreen (Hewlett-Packard Company)
UNIX (Unix System Laboratories, Inc.)
Windows (Microsoft Corporation)
Windows NT (Microsoft Corporation)
WordPerfect (WordPerfect Corporation)

Part I
Introduction

1
Universal CICS

For a mere computer program, IBM's CICS has a profound and probably surprising influence on your life. If it vanished tomorrow, never to have existed, modern society and industry would alter radically. It is used worldwide (see Fig. 1.1). Yet you are more than likely unaware of its existence, let alone its influence. Many of those around you will never have heard of it. CICS has been immensely influential for two decades, and its importance will grow as we go into the twenty-first century. This chapter explains why. It explains what CICS is, and what it does.

When it first appeared in 1968, CICS was an answer to a need of the time. Its

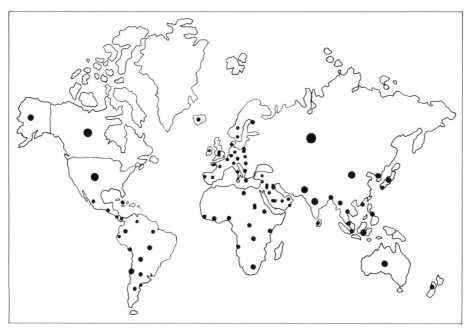

Figure 1.1. CICS around the world.

success since then has surprised many observers, including many within IBM. It has done its job so well that it has been taken for granted, treated as simply another anonymous system component. Only those working directly with CICS have understood fully its importance and value. CICS was a magic ingredient for growth in the data-processing industry in the 1970s and 1980s. Use of displays, communications hardware, storage, programs and processor power continued to grow as business needs were met by systems based on CICS. Yet CICS rarely drew attention, despite the key part it played as both supporter and driver of technology.

CICS's anonymity was helped for many years by the words used to describe it: it was a 'database/data communications system'. As its importance became impossible to ignore, in the late 1980s and early 1990s, CICS and a growing number of imitators were more commonly known as 'transaction processors'. At the end of the century, transaction processing is often portrayed as a technology in its infancy, but CICS has been processing transactions since 1968.

1.1   CICS is . . .

CICS is a special kind of enabler program, called a *transaction processor*. It acts as an adaptor between individual business programs and the powerful but complex system software supplied as standard with business computers. There are adaptor programs for different situations, but transaction processors such as CICS are purpose-built for a particular kind of activity: efficient handling of random, and usually repetitive, requests to run business programs. From this description, the key words in understanding the importance of CICS are 'efficient', 'random' and 'programs'.

Handling requests *efficiently* is essential, because transaction processors often have to cope with immense workloads. A CICS system often has to support thousands of users throughout the working day, each performing a small mix of transactions over and over again. Almost any computer system can be made to process transactions, after a fashion, but only a purpose-built system will handle large volumes of transactions efficiently.

CICS has to be able to handle *random* requests because most business transactions are performed randomly: requests arrive unpredictably, from anyone within a large user population. Other systems can handle random requests, but not usually with both the performance and added value of CICS.

CICS transactions are processed by whole *programs*, not by individual commands. Minimal input from an end-user can trigger many sophisticated processes within a single program. In addition, the program can be custom-made to suit the end-users, providing simple display screens to conceal the underlying sophistication.

CICS handles the challenges set by randomness, the need for efficiency, and the need to work with many other parts of the computer system. It leaves programming staff free to concentrate on producing high-quality business programs, without having to design the underlying transaction-processing mechanisms.

An analogy

An analogy can sometimes help in visualizing programming concepts. In the case of CICS, a suitable analogy lies in the theatre. A theatre is a building custom-built for live performance, just as CICS is custom-built for transaction processing. Other buildings can be used for live performances—village halls or sports stadiums, for example—but none can be as effective as a proper theatre.

Like CICS, a theatre can be used for an infinite variety of shows, or programs, and each show can be performed over and over again. Each will use the standard facilities—scenery, lighting and so on—in a different way, but all will use the same building, stage and auditorium. Once built, a theatre is the obvious place to stage new productions: individual production companies do not build new theatres to stage their shows. They spend their time pursuing their own business of producing high-quality shows. In the same way, business programmers use CICS to do their transaction-processing management, leaving them free to concentrate on the content and usability of business programs.

1.2   CICS in our lives

Let me illustrate the place of CICS in our lives by taking a typical example of CICS in *my* life. Before my second cup of coffee this morning I had twice used CICS, without realizing, and without leaving home. First I had called my credit card company to confirm an item on my monthly statement, then I had called my bank to ensure I had enough money to cover the total bill. I have become used to instant responses to these kinds of enquiry, so was not surprised when I received them. Only when I returned to the task of writing this chapter did I reflect on the service I had received, on the speed and efficiency with which it was given, and on the fact that CICS was instrumental in the service.

Despite having worked with CICS for fifteen years, I rarely think about my own use of this amazing computer program, just as I rarely think about electrical generators when switching lights on, or about electronic switches when making a telephone call. Nevertheless, CICS is now an essential contributor to my lifestyle, and I use it indirectly almost every day. You do too, but probably never think about it.

I can still remember the pre-CICS days. I opened my first bank account before computer terminals reached every bank branch, and can remember how bank clerks made balance inquiries for me by telephone. I can also remember the cost of such personal service. Today's service is quicker and more comprehensive, yet relatively inexpensive. My bank makes extensive use of transaction-processing systems, yet has spread the cost by attracting more customers; the same staff copes

Airlines	Accountancy	Gas supply	Shipping
Mail order	Telecommunications	Oil industry	Railroads
Electricity	Travel agency	Stockbrokers	Retail
Government	Broadcasting	Credit union	Insurance
Agriculture	Universities	Engineering	Trucking
Hospitals	Local government	Credit cards	Banking
Government	Chemical industry	Wholesalers	Military
Publishing	Motor industry	Architects	Coal
Electronics	Computer bureaux	Insurance	Steel

Figure 1.2. Some industries in which CICS is used.

with many more accounts and a greater variety of business, but the service is noticeably better.

1.3   Ubiquitous CICS

I have used my bank and credit card company as examples because my own recent transactions were foremost in my mind. However, these are just two out of hundreds of thousands of different business transactions in daily use (Fig. 1.2). Almost all business or commercial enterprises have found need for real-time transaction-processing systems. Most enterprises cannot compete effectively without the help of such systems, of which IBM's CICS is the foremost example.

Who uses CICS? Well, who does *not*? Only a handful of America's Fortune 500 top companies do not. Most of the biggest corporations and government organizations in the western world do. They use it whenever they need to provide instant access to data. Corporations first began to use CICS in situations where they had to handle communication with large numbers of clients or customers, for example the general public. Hence the name: Customer Information Control System.

As I have already suggested, CICS's omnipresence makes it almost as vital in today's world as other man-made wonders, such as the telephone or the internal combustion engine. Like both of these, it has become a key to improved communication, and to growth of commerce and industry. CICS is relatively anonymous, and most of those who have benefited from it have never heard of it. This is not surprising among the general public—and the clerical staff with whom they make daily contact—but it is surprising, and maybe a cause for concern, among decision-makers and strategists. Such people need to understand the technologies that drive their businesses.

1.4   CICS and the corporate scheme

For a quarter of a century, the systems analysts and programmers who have harnessed CICS for their enterprises have served decision-makers well. They have pioneered online systems that have made possible rapid, but controlled, growth in worldwide business and commerce. As a result, transaction-processing systems based on IBM's CICS can be the key to the survival of entire corporations. In the worldwide stock market crash of 1987, for example, major financial institutions stood to win or lose fortunes, according to their readiness to handle unprecedented volumes of business transactions. That experience taught surviving institutions how much they owed to CICS.

As enterprises grow, they need their support infrastructures to grow just ahead of them. A company that establishes a new line of business, for example, should have transaction-processing systems in place to handle normal activity: order processing, stock control, accounts management, payroll and so on. Similarly, a company that takes over another, or creates a subsidiary, needs to establish compatible, homogeneous systems. In all cases, decisions about transaction processing, usually involving CICS, will be a key part of the data-processing strategy. Executives need to understand the choices and investments to be made. This book should help them to understand the investments in software, hardware and people necessary to keep CICS systems, and hence the entire organization, vital.

1.5   The roots of transaction processing

CICS is now almost twenty-five years young. As it enters its second quarter-century, it is reaching its prime. You will see in this book that it has had a vigorous and successful adolescence. You will also see that it is poised for great things in its maturity. CICS was originally created to meet the specific needs of a few companies, but its universal, almost immediate, acceptance showed that almost every other kind of business had the same needs.

The first users of CICS, indeed the people whose needs dictated its creation, were major utilities companies in America. Gas and electricity companies needed to find a way of handling customers efficiently in a time of expansion. The American business emphasis on service to the customer meant that service levels and responsiveness were of prime importance. The vast amounts of data that were then being processed in long, sequential batches were wasted by being locked away when they could be used to provide better service.

For example, a consumer needing to query an account might have to wait for an overnight run for information; either that or accept the previous day's information. Another customer asking for a visit by a service engineer would have to wait until diaries and workloads could be compared, probably waiting for an appointment card to be mailed several days later. The data needed to handle queries or schedule work existed, but processing it still took minutes or hours rather than seconds. Furthermore, such data could be guaranteed to be only *almost* up to date, because it was not updated continuously.

Handling customer-related data should be fairly straightforward. Consequently, delays are frustrating for customers, because they seem unreasonable.

They give an impression of inefficiency, and can lose business. The kind of processing needed to provide up-to-date customer data is nowadays called *transaction processing*, because it is most commonly used to carry out business transactions. After more than twenty years of existence, CICS transaction processing has been adopted so widely that it now takes many forms. Some transactions have lost their strict customer/supplier nature, and interaction is simply between a terminal operator and some data.

Partnership with technology

CICS emerged by design, not by accident, though it could not have been implemented earlier. Its creators built it to use the technology of the moment. Their successors have followed this example, keeping the evolving CICS close to the state of the art in information technology.

The original development of CICS was made feasible by a combination of technological advances, initially those of magnetic disk storage, cathode ray tube displays and advances in communications technology. The first removed the need for sequential access to data on tapes, allowing more rapid searching for scattered data. The second and third provided almost instant, silent delivery of the data to both local and remote operators. Suddenly, a clerk equipped with a telephone and a terminal could ask for a name or account number, and immediately start to use the supplied information to get information from the computer, put information into the computer, or both.

In addition, many employees could have access to the same data, to satisfy many customers at the same time. Other employees could make changes to data— even *the same* data— at the same time. Most importantly, they could get access to data in 'real time'. This was something that scientists and engineers had been used to for years, but that commercial users had been denied. This ability to get up-to-the-minute information is vital for modern computing tasks, such as credit authorization, point-of-sale, control of retail transactions and so on.

Of course, CICS did not create the complementary hardware and software technology. Instead, it was a catalyst that made it possible to use the technology effectively. It acted as middleman between the programs that controlled the disk drives and the programs that controlled the new 'glass teletypes'. In return, the popularity and effectiveness of these devices helped to drive the popularity of CICS. Each arrived at the right time and place for the other. This has remained the story of CICS, even to the present day.

Universal appeal

Not surprisingly, corporations in almost every segment of industry and commerce recognized the value of CICS when it appeared. What initially seemed to be a requirement of the utilities companies became a universal need. CICS was the

Abu Dhabi	Angola	Argentina
Australia	Austria	Bahrain
Bangladesh	Belgium	Bolivia
Brazil	British Honduras	Chile
China	Colombia	Costa Rica
Cyprus	Denmark	Nigeria
Ecuador	Egypt	Ethiopia
Finland	France	Germany
Ghana	Greece	Guiana
Honduras	Hong Kong	Hungary
Iceland	India	Indonesia
Iraq	Ireland	Israel
Italy	Japan	Jordan
Kenya	Korea	Kuwait
Lebanon	Liberia	Libya
Macao	Malaysia	Mexico
Netherlands	New Zealand	Nicaragua
Norway	Oman	Pakistan
Panama	Paraguay	Peru
Philippines	Poland	Portugal
Qatar	San Salvador	Saudi Arabia
Singapore	South Africa	Spain
Sri Lanka	Sudan	Sweden
Switzerland	Taiwan	Thailand
Turkey	Uruguay	USA
USSR	UK	Venezuela
Zaire	Zambia	

Figure 1.3. CICS around the world.

universal answer, its flexibility and power meeting almost all individual requirements.

As you will see later, the main appeal of CICS lies in the ability of its application-programming facilities to adapt it to any business situation. Its appeal has always been broader than many alternative systems because even from the start IBM made it available in two forms: for the main operating systems, OS and DOS. It therefore reached a very wide range of users, small, medium and large, and stimulated production of much packaged software. The resulting popularity has been self-sustaining, as it has encouraged the development of countless packages and utility programs. These in turn have attracted additional users to CICS.

1.6 CICS as a family

Until now I have been talking about CICS as though it is one indivisible program. In fact, it is a family of related programs, and the family is growing. The majority of the long-established and growing population of CICS systems runs on System/370 IBM and IBM-compatible mainframe computers. It has been estimated that, worldwide, more than ten million terminals are connected to such CICS systems (Fig. 1.3). Some rough calculations show the scale of CICS transaction processing today.

There are more than 10 000 CICS installations using large MVS computers, and many of the machines running CICS have 100 or more systems running at the same time. As CICS systems on MVS machines probably average 0.5 million transactions per day, you can see that maybe 5000 million MVS transactions are being processed every working day. A further 5000 million may be performed on the smaller, but more numerous, VSE systems. So the worldwide total could conservatively be estimated at 10 000 million online transactions per day. It is thus no wonder that I felt able earlier to state that both you and I are CICS users.

Despite this immense scale of use of host CICS systems, System/370 systems account for only a fraction of overall business processing capacity. Until now, the rest of the business community has had to manage without CICS. This is now being corrected, first by extension of the CICS family to non-System/370 IBM systems, and in future by further extension to non-IBM systems.

The growing CICS family

CICS has a large-system image, with its history of success on the IBM System/370 hardware and software platforms.[1] Despite this history, it is spreading to other IBM platforms, forming a family of compatible products; or, rather, a family of offerings of the same product for different platforms.

The old favourites, CICS/OS/VS and CICS/DOS/VS, have been succeeded by advanced versions for the 1990s, designed to work with the MVS/ESA and VSE/ESA operating systems. At the same time, companion products have emerged to run on other IBM operating systems: AIX OS/400, OS/2, DOS and VM. In producing a CICS system for AIX, IBM's version of UNIX, CICS is close to becoming a truly open system. In time, as we will see later, CICS will almost certainly become available on a wide range of non-IBM platforms.

Master becomes servant

Host CICS systems have long set the pace of transaction processing, and they are certain to continue to do so. Nevertheless, over time, many mainframe-based systems will spend more of their time serving smaller, connected systems. As you will see in Chapter 3, where I describe the different CICS systems, the technology is already available for members of the CICS family to work cooperatively.

As new CICS systems emerge and enter common use, the need for central, very high capacity 'hub' systems becomes more apparent. In many enterprises, it is convenient to distribute data to computers close to where it will be used. However, every corporation needs a headquarters, and satellite locations need to communicate with the headquarters. As each satellite increases the amount of data it communicates, so it will require more transaction-processing power at the hub to handle communication and data.

Much of the data processed by a corporation is vital to the continued success, and maybe even existence, of the corporation. The data must therefore be handled safely and effectively. Reliability, security and protection from damage are best achieved through use of professional staff, grouped together for efficiency, probably at a single central site, or at a central site plus one or more back-up sites (in case of fire or other disaster). Generally, central sites continue to use System/370-based CICS systems such as CICS/ESA, which offer great power, reliability and security. Programs created on such a system can be distributed to similar systems on computers at satellite locations or can be distributed to CICS systems on other platforms.

The demise of mainframe-based systems has long been prophesied by commentators on the data-processing industry. The distributed power of the workstation has been held up as the greatest threat, and 'downsizing' or 'rightsizing' has been seen by some as the fashion of the 1990s. In the world of CICS, rightsizing has long been an option, as CICS/VSE and CICS/ESA systems have offered a range of system power. With the extended family, the range is enormous: from systems based on OS/2 to others based on ESA/390. Nevertheless, successful businesses look for growth rather than contraction, and the CICS family offers them the most options for growth.

1.7   What keeps CICS vital?

CICS is twenty-five years old, so you may be forgiven for wondering if it has not passed its prime. In fact, it is still maturing. It has changed almost beyond recognition over the years, but only where change brought benefits. It retains the unique architecture that has made it the best purpose-built transaction processor in the world.

We have come a long way since the first CICS customers used the first CICS systems. We have seen better and bigger screens, colour terminals, personal systems. We have magnetic and optical disks that hold phenomenal amounts of data. We have communications networks that make global communication commonplace. Throughout these advances, the need for CICS transaction processing has remained. And the core requirements remain the same: the ability to store and retrieve shared data quickly and with integrity, and the ability to communicate the data to others. CICS continues to meet the core requirements, yet has adapted to all technological advances. For this reason, CICS is still foremost in the world of transaction processing.

The things that have changed since those early days are almost countless. CICS transaction processing has helped to generate need for new technology. As users have discovered the advantages of online transaction processing, so they have identified new things that need to be done in a hurry. They have become critical of the displays they had to use, and of the speed of response of their systems. Originally concerned about the minutes it took for a teletype to finish its message,

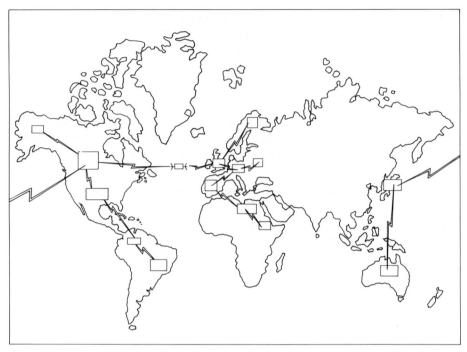

Figure 1.4.   Global CICS networks.

users are now critical of two- or three-second delays. Taking for granted almost-flawless local communication, they expect global access to other systems, around the clock, from the same familiar local CICS system (Fig. 1.4).

Continuous evolution

Growing demand has therefore required CICS's capacity for work to increase continuously. The growth needed has been more exponential than linear, caused by increased expectations as well as a rapid growth in the number of terminal users. The community of terminal users no longer consists only of dedicated data-entry clerks; in some organizations, operators now include almost all members of staff. The terminal-per-desk age has been with us since the early 1980s, and for most industries the definition of 'desk' has stretched. Terminal operators now include: members of the public using teller machines in banks; operators of production control equipment in car plants; car rental clerks with hand-held radio terminals; nurses and doctors in hospitals.

Now that many millions of people worldwide have access to CICS systems all year round, the nature of the system, if not its basic structure, has changed. The current system is a highly-evolved successor to the original. It uses the latest-technology computers, communications equipment, displays and workstations, and data-storage devices. Yet one of its attractions has been that it continues to support older technologies while adapting to the new. So, for example, corporations that invested large sums in non-programmable terminals and associated transactions continue to use them despite the emergence of programmable workstations. Programs that were written ten years or more ago continue to run unchanged.

CICS systems are the engines of much of the banking business in the world; CICS systems underpin, if not underwrite, the insurance industry; CICS systems help brokers to wheel and deal on world markets. This means that millions, if not billions, of dollars are being handled by CICS at any time. So CICS needs to be able to provide levels of security and protection from failure unheard of in the 1970s. At the other end of the spectrum of business, thousands of small companies use CICS systems as low-cost, reliable and proven real-time systems for uncomplicated day-to-day transaction processing. They too need security and reliability, but they also need greater ease of use. We will discuss these and other needs, all met by CICS in its different forms, in the following chapters. First though, let us consider why you need CICS at all. Why can't your expert teams of system and application programmers do this themselves?

1.8   Do it yourself?

At first glance, the challenge of producing a transaction-processing monitor does not seem too daunting, and you might consider creating your own.

It would certainly be possible for your staff to write your own in-house substitute for CICS. In fact, in its early days, a home-grown system would probably match your specified needs more closely than any other system. However, as you will see throughout this book, creating a transaction processor is a much more complex undertaking than it first seems, and you will need a dedicated development team to create one effectively, and to maintain and extend it once it is complete. Many organizations have, in fact, entered transaction processing in this way, creating their own 'roll-your-own' systems. With few exceptions, they have rapidly recognized the cost and inflexibility of staying with such systems, and many have replaced their systems with CICS-based equivalents.

Computer suppliers like IBM have traditionally tried to provide general purpose systems that their customers can tailor to provide solutions for their businesses. Volume production of general-purpose systems makes their design, development, production and maintenance cost effective. CICS is an excellent example of a generalized system designed by a team that is expert in aspects of transaction processing. The team adapts CICS to respond to changes in technology, industry standards and business needs. It cannot focus on the day-to-day business needs of your end-user departments; that is the responsibility of your programmers or programming analysts, or of qualified facilities management consultants. CICS developers observe and interpret the needs of *all* industries, developing products that are building blocks from which individual users can create tailor-made systems.

IBM spends many millions of dollars every year ensuring that its CICS products keep abreast of modern technology. If you, and every other user, tried to do this yourself, the cost to business and industry worldwide would be billions, not millions. And this would have a further effect: each implementation would be different, and incompatible. Each would have to develop its own interfaces with other system software products, such as databases and telecommunication programs. And each would impose different rules on programmers. This would immediately eliminate one of the most important aspects of CICS—its infrastructure.

The CICS infrastructure

In its early days, CICS worked with its operating system and one or two other subsystems to create a transaction-processing system. Over the years its increased use has created a demand for greater sophistication. Some of this has, rightly, been built into the product or left for the operating system to handle. Other improvements have been provided as optional software packages by specialist software companies. As CICS and its environment have become more complex, these packages have become more important, freeing CICS customers' staff to focus on matters more directly related to business. The packages, providing both ready-made transaction programs and system-management utilities, have been widely successful. The success of early packages has encouraged further enterprise, spawning a major industry of related programs and services: program packages, utility programs and consultancy and educational offerings. As always, a successful industry is a sign of a very real need. And the industry surrounding IBM's family of CICS systems is very successful; from monitoring programs and security packages through to payroll and accounting packages, CICS users employ ready-made programs and offerings to achieve high levels of productivity at reasonable cost.

Where CICS provides a general-purpose transaction-processing system, these other products and services add the layers that turn it into a special-purpose system to meet specific business needs more precisely. At the simplest level, independent suppliers provide utility programs, or ready-made business packages, that make life easier for your system support or application-programming organization. At the most sophisticated level, facilities management teams can take responsibility for all aspects of the system. However, most organizations have in-house data-processing departments running their systems. Where CICS is used, there will be a team devoted to it and its programs. As Parts II and III of this book consider CICS in terms of parts of the team, it is worth now taking a look at the team.

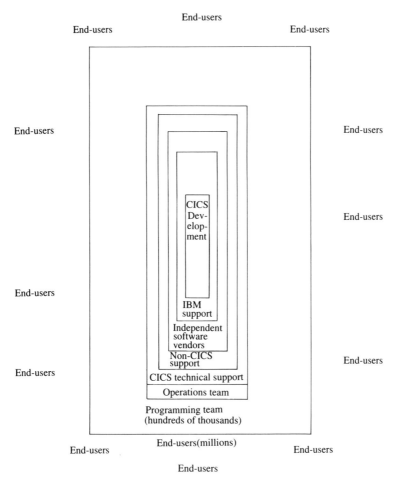

Figure 1.5. The CICS community.

1.9 CICS people and their work

CICS is a very people-oriented product. Its purpose is to provide services to thousands of end-users,[2] most of whom do not even know that it exists. Behind the scenes it is designed, set up and maintained by a team of data-processing staff. These people are specialists, often enthusiasts.

The people who work with CICS combine to form an efficient and cost-effective team. Although the composition of a CICS team varies from one organization to the next, the elements remain the same. The team consists of several layers, each containing people with different parts to play (Fig. 1.5). Their relationships can be illustrated by returning to the theatrical analogy we used earlier.

Just as earlier we considered CICS as analogous to an all-purpose theatre, capable of staging almost any show, so CICS people can be likened to a theatre company and its audience. As you would expect, an end-user is equivalent to a member of the audience, and the transaction program that runs on the CICS system is like a show. Programmers, like performers, interpret the master design and present it in a way that the audience can understand. The finished program is presented on a stage that has been 'set and dressed' by system programmer designers and builders. After full testing or rehearsal, the live show runs under control of the operations team, which tries to keep the show running without pause, keeping the audience fully occupied.

The purpose of the transaction-processing system and its support team is to give an elegant, polished and convincing performance as viewed from 'front of house' while concealing the relatively crude and confused-looking appearance of backstage reality. The director, stage manager, designers, builders and crew are vital to the success of the show, but both they and their activities should be transparent so that the audience can become and remain engrossed in the performance.

The theatre analogy to transaction processing is surprisingly effective, reflecting many of the relationships between the layers around CICS. It works on several levels.

Numbers

Just as a theatrical company hopes to have many more audience members than cast and crew members, so the population of CICS end-users is usually much larger than the population of support staff and programmers. A CICS system can have thousands of end-users, yet it is probably developed and maintained by a team of only tens of programmers and systems-support staff. In stable systems that are dedicated to running small numbers of major applications, the number of staff can be in single figures.

Within the organization, the same correlation exists between the theatre analogy and the CICS team. The largest element of the CICS team is often the programming team—the performers—producing the programs that handle end-user transactions. Their programs, like the actors' performances, are the reason for the whole system. There are probably twenty programmers in an average installation. The largest installations have hundreds, and worldwide there are probably 300 000 CICS application programmers.

The smallest groups of all are the groups of CICS system programmers and the operations teams, probably both in single figures. In the largest organizations, there will be correspondingly larger teams—perhaps tens of system programmers and a similar number of operations staff. Worldwide, there are probably about 40 000 CICS system programmers. The number of CICS operations staff is difficult to estimate, as few are dedicated to operating only CICS, most having responsibility for all programs in the system.

Responsibilities and expectations

End-users are responsible for doing their everyday jobs, and they expect systems to serve them transparently. End-users can be office workers, factory supervisors, nurses, engineers, or even the general public. They become end-users when they use the transaction programs provided by a CICS data-processing team. They may use CICS from a desk, a production line or a teller machine. They need to know nothing about CICS itself and, if your staff design systems and applications well, should not even know that it exists. The modern CICS end-user includes members of the general public. For example, anyone entering the US Library of Congress can walk straight to a touchscreen display to start a CICS transaction, without instruction or help.

Programmers are responsible for making the end-users feel 'at home' with CICS transactions, constantly giving each end-user the impression that CICS is dedicated solely to satisfying his or her needs. At the same time, the programmers are responsible for ensuring that their programs are safe enough and efficient enough for use in a multi-user system.

The system-programming team is responsible for designing and building a system that will serve the required number of users. This may involve selecting the underlying hardware and software systems on which to run CICS, or simply determining how to get CICS running within existing systems. In this they are directly analogous to set designers and builders. Also like backstage designers, they prepare operating procedures, even actual scripts, for the operations team to use during a run. They then remain on standby to advise in case of emergency.

Interdependence

The different elements of the CICS team are as interdependent as are the groups within a theatrical company. The best CICS application programmers can achieve nothing without the help of the backstage crew of system programmers. They need them to build CICS systems tailored to provide the necessary program services, and to keep those systems running efficiently. They need operations staff to keep the same systems running smoothly. At the same time, the system-programming and operations staff need application programmers; they have no purpose without programs to support.

1.10   CICS people and this book

So far, I have talked about CICS people in general terms such as system programmers, programming staff, operations staff and so on. In Part II of the book I shall look more closely at the work of system programmers. I shall start to distinguish between different kinds of application-programming staff. In Part III I shall introduce different kinds of system programmer. My distinctions will not necessarily correspond exactly to those that you will find in your own organization. However, they should be largely similar, and they help to support the introduction of new technical subjects throughout the book.

Here we will look briefly at the different kinds of staff to be introduced later.

Programmers

Many organizations maintain a sizeable programming department that develops in-house programs. The department will contain systems analysts who will research and specify the underlying requirements for new online programs, and programmers, referred to as 'application programmers', who will write, debug and verify the code to satisfy the requirements.

There are almost as many definitions of the jobs of CICS application programmers and systems analysts as there are companies using CICS. In some organizations you can find the same person doing all parts of the job; elsewhere, you will find a string of people tackling successive stages in the development process.

System programmers

CICS system-programming teams vary enormously in composition and duties from company to company. The different roles in the team are sometimes performed by only one or two people, and sometimes by very large groups. In organizations with stable CICS systems, the teams may simply be occupied applying routine maintenance. In the most adventurous installations, large teams may work at several levels at once: maintaining working business systems at one level; planning medium-term developments at the next; researching and developing advanced systems at the highest level. Throughout Part III of this book I discuss system-programming work in terms of these three levels. This allows us to consider more routine functions first, going on to look at more advanced topics later.

I shall describe the system programmers who maintain working systems and develop medium-term developments as *system-support* personnel. I shall describe those who take the longer-term view as *system strategists*.

The operations team

The operations team runs your computer systems. In a mainframe computer installation it is usually responsible for all systems, including CICS systems. Members of the team usually work with all systems equally, with no-one having particular responsibility for or expertise with CICS. CICS is treated simply as an element of the overall system.

The composition and duties of the operations team depend upon the size of the whole organization, the system availability requirements and similar factors. Very large organizations have teams working in shifts around the clock, dedicated to keeping systems running continuously. Smaller organizations have a small number of operators working under the guidance of systems programmers, and either restart systems each working day or leave them unattended outside main business hours. The smallest organizations may have no operators and only a small number of system programmers. Modern departmental CICS systems, based perhaps on CICS/400, need very little attention. Operation, if any, may be the responsibility of ordinary end-user departments, supplemented by periodic visits by the technical staff who installed the systems.

In this book we shall treat operation as part of the system-programming job, as system-operation procedures are usually designed and supervised by system programmers.

The non-CICS team

The CICS team has to work with other groups. These include client departments, operating-system specialists, telecommunications specialists, database administrators and security administrators.

A client department is one that decides that a new transaction is justified by the needs of business. The client has to be helped to clarify the transaction requirements and to understand the cost and timetable for implementing them. We will discuss clients and their requirements in Chapter 4.

Operating-system specialists exist mainly for very large MVS/ESA systems, which require special levels of support and maintenance. The CICS team works with operating-system specialists whenever there are special CICS-related requirements, such as maintenance, or when pooling of knowledge will be mutually beneficial, for example when doing capacity planning.

Telecommunications specialists, database administrators and security administrators work with the CICS team whenever the products for which they are responsible interact with CICS. As you will read later, CICS 'subcontracts' specialist tasks to subsystems that are specifically designed to perform them. As these are separate, generalized program products, they and CICS need to be tuned to work together optimally.

We will discuss these matters in Part II, which covers system-programming matters.

Non-staff CICS support

As you can see, there is room for wide variation in the composition of a CICS team. Modest needs can be met by a simple but effective CICS system run by two people. The more demanding requirements of a large corporation need a team of tens, or maybe hundreds. In the largest organizations, including conglomerates or multinational corporations, CICS teams employ complementary products, and sometimes expert consultants, to get the best from their systems and transactions. We shall see more of this in Chapter 11.

1.11   Real people—real time

In summary, CICS transaction processing allows large numbers of ordinary people to carry out a variety of business transactions on demand. CICS's design permits a clear separation of programming and system design and control. Its services provide programmers with all they need to create real-time business programs. To understand CICS fully, you need to know why real-time transactions are different from other sorts of computer program. That is the subject of the next chapter.

Notes

[1] Throughout this book the word 'platform' is used to mean the complete combination of hardware and software that supports CICS. For CICS/ESA, the platform consists of a System/370 or System/390 processor plus a suitable level of the MVS operating system.

[2] An *end-user* of CICS is anyone who uses a CICS transaction for its intended purpose: for example, a bank clerk who uses a terminal to query a customer's account balance on request or a cinema booking clerk who uses one to check seat availability.

2
CICS in the DP scene

This chapter shows why CICS is not merely another personal-computer program or mainframe batch program. In developing the theme, the chapter shows how CICS has evolved to exploit new technology throughout the years, and explains the significance to businesses of CICS's use of the technology.

2.1 End-user's view of transaction processing

CICS transactions are designed to make possible, or more economical, rapid processing of customer data. As CICS systems have become more sophisticated, they have been expected to become easier to use, to the point where unskilled users are expected to use them directly. To make this possible, your programmers have had to design very user-friendly programs. The result has been the creation of transactions that make it look as though each user has the system to himself or herself.

This is probably the image to keep in your mind as you consider what a good transaction-processing system should be. That is, it should have the appearance of a typical personal-computer program. The user should think that he or she has sole access to the system, its storage, its printers, its files and databases (Fig. 2.1) and to any other resources it owns. The user should also be shielded from anything technical and anything that needs technical understanding. For example, if a program fails for any reason, the user should either not know of the failure or should be left totally clear about its nature, its consequences and what to do next. Ideally, every user should be able to view a CICS transaction as though their terminal is a dedicated computer (Fig. 2.2).

If your programmers achieve this aim, your CICS systems will become very much easier to use than the average personal computer, because users do not have to think about such things as disk file maintenance, backup, software upgrades, configuration and so on.

(a)

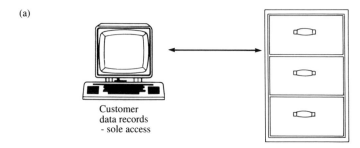

Customer
data records
- sole access

(b)   End-users

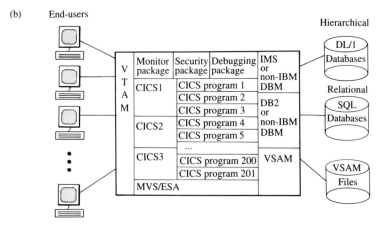

Figure 2.1.   CICS user's view. (a) Illusion—one user, one filing system. (b) Reality—
many users, programs, databases . . . .

2.2   The nature of a CICS transaction

Reduced to basics, the ideal CICS transaction is a combination of terminal
dialogue and data access, linked by a minimum of additional processing program
code. Although CICS transactions can be designed to be very complex, most are
relatively small and uncomplicated, and contain a minimum of calculation or
other data manipulation.

A transaction is started when an end-user types something into a terminal. This
is the first step in what becomes a dialogue with a processing program. The
transaction should be designed to be as economical as possible, both for the end-
user and for the CICS system. At the same time, it should not tie up system
resources for longer than is absolutely necessary.

At the simplest level, the transaction is an electronic filing clerk, finding and
opening customer files immensely quickly. At a more complex level, the system
allows the same clerk to open and adjust many files at the same time, culminating
in dispatch of goods, billing of customers and ordering of more stock.

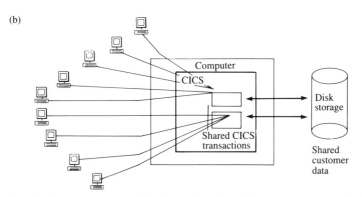

Figure 2.2. Order entry system—illusion and reality. (a) Appearance—a single-user system. (b) Reality—many users competing for programs and data.

Order entry example

Consider a simple task given to the computer when a customer telephones to order an item from a warehouse or store. For simplicity, we will start by assuming that the computer really is a single-user system. The task is:

1 To run a program that checks that the item is in stock in the warehouse
2 To tell the person taking the order that the item is in stock, so that he or she can confirm the order with the customer and get credit card or account authorization details
3 To generate an invoice for the customer and update billing records and other accounting records
4 To generate a shipping order
5 To revise the stock data to show that one less item is now in stock
6 If stock is low, to notify inventory-control personnel that reorder may be necessary

7 To tell the person taking the order that it has been accepted, is being
   processed, and that the item will be delivered within a given period.

For a single-user system, such as a personal computer, this is a fairly straightforward program. Now imagine twenty telephone operators in the office, all
receiving telephone orders at the same time and starting transactions on the same
CICS system, instead of on a personal computer. Each operator may run the same
program, enquiring about and ordering the same item. Any program coordinating
their work must ensure that they do not interact in ways that create errors. For
example, Operator 2 must not be allowed to allocate the last item in stock to
Customer 2 if Operator 1 is already doing the same for Customer 1. Under old
batch systems, this was never a problem, as orders would have been processed in
batches, but always one after the other, typically overnight. Processing of Order 2
would not have started until Order 1 had been fulfilled. But then the customer
would not have had the satisfaction of placing an order by telephone, receiving
confirmation of the order at the end of the call.

2.3   CICS framework of services

The challenge of providing the single-user view of the system and its data while
maintaining data integrity is met by a combination of programming and CICS
services.

The requirements sound fairly straightforward, but the implications for system
and program design are considerable. Moving from batch or single-user systems
to online real-time systems forces program designers to consider more seriously
than before such things as data management, data communications, data integrity
and recoverability, task management, system resource management, program
services, security and system-usage monitoring.

CICS works with underlying subsystems to coordinate data updates on behalf of
all programmers using the system. At the same time, it provides most of the
framework facilities for all of the above considerations. Nevertheless, as CICS is a
general-purpose system, most users employ technical support specialists to tailor
it to their exact business needs.

It is important to free application programmers from the need to worry about
the online aspects of all these things. After all, the most important consideration
for them must be the design and coding of effective commercial programs, often to
tight schedules. CICS provides the means to shield programmers from the
complexities, allowing them to focus on actual programming. As you will see in
Part II, the programmers still need to think differently when designing real-time
programs, but many of the complexities are hidden.

Data management

As part of its function, CICS provides data-handling services designed to make
life easier for programmers in the dynamic world of real-time transaction

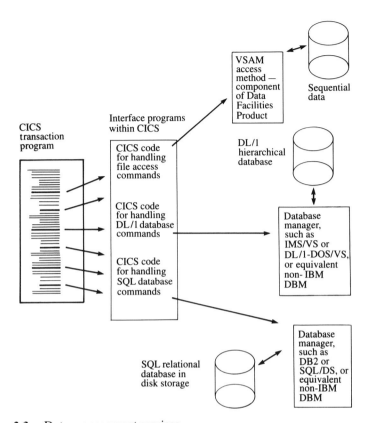

Figure 2.3.   Data-management services.

processing. It uses data-management systems, such as database managers, to do most of the work (Fig. 2.3), but provides the additional services vital for online processing.

These additional services, and the associated new responsibilities for data processing staff, are reviewed in Part III. However, you can understand the sorts of things needed by imagining the challenge of keeping shared disks up to date, backed-up in case of damage and fully accessible at all times. Furthermore, you can visualize the difference between the simple case of a single user updating one or more files on a personal computer's disk, and many users trying to update the same two or three files at the same time. In the former case, the program is in no doubt about which user and which program is updating the file. In the second case, the system needs to perform very careful logging and tracking to ensure that no conflicts occur.

Data communications

In the same way, there is a fundamental change in complexity of communications when you move from a single-user system to a multi-user shared system. With a

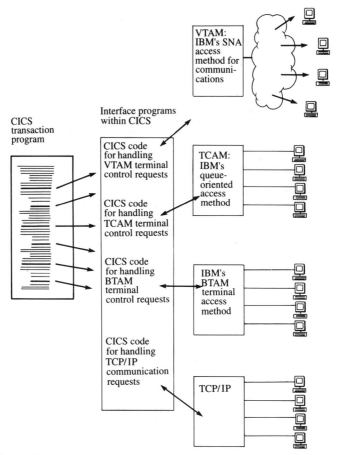

Figure 2.4. Data-communication services.

personal computer, there is only one keyboard/mouse/screen set to represent the user, so communication is simple. In a multi-user environment, the program has to recognize which user has sent a particular message, and to whom a message must be returned. Data for one user must not get routed to another. At the same time, it must ensure that display data is presented in a way that is compatible with the end-user's terminal. Many CICS systems have to work with a variety of terminals, each having different data requirements and screen formats. CICS manages all of this data handling and transmission, leaving application programmers to concentrate on business logic.

CICS monitors all incoming communication sessions for activity, so that no one is left waiting for access to the system. It works with a communications subsystem, such as VTAM or TCP/IP, to manage incoming and outgoing data, finding storage for the data while it exists and then relinquishing that storage for reuse when the data has been processed (Fig. 2.4). It leaves the actual communication to the

VTAM program, but does the work necessary to provide the dynamic environment for real-time programs.

Data integrity and recovery

From the discussion of data management earlier, you will appreciate that with hundreds of users able to change data at the same time there could be significant problems if something goes wrong. In most cases, the problems will be far too complex for the human brain to tackle with anything like the required speed.

So, for example, if your system handles seating allocation at a large event, with many outlets releasing seats, chaos would reign if the computer broke down at a time of peak activity. To recover from such a situation, you would need to know what had been promised, what had been confirmed, and which seat allocation transactions failed even to start. Your business could not afford mistakes or uncertainty.

Equally, if for some reason your data disks were destroyed, say by fire or accidental damage, you would need to be able to recreate their contents up to the moment of failure. This might mean recovering the results of transactions completed in the last day, hour or even second.

CICS provides a lot of help in addressing these challenges, recording the data you would need to recover from the situations described. In some cases, CICS can continue after such an error without needing intervention. In other cases, staff would have to start special procedures. In either case, system-programming staff need to plan for such events, to minimize their effects. Application programmers may also need to consider such matters when developing programs and their data. Part III will look at this subject in greater depth, in a section on recovery and restart.

Task management

One of the main activities for a mainframe CICS system is scheduling and dispatching transaction-processing tasks.[1] At any time there are likely to be hundreds of CICS tasks to be performed concurrently, all requiring use of the same resources. CICS controls the rate and order in which tasks are handled, thereby minimizing the chances of conflict or system overload.

You are probably already aware of the function of the operating system, the program that controls the basic operation of your computer. This program controls the operation of programs running within the computer. It controls the operation of CICS itself, and allocates storage, computer cycles and other resources that enable CICS to do its work.

However, the operating system does not provide control to the level of granularity required by individual real-time transactions. This is the job that CICS was originally designed to do. CICS lobbies the operating system for computer

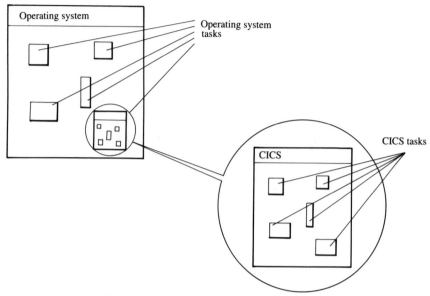

Figure 2.5. Mainframe CICS—an operating system within the operating system.

execution time, or resources, then reallocates them to the programs that have to run on behalf of user transactions. It sets each program running, and intervenes whenever the program has to stop for any reason—for instance, to wait for data or operator input. At such a time, CICS starts another program, to keep work flowing through the system.

CICS's aim in scheduling system tasks is to keep itself fully busy, giving it no chance to wait idle. If it cannot provide enough work itself, CICS will give control back to the operating system to let other programs run to fill the time. The operating system sees CICS and all the transaction programs that it controls as a single program; it cannot detect individual transaction programs. Working in this way, CICS does not duplicate the scheduling functions of the operating system. It provides nested scheduling for a special class of programs (Fig. 2.5).

System resource management

Whenever CICS schedules a new task it is using processor cycles. It is also using processor storage for the programs that process the transaction data, and for any customer data. It needs smaller areas of storage for scratchpad-type calculations and, from time to time, it needs access to data-communications channels and data files and databases. For all of these, CICS acquires the necessary resources from the operating system. It then allocates them to its own transactions as it starts or restarts them. It takes the resources back when transactions complete their processing. As with task scheduling, CICS does not duplicate services provided by the operating system.

What you are getting from this is simplicity for the programmers. Without the intervention of CICS, every transaction's program would have to contain code to negotiate with the operating system to acquire and release resources. This would require every programmer to understand operating-system interfaces. Poor design, or lack of load balancing, would quickly overload the system.

As with task management, the operating system does not provide the necessary granularity of storage management needed to satisfy the needs of a busy transaction-processing system, so CICS provides the granularity.

Program services

In the previous section we saw how CICS removes the need for programs to acquire system resources for themselves. This is just one of the ways in which CICS tries to simplify or hide aspects of real-time program design, so keeping transaction-processing programs similar to traditional programs. The following paragraphs identify some of the other services CICS provides. The services will be described in more detail in Chapter 6.

CICS offers screen-management services, which remove the need for every application programmer to be familiar with the detail of communications data streams used by each kind of terminal used in the installation. As a side-effect, this 'device independence' saves your programmers from having to change every program in the inventory every time a new kind of terminal is put into service.

As well as managing the use of working storage for programs, and storage for data files, CICS manages special kinds of storage: that needed for queued data. Data of this kind, transitory in nature, is needed because of the very dynamic nature of the CICS environment. For example, data produced as part of a CICS task is usually not printed until well after the task has been completed; it waits in a queue for a print program to process it when there is no more urgent work to be done. Queuing is also used for data passing through multiple processes. Such data will wait in a storage area within a CICS queue until needed for the transaction that executes the next process. In all cases, the programmer needs to know of the facilities provided, and when to use them. However, CICS manages the data queues and their storage, and handles any errors, providing the programmer with simple commands to use within programs needing storage.

Other services include those concerned with time management: for example starting a task at a particular time of day, logging events on disk for accounting purposes or to ensure data integrity, or checking or controlling part of the system to provide a degree of automation.

In each case, the CICS programming interface is designed to make it easy to get the required services, using commands that can be learnt relatively easily (Fig. 2.6). So CICS does a lot to minimize the impact of the special program-design

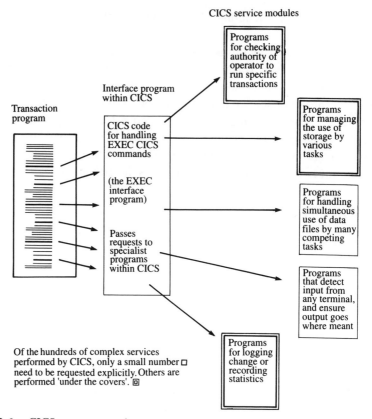

CICS service modules

Programs
for checking
authority of
operator to
run specific
transactions

Interface program
within CICS

Transaction
program

CICS code
for handling
EXEC CICS
commands

(the EXEC
interface
program)

Passes
requests to
specialist
programs
within CICS

Programs
for managing
the use of
storage by
various
tasks

Programs
for handling
simultaneous
use of data
files by many
competing
tasks

Programs
that detect
input from
any terminal,
and ensure
output goes
where meant

Of the hundreds of complex services
performed by CICS, only a small number □
need to be requested explicitly. Others are
performed 'under the covers'. ◙

Programs
for logging
change or
recording
statistics

Figure 2.6. CICS program services.

challenges on the application programmer. However, as you will see in Part II, to
be effective a CICS application programmer (indeed any real-time programmer)
needs insight into the working of the system as a whole. The success of CICS in
concealing many of the complexities of real-time operation makes it easier to
absorb the residual concepts.

As you will see in Part III, some of the programming considerations are hidden
from the programmer at the expense of the system-programming team. Special
system-configuration options push the complexity down to a lower level, where it
is handled either by technical support staff or by special-purpose software
packages.

Security management

CICS's reason for existence is to give people in, or associated with, your
organization free access to the information needed to conduct your business.
However, you will want to restrict such free access to those entitled to it. CICS
itself does not try to provide a secure environment. Instead, it provides interfaces

that allow special-purpose security packages to manage all aspects of system security. IBM's RACF package is one such package. Others include TopSecret and ACF2.

Most packages provide security against unauthorized logon, then protect individual resources (programs, files and so on) from use by all but specifically-identified system users.

As well as providing an attachment interface for security packages, CICS provides special-purpose transactions and programming commands for controlling security functions.

System usage monitoring

Online system resources are valuable company assets, and most users gather data to help them ensure that the resources are well-used and trouble free. Monitoring data allows you to monitor all aspects of the system's performance. Statistics allow you to determine how often particular resources were used or particular operations were performed in a given period.

Monitoring helps you to charge client departments for their use of systems. The effectiveness of online systems based on CICS often ensures that they become heavily used, and creates demand for additional systems. To fund growing investment in hardware, software and staff, you need to charge your clients in proportion to the workloads they generate. CICS gathers data that helps you to do this. It also gathers performance data that allows you to assess the level of service you are giving your clients.

CICS gathers monitoring and statistics data and stores it for offline processing. You can use supplied offline programs to process the data that has been gathered, or you can write your own routines. Whatever the method, you need experienced staff to interpret the data in the light of your installation's program portfolio, its goals and agreed service levels, and the expectations of users.

Some programs are so resoundingly successful that you need to monitor their effect on system usage and to detect possible overloads and bottlenecks. Most online systems have regular patterns of workload peaks and troughs, and it becomes very important for capacity planners to have good statistics on which to base their growth projections.

2.4   Working with other systems

It is no accident that CICS remains the leading commercial transaction-processing system, even after 24 years of use. The reasons for CICS's continuing success are that its developers have ensured that (a) it does its own job well and (b) it does not try to do the jobs of other system components. It has been successful because CICS Development's commitment has always been to give timely support to new technology, not to duplicate that new technology. In addition, CICS Development has always remained sensitive to the need of customers to protect existing investment in DP equipment and programs.

Technological advances

In its 24 years, IBM's family of CICS systems has evolved from CICS OS Standard, through CICS/VS and CICS/XA, to CICS/ESA, CICS/VSE, CICS/6000, CICS/400 and CICS OS/2. It has grown onto successive generations of processors and operating systems, taking advantage, with minimum change, of each new architecture change or new function. It has become independent of DASD subsystems, accommodating any that can be used by data-management subsystems such as DFP and the database products. Similarly, it is independent of communications hardware, leaving network management to VTAM or other communication managers. As a result, it has been able to take advantage, with only incremental change, of new technology.

CICS reinforces its independence of hardware by leaving it to program packages to provide layers of support on top of CICS. For example, in recent years CallPath products have provided a way of linking telephony services to CICS transactions. They can be added to any existing CICS system. CICS has not had to be modified to support this capability, yet is immediately able to take advantage of the capabilities of telephone switching gear. And because such packages are designed to use CICS's external programming interfaces, CICS will transparently support any extensions to them.

Specialization

Throughout this chapter, you have seen how CICS subcontracts work to other subsystems wherever possible (Fig. 2.7). It gives the operating system the work that it is best at, such as overall storage management, job scheduling and so on. In the same way, it leaves telecommunication to VTAM, sending it data streams for packaging and transmission; data management to DFP and database products, sending them data records to be stored; resource security to security managers such as RACF.

Language products are best at providing business-related programming languages and their associated compilers. CICS does not try to replace them, but complements them by providing special processing commands for the transaction-processing environment. It provides a translator that turns the coded CICS commands into command sequences written in the language of choice. What is most impressive is that CICS supports the most common commercial programming languages, and is extended from time to time to accommodate new languages.

Beyond these, there are products that complement CICS, being produced by experts in particular niche fields: for example systems management, monitoring,

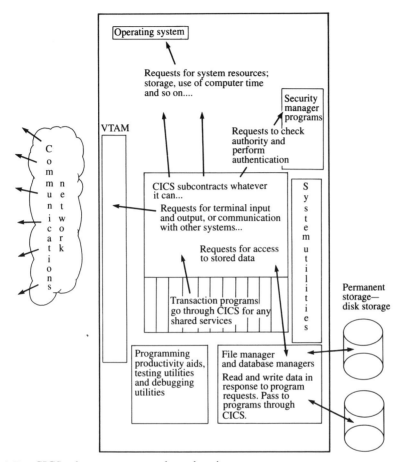

Figure 2.7.   CICS subcontracts as much work as it can.

front-end, screen definition, program generators, communications adaptors and all kinds of end-user programs.

As a result of CICS's modest practice of doing only what it excels at, you may end up with an array of complementary products in building a CICS-based system. Yet by doing so, you will be able to construct the optimum configuration to meet your business's needs.

2.5   All things to all people

In this chapter, you have seen the range of services that CICS provides. Its attraction comes from the fact that it is a truly comprehensive system, offering all of these services either directly or through another subsystem. At the same time, CICS is highly tailorable: you can choose whether or not to use many of its functions. You can select alternative subsystems to provide the subcontracted functions.

CICS has been such a powerful general-purpose system that it has been easy to develop programs to carry out the normal transactions of businesses. In addition, the widespread acceptance of the CICS products has made CICS programming skills highly marketable, and readily available. Furthermore, it has proved cost-effective for software development companies to write general-purpose program packages, such as payroll or accounts receivable, for sale to businesses. This phenomenon of a major infrastructure of vendors and packages and consultants is commonplace nowadays, as DOS, OS/2 and AIX systems have generated self-sustaining industries of their own. It is easy to ignore the fact that CICS has had such an infrastructure for the past twenty years.

Before we go on to look, in the next chapter, at the CICSs that have proved so successful, it is worth remembering another reason for CICS's enduring success: its ability to evolve. Remember that CICS emerged in 1968, running on OS/360 and DOS/360, in the days before virtual storage was generally known. It adapted to virtual storage, then later to extended architecture (XA), then most recently to enterprise system architecture (ESA). Each adaptation helped to break through perceived barriers to growth.

CICS has made use of extensions to the operating system, through such advances as PR/SM and data spaces, and to advances in other subsystems, such as SNA's LU6.2 through VTAM and DBCTL through IMS. It has given users access to data on successive releases of IMS, DB2, VTAM, DFP and RACF. It has supported emerging languages, most recently C/370. It is always among the first to accommodate new architectures, such as SNA, ESA, SAA and OSI.

It has therefore remained at the forefront of technology. Yet it has managed to provide a remarkable degree of stability for its users and their programs. This has given businesses confidence in their investments in hardware and software.

Note

[1] It is worth noting the distinction between a task and a transaction. The terms are often used as though interchangeable, but the difference is important.

A CICS transaction is a predefined sequence of data processing that corresponds to a business transaction. The sequence involves the execution of one or more CICS application programs.

A CICS task is a particular instance of the performance of a CICS transaction. Two terminal operators may start the same transaction simultaneously, from different terminals; each is setting the CICS system a separate task and will be given separate treatment. A task is often referred to as an 'execution unit'.

3
Meet the CICS family

This chapter introduces the different products in IBM's CICS family, describing some of their similarities and differences and how they can be used together.

Many current users have grown with the CICS systems provided by IBM since the early 1970s, but have no experience of IBM's new systems that have emerged in the 1980s and 1990s. This chapter describes each of the CICS systems, and shows the place of each in the transaction-processing world.

3.1   Family history

The majority of CICS systems in productive use today are still running on the IBM proprietary operating systems for System/370 computers, MVS and VSE. As a vital element of most business systems, transaction processing has to be entrusted to reliable, known and powerful systems. The new systems that have been emerging during the 1980s and 1990s adopt the best and most appropriate features of the established mainframe-computer-based systems.

CICS on the big mainframe systems survives and thrives, as we have seen, because it can be moulded to meet almost any business need for real-time processing, and because it evolves with related technologies. Its success as a general-purpose transaction-processing platform is proven by its acceptance across the range of systems on which it is available: from the top-of-the-range MVS systems to the small-user VSE systems. However, this is the traditional CICS, the System/370 mainframe CICS. It often coexists with other mainframe systems, sharing systems resources with batch and interactive systems that support your organization's other processing needs.

In the 1960s, any new commercial computerization project was based on mainframe systems—there was no real alternative. Nowadays, though, medium and small computer systems have become powerful enough to offer alternative solutions to business needs.

The CICS systems for MVS and VSE, currently CICS/ESA and CICS/VSE, have been joined over the years by IBM's CICS systems for VM, OS/2 and DOS, AIX (IBM's implementation of UNIX) and OS/400. Versions of IBM's CICS system are therefore available on all of its strategic operating systems. Meanwhile, old versions of CICS are still in common use, and users have upward migration paths that they can use to upgrade in the future.

Anyone planning a new project will consider the merits of different system configurations. Sometimes, systems based on non-System/370 computers will meet the needs best. Although installed and maintained by experienced data-processing staff, they are often left to run for long periods without special attention. Their users understand how to perform only routine administrative tasks, but technical staff may be based many miles away, at a headquarters location—or in the offices of a facilities management company that is contracted to provide support. Typical of this kind of system is IBM's OS/400 system, for which many ready-made program packages have been developed. Other systems have been designed to run on clusters of DOS or OS/2 workstations, or on IBM RISC/System 6000 workstations.

Often, this kind of 'departmental' system is preloaded with programs designed to do the single job for which it was bought. Other programs can be added as the need arises. In large enterprises, users of departmental, or distributed, systems can link them to central mainframe systems, allowing company-wide communication, centralized control and some degree of remote maintenance. Such linking is now commonplace, but its full potential has not yet been exploited.

One way of helping to realize the potential is to use programs and data that are portable between systems. Another way is to provide ways for different systems to communicate with each other. By expanding to cover different operating systems, the CICS family is helping its users to make better use of their resources. By installing a CICS system for each platform in your enterprise, you provide a transaction-processing bridge between a variety of different systems. Programs written to appropriate standards can be compiled for each of the separate platforms. At the same time, proven CICS-to-CICS communication facilities unify the different systems. The same facilities can give remote users access to central mainframes, if necessary without them realizing that they are using several different systems at once.

In this chapter, we will look at the products for each platform, and at their places in the family. In Part II we will consider how programs bridge the gulf between different systems. In Part III, we will see how CICS systems can be connected to each other.

Terminology

If you have much experience of software from any supplier, you will be familiar with the concept of versions or releases of a program. IBM products are presented as different Versions, Releases and Modification levels. These terms appear frequently throughout this book, and it is worth briefly stating the significance of each.

IBM strategic software products are expected to have long life spans, evolving to keep pace with technology and with users' additional demands. So, IBM develops a product, *releases* it for customers to use, develops it some more, *releases* it again, and so on. Each time the product is released, it is given a new number to distinguish it from the existing release. A new release usually contains significant new function.

From time to time, IBM considers it appropriate to make minor improvements to a product, which are not in themselves enough to warrant a new release. In this case it issues a *modification release*. Such releases are usually relatively easy to install, and usually offer as much in the way of maintenance improvements as in new function. Typical reasons for a modification release are support for additional devices (say, new kinds of display), or conformance to new standards or architectures.

After a number of years, IBM may decide to invest in a major overhaul or redesign of a product. After this, it is considered to be a new product, rather than a new release. It may have the same name as the old product, but now will be called Version 2 (or 3, or whatever). It will have a new product number.

IBM products are therefore identified in terms such as: CICS/MVS Version 2 Release 1 Modification 2. In shorthand, this can become CICS/MVS Version 2.1.2, or even CICS/MVS 2.1.2. You will see this notation throughout the rest of the book, as there have been many versions and releases of CICS, and a few modification releases too.

Sometimes, the first release of a product is given an unexpected number. For example, the first release of CICS/400 was called CICS/400 Version 2 Release 2. This leap of both version and release number was for consistency with OS/400: to associate the product with the correct levels of related OS/400 products, including the operating system itself.

3.2 The MVS systems

The CICS products for the MVS operating systems are known as CICS/ESA Version 3, CICS/MVS Version 2 and CICS/OS/VS Version 1. Together they represent the history of state-of-the-art transaction processing. Use of CICS/OS/VS has diminished rapidly since the end of the 1980s. Most users have migrated to CICS/MVS or CICS/ESA. At the beginning of 1993, the majority were still based on CICS/MVS but were transferring in large numbers to CICS/ESA.

The MVS CICS systems are designed to conform to the System/370 architecture, and run on System/370 and System/390 processors that support the architecture. In this, they have much in common with the VSE systems, which we will

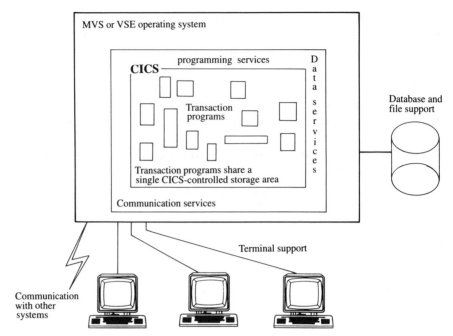

Figure 3.1. CICS controls its own region.

consider next. It is worth looking briefly at the basic structure of System/370 CICS, as that can help understand what follows.

A System/370 CICS system runs as though it is a single program in its own address space in the computer. The computer sees, and deals with, only one program—CICS. In its turn, CICS monitors and controls all activity within its address space; it runs control code of its own, maintains control blocks of its own, and starts, stops and handles the needs of business transaction programs. CICS alone is responsible for communicating with the world outside its address space. The programs that it permits to run within its address space share that address space quite freely, with very few limitations (Fig. 3.1). In this, MVS CICS systems are similar to CICS/VSE systems, but different from the other members of the CICS family, as you will see later.

CICS/ESA

CICS/ESA (as the third version of CICS is known) was announced in June 1989, and two further releases have since been produced. As a result, the new version has reached maturity, and its full worth is becoming apparent to those that are using it. IBM refers to CICS/ESA as its 'flagship' transaction-processing system, as it usually sets the direction for the whole family, using new technology and providing new facilities before other family members.

Beneath the surface, the product has been restructured since Version 2. After twenty years of evolution, CICS had a structure that made continued development difficult. It was becoming more difficult to service, yet less able to adapt to advances in hardware and architectural technology. The nucleus of CICS Version 3 has been redesigned according to object-oriented principles. At the same time, old and error-prone code supporting obsolescent function has been removed. Most notably, CICS's macro-level programming interface has been removed. Besides removing a basic cause of fragility, this has allowed IBM to optimize the performance of CICS in certain functional areas, and to introduce new system capabilities. Most notable among these is the ability to use the MVS/ESA facility known as subsystem storage protection. This allows you to ensure that programs are unable to damage CICS code and its vital data areas.

Changes in CICS/ESA have removed much of the need to understand and use information about the product's internal design and operation. In the past, your CICS team needed to understand the operation of parts of CICS in order to be able to add special routines of their own. New interfaces give them programmed access to the most commonly used information.

Other changes have been aimed at reducing the need for what are referred to as 'scheduled outages' (planned shutdowns for maintenance and administration). It has always been necessary to stop CICS to update or extend it in certain ways. It is now less necessary, as more changes can be made dynamically while the system is running. At the same time, the system has been made more robust, so that errors in transaction programs are less likely to affect the entire system. The internal restructure has contributed to this robustness, but the removal of support for macro-level programs and the introduction by MVS/ESA of subsystem storage protection guards against the most damaging—usually self-inflicted—programming errors.

Among the most important improvements are those that extend CICS/ESA's ability to communicate with other systems—both CICS and non-CICS. The extensive CICS-to-CICS communication capabilities will be reviewed in Chapter 9. As well as these, CICS/ESA provides improved communication with IMS database subsystems, through use of IMS Database Control and a new front-end programming interface.

Producing CICS/ESA Version 3 was a major project from IBM, involving almost ten years of research and development. The last year was devoted to field trials with customers and manufacturers of CICS-related utility programs. After the first release became available for general use, testing and development continued; the first release of Release 2 had the same field-testing. Release 3 had further field-testing, less widespread but more intensive. So new users of 3.3 get a system with more than three years of accumulated and intensive testing, of the system itself and the supporting infrastructure products.

CICS/ESA has the same programming superstructure (at the command level) as its predecessors; but this superstructure has grown, being more complete and better-defined. Yet all the time, it has remained compatible with existing languages, so that you should not have to update your business transaction programs to move to CICS/ESA.

CICS/MVS

CICS has a long history of evolution, and each new version builds on the strengths of its predecessor. CICS/ESA Version 3, described in the last section, inherited the improvements produced in Version 2. Version 2 was based on CICS/OS/VS Version 1, but included an extended recovery capability that allowed a failing system to hand control to a standby system. It improved system availability both by detecting failure before a human operator could, and by starting a replacement system faster than normally possible.

Version 2 was also a platform on which IBM introduced new ways of providing functional enhancements and maintenance. This is always a problem with major software products, especially those with as many users and with as complex a structure as CICS. As a result, CICS/MVS users have seen many enhancements and modifications. Among these is the Data Tables feature, which allows users of the largest CICS systems to perform very low-cost, high-performance transactions alongside normal CICS transactions.

The end result of the CICS/MVS program of enhancements has been a high degree of system stability and a relatively straightforward migration, both from CICS/OS/VS and between modification releases of Version 2.

The reported good stability is appropriate, given CICS/MVS's other role: that of migration and coexistence platform. As you have seen already, CICS/ESA has developed rapidly since its first appearance. Some of its improvements have necessitated removal of the macro-level programming interface, so some users migrating to Version 3 need a supported way of continuing to run very old, but still important, programs. IBM allows this by continuing to support CICS/MVS so that you can run it alongside CICS/ESA during the lifetime of your old macro-level programs. As is usual with IBM software products, CICS/MVS can run on new releases of the operating system as they emerge, though usually without being able to use new function. CICS/MVS Version 2 runs on both MVS/XA and MVS/ESA, so can run on the same machine as CICS/ESA.

CICS/OS/VS

CICS/OS/VS is Version 1 of the CICS product for the MVS operating system. It has been enormously successful, evolving from the original CICS/VS product in 1968, through seven major releases, and a couple of minor ones, to the final release in 1985. During its lifetime it grew to include the command-level programming interface, intersystem communication and multiregion operation, and resource definition online. At the same time it adapted to successive generations of SNA, to new database subsystems, and to new hardware—storage, displays and communications, and processors. It has been such an effective programming platform that enormous numbers of transactions and packages have been developed for it. All of these can be migrated to run on CICS/MVS Version 2.

It is a credit to the designers of the original CICS system that it has been able to evolve in this way for so many years. However, the changes and extensions introduced over the years produced a product that has become difficult to extend or maintain at the rate required by its users. Advances in software engineering methods allowed the CICS development team to produce a new product designed to provide the function required of a CICS for the twenty-first century, but with an architecture to match. The new product has already largely replaced CICS/OS/VS Version 1.

Use of CICS Version 1 is declining, and it is no longer being improved; the last improvements were made in 1990, when changes were made to improve the way CICS/OS/VS communicated with CICS OS/2. Just as the emergence of virtual storage made the first CICS products obsolete, so the coming of ESA/370 is making CICS/OS/VS become part of history.

Many users are migrating directly to Version 3. Some are using Version 2 until they prepare a strategy for handling transactions that depend on the macro-level programming interface. In some cases, these transactions are supplied by third parties, so users are not in direct control of the situation. Nevertheless, it seems that Version 1 will have disappeared from use by the turn of the century. Long before that, IBM will have ceased support of the product.

Connectivity

The System/370-based family of CICS systems has been at the forefront of communications technology for all of its life. In fulfilling its basic task of communicating with terminals, it has always been among the first to support new device types, and to implement new communication protocols. For example, it was among the first systems to support colour display terminals, and was quick to implement SNA's application-to-application (LU6.2) protocols.

Version 1 and CICS/MVS Version 2 communicated with terminals through BTAM, TCAM and VTAM. CICS/ESA no longer uses BTAM, concentrating mostly on the strategic VTAM program, which implements IBM's systems network architecture (SNA). In addition, CICS systems have been tested successfully with both OSI networks and TCP/IP networks.

Through VTAM, CICS systems can communicate with each other as well as with other subsystems. So CICS/ESA can communicate with other CICS/ESA systems, with CICS/MVS, CICS/VSE, CICS/DOS/VS, CICS/6000, CICS/VM, CICS OS/2 and CICS/400. In addition, it can communicate with other subsystems, for example IMS TM.

Further, CICS systems operating under the same operating system, on the same computer, can communicate with each other using private protocols, a process known as multiregion operation. You will read more of this in Chapter 9.

Data management

CICS systems delegate some special functions to other subsystems. Data management is one of the best examples of this. For ordinary file management, MVS CICS systems delegate the work to DFP, IBM's Data Facility Product. For sophisticated database facilities, they delegate the work to any suitable database product. IBM's preferred products are of course its own long-standing partners of CICS: IMS for hierarchical databases and DB2 for relational databases.

CICS's support for databases was, in early releases, closely woven into the product, with individual customers having to include pieces of database code in their CICS systems before running them. This meant that products were quite interdependent. Later releases introduced new, formal interfaces allowing attachment of subsystems such as database managers. DB2 was the first to use the interface. With CICS/ESA Version 3, IMS can also use the interface. One consequence of this is an increased independence of operation, giving improved system availability.

Security facilities

The MVS CICS systems provided their own internal security capabilities over the years. However, these were limited mainly to controlling access to the system itself, through sign-on control. CICS/ESA Version 3 has no internal security facilities. Instead, it relies upon external security management products, such as IBM's RACF, to provide protection against unauthorized access to data and other system resources, including CICS itself. CICS now provides a specialized interface for such security managers.

Programming support

It has been estimated that more than 300 billion lines of program code have been written for CICS transaction and that there are 300 000 application programmers, worldwide, currently developing and supporting CICS. A large proportion of that code and those programmers will be working on MVS CICS systems.

Programs can be written for CICS in assembler language, COBOL, PL/I or C. Many of the oldest programs will have been written in assembler language, but nowadays most are written in one of the high-level programming languages.

CICS/ESA is the senior member of the CICS family, and usually sets direction and offers new function first. It presents almost a complete superset of the CICS interfaces. There are a few exceptions to these rules: it is sometimes second to implement new function, as it was when it followed CICS OS/2 in implementing distributed program link. Secondly, there are a few functions that it has never implemented: for example the report controller feature provided by CICS/VSE. Thirdly, it has discontinued certain support that continues to be available on CICS/VSE: for example BTAM communications and the macro-level programming interface.

Nevertheless, CICS/ESA users have seen extensive additions to the interfaces provided. There are now new commands for controlling the system from within programs, new commands that remove the need to examine system internal control blocks and a new interface for security programs.

3.3 The VSE systems

This section discusses CICS/VSE Version 2 and CICS/DOS/VS Version 1. These systems are very closely related to CICS/MVS Version 2 and CICS/OS/VS Version 1 respectively, in many places sharing a common code base. They are designed to run on System/370 and System/390 computers, and have a similar underlying structure to that shown for MVS CICS in Figure 3.1. They are typically used as the 'mid-range' systems, whereas CICS/MVS or CICS/ESA are used as 'large' or 'high-end' systems. In large enterprises, VSE-based CICS systems running on smaller IBM System/370 processors are often used as departmental or branch-office distributed systems, connected to a head-office system based on CICS/MVS or CICS/ESA. In turn, a CICS/VSE system sometimes serves as a hub for CICS OS/2 distributed systems.

CICS/VSE

The first release of CICS/VSE Version 2 was announced in 1990, succeeding the long-standing CICS/DOS/VS. The second release of CICS/VSE was announced in June 1992, and became available in 1993. Unlike CICS for the MVS platform, a restructured CICS has not yet been provided for the VSE user. However, Version 2 provides major extensions to system capability, and has in many ways exceeded CICS/MVS in the range of improvements it offers.

CICS/VSE is delivered as an integral part of the VSE System Package. It plays an important part in VSE/SP installation, controlling the initial dialogues. It is then an integral part of the basic system. Almost all VSE/SP users use CICS, but many take it almost for granted, running packages without need for intervention.

The functional improvements in CICS/VSE Version 2 match quite closely those in CICS/MVS Version 2. In addition, they include some improvements over CICS/DOS/VS for the VSE user that are not applicable to the MVS user.

The headline improvements on Version 2 are: support for the extended recovery facility (XRF) that was originally provided for CICS/MVS and later adopted by CICS/ESA; support for the Data Tables feature that was originally provided as a feature on CICS/MVS and later integrated into CICS/ESA. Version 2 also provided much-requested improvements to the report controller feature (for handling printing) that was originally provided in CICS/DOS/VS 1.7.

CICS/DOS/VS

Like CICS/MVS Version 2, CICS/VSE replaces an earlier Version 1 product with a considerable history. CICS/DOS/VS was for many years an almost identical system to CICS/OS/VS. The differences between the two products were caused by the design and operational differences between the underlying operating systems, and their associated access methods. Such differences were minor at the level of user interfaces, especially the programming interface. However, they were more significant at the system programmer's level, showing up particularly in job-control language.

Over the years, CICS/DOS/VS and CICS/OS/VS users developed a friendly rivalry. Certainly, VSE users have remained determined to resist suggestions that they should migrate to the MVS platform. In part they are convinced that their VSE-based systems are better; in part they feel they have a cost-effective and usable system more suited to their scale of operations. They are comfortable with the level of function and power provided by the CICS/VSE system. VSE-based CICS users are usually viewed as 'mid-range' systems. However, some installations are very large, matching many MVS-based systems in the volumes of work handled. Nevertheless, the majority of users tend to be smaller in scale and are less likely to have large data-processing departments. They tend to view the VSE/SP system, including CICS, as a very effective layer of enabling software, rather than as a system in its own right.

CICS systems for OS and DOS operating systems had developed side by side since the CICS program product was first announced in 1969. Since then, the two operating systems have evolved side by side, but in different ways. CICS products for the two platforms have also evolved, keeping closely in step until the emergence of the much-changed CICS/ESA, for which there is not yet a VSE-based equivalent. The relationship between CICS/VSE and the VSE System Package (VSE/SP) has been a key factor in the development of CICS/VSE. In some ways it has introduced differences between CICS/VSE and CICS/MVS. At the same time, it has had a positive influence on the packaging, delivery and usability of CICS/VSE.

Looking back, we can see that the report controller was the first major functional difference between CICS/OS/VS and CICS/DOS/VS, apart from their support for different subsystems for such things as data management and security. MVS CICS systems still have no equivalent to the report controller.

Relationship with VSE/SP

This is almost a symbiotic relationship: VSE/SP needs CICS to run ICCF as part of its installation process, yet CICS needs several of the VSE/SP components to provide the services it uses. At one time, CICS and the VSE operating system had different schedules. However, this has changed since the VSE system package came into existence. Originally called a SIPO, the package was designed as a 'productivity option'. This meant that a popular set of software products were configured and packaged by IBM, to simplify the process of choosing and installing them. The packaged option was exactly that at first: optional. However, over time it has become so popular that it has been made almost the only way of receiving VSE components. It has also been renamed VSE/SP, and more recently VSE/ESA.

The VSE system package caused CICS/DOS/VS 1.6 to be delivered some time after CICS/OS/VS 1.6. It also delayed delivery of CICS/DOS/VS 1.7 until it could be packaged and tested with other VSE components. Generally, after CICS 1.6, CICS/DOS/VS development was influenced very much more by the need of its users for a transaction-processing capability integrated into the VSE System Package than by the pressures for enhancement of MVS CICS systems. CICS/VSE development continued in parallel with CICS/ESA development, and ensured compatibility, but timing of new development was driven more by VSE than by CICS. Nevertheless, as has been shown by the development of the two Version 2 systems, CICS/VSE will continue to adopt many of the changes pioneered by CICS/ESA.

CICS/VSE users should consider following some of the steps taken by their CICS/ESA opposite numbers. So, for example, although CICS/VSE has not dropped support for the macro-level programming interface, CICS/VSE users should consider converting existing programs and packages to command level. It has been shown that these are more robust and reliable than the macro-level programs they replace.

Connectivity

Both CICS/DOS/VS and CICS/VSE support communication through BTAM and VTAM. Ongoing enhancement of the VTAM support ensures that CICS/VSE will continue to be able to communicate with terminal devices as they are developed.

VTAM communication also enables CICS/VSE to participate in intersystem communication with other CICS systems and, through distributed transaction protocols, in distributed processing with non-CICS systems.

CICS/DOS/VS and CICS/VSE systems running in different partitions within the same operating system on the same computer can also communicate using multiregion operation. This is the same facility as provided for MVS CICS systems, and is described in more detail in Chapter 9.

Data management

CICS/DOS/VS and CICS/VSE delegate data management to other subsystems. Management of files is delegated to VSE/VSAM, and database facilities are provided and handled by database managers such as DL/I DOS/VS or SQL/DS.

Programming support

I said in the section on MVS CICSs that an estimated 300 billion lines of program code have been written for CICS transactions. Many of the programs this represents will be able to run on VSE-based systems. CICS/DOS/VS and CICS/VSE provide almost the same programming facilities as the MVS CICS systems, so most programs written for a VSE system can be retranslated and compiled to run on an MVS system. Similarly, MVS-based programs will usually run on VSE systems after being recompiled. Currently, both CICS/DOS/VS and CICS/VSE continue to support the old macro-level programming commands for compatibility with earlier releases. In this they have more in common with CICS/MVS than with CICS/ESA, which no longer supports macro-level programming.

The main differences between the programming interfaces of CICS/VSE and CICS/MVS are caused by underlying differences in the operating systems. However, the system-programming commands introduced by CICS/ESA have no equivalent in CICS/VSE, and the report controller facilities provided first by CICS/DOS/VS and now by CICS/VSE have no equivalent in the MVS systems.

The other main advantage offered by VSE-based CICSs is that they support the RPGII programming language. Since CICS/VSE began to support VS COBOL II, this is the only difference in the support for languages.

3.4   CICS OS/2

CICS OS/2 is the smallest of the CICS systems provided by IBM, but it makes up for its size by its versatility, as you will see. It was announced in 1988, and has been subject to progressive change since then. With the emergence of CICS OS/2 Version 2, it has become a full-scale transaction processor. This, combined with the growth in use of local area networks, and the availability of suitable business transaction packages, makes CICS OS/2 an excellent entry-level system for business transaction processing. Having begun life as a system used by subsidiaries of large corporations or cooperatives, it is now ideal for smaller enterprises starting out in transaction processing.

CICS on OS/2 has been seen by many as a contradiction in terms. How, they ask, can you sensibly put transaction processing onto a single-user system? Such a question underestimates both the untapped potential of the personal system and the true nature of transaction processing.

The challenge for transaction-processing systems is to provide a way of letting more than one terminal user run the same programs, and use the same data, at the same time, and with full protection against system failure or access contention that could corrupt the data. Traditionally, CICS has provided this by allowing multiple users to share the processing power and data-storage facilities of a mainframe. With CICS OS/2, a small number of users can get a similar service by sharing the power and storage of one or more Personal System/2 machines. In effect, the CICS OS/2 user is creating a powerful centralized system by pooling the distributed power of individual workstations. In contrast, the traditional CICS user used an intrinsically powerful central system to relieve many non-programmable terminals from the need to do complex processing locally.

In addition, individual workstations can engage in client/server sessions with host CICS systems, either directly or through a local area network. The ability to choose where to run parts of a transaction, and where to store parts of the data, gives a designer great flexibility.

CICS OS/2 is a very exciting addition to the CICS family of transaction-processing programs. So far, its power has been fully harnessed by a relatively small number of users. However, this number is likely to grow explosively now that the number of program packages adapted and tested for it is reaching a critical mass. As you can see from the following description, CICS OS/2 is already a full-grown CICS system.

Configurations

CICS OS/2 is a very flexible system, offering several alternative ways of combining system elements to provide a viable transaction processor (Fig. 3.2).

The most sophisticated way of using CICS OS/2 is to use it as a server system on a local area network, thereby providing CICS transaction processing for a number of client workstation operators attached to the LAN. The server machine provides the focal point for sharing resources, and an intermediate node for change control, allowing greater control of software distribution and change. With CICS OS/2 Version 2, multiple-server machines can cooperate across both local area networks and wide area networks to form an expandable multi-user CICS system. At the same time, CICS OS/2 Version 2 can accept existing personal systems as clients. Each client runs a small client program, which can be either stored locally on the personal system or loaded from the LAN server when needed. The client systems on which server programs run can be OS/2, DOS or Windows. Consequently, CICS transactions can be blended into a variety of different workstation 'desktops', driven with familiar icons or menus.

A second way of combining CICS OS/2 system elements is to copy the approach of the host system, using the capabilities of OS/2 to support multiple low-cost ASCII terminals, or diskless personal systems, from a single, powerful PS/2 processor. In effect, this produces a miniature version of a host-based CICS system. Up to eight ASCII terminals can be attached through an ARTIC card in

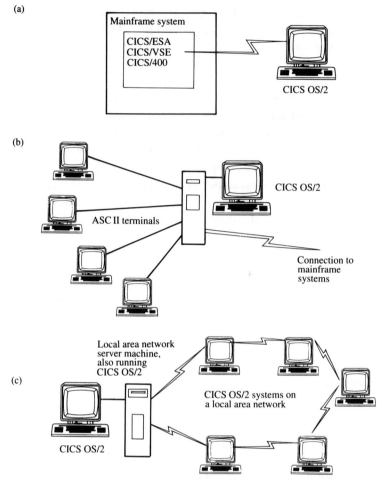

Figure 3.2. CICS OS/2 configurations. (a) Stand-alone CICS OS/2 system, with connection for host services. (b) CICS OS/2 as a server for multiple ASCII terminals. (c) CICS OS/2 systems on a LAN.

the PS/2 processor. Larger models of the IBM PS/2 family of machines can contain five such cards, producing 40-user systems. This gives a low-cost multi-user system for small businesses or remote locations, such as branch offices, workshops or individual retail stores.

A third way of using CICS OS/2 is in the stand-alone mode, as a single-user system. As we have already discussed, this does not at first seem particularly useful as a base for a business solution. However, the original requirement for CICS OS/2 came from a user who needed exactly that. In this mode, many highly-dispersed end-users can achieve high levels of system availability, dealing with the workstation-based CICS when no host connection is available and with the host CICS system at other times. Routine communications ensure that data updates can be exchanged as often as necessary to achieve accuracy and currency. Individual workstation users use traditional CICS programs compiled for the workstation, or can execute host-based programs when the connection is available. This is particularly useful when access to the working data is needed more at outlying sites than at the central site, for example when account data is needed primarily in a branch office and only occasionally for cross-branch or centralized processing. As laptop and notebook computers grow in power, the same model of working applies to a greater number of highly mobile employees. For example, meter-readers for utilities companies now often use hand-held data recorders, which need to be connected twice each day for data exchange.

A stand-alone CICS OS/2 system can also be a useful platform for CICS program development and testing. CICS OS/2 is an effective unit test system; programming errors during testing will not cause expensive loss of test system availability, and will need a system restart on only the failing CICS OS/2 system. The programming interface subset available on CICS OS/2 is sufficient to test most programs.

Regardless of the CICS OS/2 configuration you use, the system can simultaneously be connected, for client/server operation, to CICS/ESA or the other MVS CICS systems, and to CICS/VSE, CICS/DOS/VS, CICS OS/400, CICS/6000 or CICS/VM.

Connectivity

So, CICS OS/2 can communicate with other CICS systems. These can be other CICS OS/2 systems or they can be CICS systems running on an entirely different operating system: MVS, VSE, AIX or OS/400. In almost all cases, communication has to take place using the SNA protocols known as LU6.2, though limited communication can take place if the workstation is connected as a device using the LU2 protocols.

CICS OS/2 systems can communicate among themselves using either LU6.2 protocols or the NetBios protocols of a token ring network.

Data management

CICS OS/2 programs can use EXEC CICS file control commands and EXEC SQL database commands identical to those used in programs designed for the System/370 CICSs. The file control data can be held by the OS/2 system itself, in the form of BTrieve files, which emulate VSAM files. The SQL database access is provided through the OS/2 Database Manager.

CICS OS/2 programs can also be given transparent access to files and databases held on other systems, using CICS intercommunication. You will read more about this in Chapter 9.

Programming support

CICS OS/2 has an EXEC CICS programming interface that provides most of the facilities offered by CICS/ESA. This suggests that programs developed for CICS OS/2 will be readily portable to other platforms, and vice versa. Early experience supports this, with some users porting large amounts of code successfully. In addition, communication with other CICS systems allows it to request other function from them.

CICS OS/2 and CICS/6000 programs have another advantage over their counterparts on other platforms: their ability to use either a graphical user interface or traditional text-based maps to build screen images. This allows program designers to create displays that fit in with the users' normal environment.

Many CICS OS/2 users are still discovering the full potential of the system. Some are developing entirely new transactions, while others are porting existing programs to run on CICS OS/2. Others are using the system mainly as a program development and test environment. Experience so far shows that program development on CICS OS/2 requires only a small learning curve, but can provide large productivity gains.

3.5   CICS/400

CICS/400 is the CICS system designed to run under the OS/400 operating system on all members of IBM's AS/400 family of computers. This family ranges in size from small entry-level systems, which overlap in power the LAN-based OS/2 systems, to large systems that support hundreds of terminal users.

In itself, the AS/400 family of systems provides an impressive growth path for users. However, provision through CICS/400 of the common CICS programming and intercommunication interfaces allows CICS/400 to fit into a broader systems strategy. CICS programs can be shared between CICS/400 and other CICS systems, while CICS intercommunication allows CICS/400 to share processing and data resources of other systems. A user who already uses CICS on other platforms can transfer existing programs relatively cheaply, saving much of the cost of developing them. Ready-made CICS/400-unique and portable CICS family packages from third-party vendors are already being prepared.

The OS/400 operating system already provides integrated transaction-processing capabilities, so you may wonder why you would consider installing CICS too. The main reason is that you can capitalize on your enterprise's existing investment in CICS programs and staff training and experience. As you install easy-to-use departmental or distributed AS/400 systems, you can continue to run established corporate transactions, or vendor packages, without having to recode them from the beginning for the new environment or retrain your staff. At the same time, you gain access to the inventory of packages available from the worldwide community of CICS package vendors. As an existing CICS user you can blend CICS/400 systems into your existing network of systems, using them to support your established business transactions. You do not have to distort existing systems to accommodate the new hardware and software.

If your CICS/400 systems are used in conjunction with an existing System/370 host system, you can use the power of the distributed systems to relieve the host of some of its workload. Looking at it another way, you can use CICS/400 where it is more appropriate, but still be able to link to System/370 or System/390 systems for centrally-provided services such as database support. By using the full range of CICS communications, you can retain flexibility, running programs on the host or CICS/400 according to circumstances.

CICS/400 characteristics

CICS/400 complies with the AS/400 interface standards, so CICS programs can be mixed freely with native OS/400 programs and can be invoked from standard menus. CICS transactions can therefore blend seamlessly with other elements of the system.

From a system-management point of view, administration can be undertaken by either OS/400-trained personnel or CICS-trained systems programmers. CICS/400 provides administration facilities to suit either or both. So you can make the most of your investment in people as well as programs.

The architecture of the CICS/400 system provides considerable application storage protection of a kind not yet available on System/370 or System/390 systems. A CICS/400 system comprises a series of OS/400 jobs (Fig. 3.3(b)). One job is dedicated to running the control region, effectively a system nucleus. The other jobs, one for each terminal user, run transaction programs, controlling both the programs and their immediate environments. As each invocation of a CICS/400 program occupies a different *shell*, it is isolated from both the control region and other programs and their data. Consequently, it is almost impossible for programs to write over each other, over each other's data, or over the system itself.

In a multiprocessor AS/400 system, it is possible for several CICS programs to be running simultaneously, each being a separate AS/400 job.

Connectivity

As with the CICS OS/2 system, you can use CICS/400 or its programs to communicate with other CICS systems, gaining access to remote data or programs owned by CICS/ESA, CICS/MVS, CICS/6000, CICS OS/2 or CICS/VSE (Fig. 3.3(b)).

CICS/400 uses AS/400's ICF to communicate with other CICS systems. This

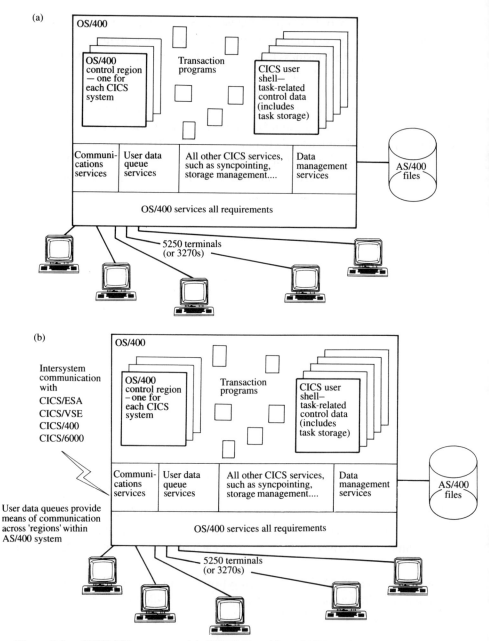

Figure 3.3. CTCS/400 structure. (a) CICS/400 and its AS/400 environment.
(b) CICS/400 intercommunication.

uses LU6.2 communication, a standard communications protocol. It is an established protocol, and should be understood by your CICS and networking specialists. Through the inbuilt intersystem communication, CICS/400 can use transaction routing, function shipping, distributed transaction processing and distributed program link to share its workload with other CICS systems. All of these will be described in more detail in Chapter 9.

Use of intercommunication is concentrated on intersystem communication rather than multiregion operation. The most common traditional reasons for using multiregion operation in the System/370 environment do not apply to CICS/400. In particular, the original 48-bit architecture of the AS/400 family ensures that users do not experience virtual-storage constraint, so do not have to replicate systems to cope with workload. Furthermore, as you saw earlier, the design of CICS/400 ensures that each user's storage is protected from interference by other users, removing the need to run several CICS systems in parallel, another common reason for multiregion operation.

Data management

CICS/400 uses AS/400's file-management and commitment-control facilities to emulate host CICS VSAM file control. This allows your programmers to code CICS file-control requests in the traditional way. They can also code EXEC SQL commands to access SQL databases, just as they can under CICS/ESA or CICS/VSE.

Security facilities

CICS/400 uses the available OS/400 security facilities: password security and control over use of particular functions or access to particular system resources, such as files. In addition, CICS/400 ensures that users communicating between systems, either to or from CICS/400, have access only to those functions or resources to which they are entitled.

Program inventory

Although CICS/400 was announced only in 1992, the existing program inventory, written for System/370 CICS systems, is enormous, and can be converted for CICS/400. Utility programs, such as debugging aids, monitors and statistics programs, are being adapted and developed to run on CICS/400.

Completeness of programming interfaces

The CICS/400 programming interface for the first release is a comprehensive subset of that for CICS/ESA 3.2.1. If you plan to create a system by moving existing CICS programs to CICS/400, you will have to review existing programs to ensure that they comply with the command subset supported by CICS/400. You will also have to review your applications' use of special characteristics of terminals. The AS/400 supports a limited range of terminals, using the IBM 3270 and IBM 5250 datastreams.

3.6   CICS on AIX

IBM has also developed a CICS system for the UNIX environment: a CICS for AIX. Designed for systems based on IBM RISC/System 6000 machines, it has potential for running on other UNIX platforms, both IBM and non-IBM.

CICS/6000, as the first UNIX-based CICS system is known, is a full-function CICS system. It offers most of the functions of CICS/MVS and CICS/VSE. It supports programs written in the COBOL and C languages and containing CICS command-level programming statements. It can communicate with CICS systems on all of the other platforms.

CICS/6000 has a modular structure, with modules communicating by using the DCE-defined remote procedure call. As a result, a single CICS/6000 system can be distributed across a local area network (LAN) of IBM RISC/System 6000 machines, with individual machines acting as specialist servers (Fig. 3.4(b)). This distributed structure allows you to build large, highly expandable systems. You can use a range of processors of different powers within the network, placing the most powerful where they can be most effective. So, for example, relatively low-powered machines can act as 'terminal concentrators', while very powerful processors can act as 'program processors' or 'database servers', handling very high workloads.

CICS/6000 can also run as a single system on a stand-alone IBM RISC/System 6000 machine. In this mode, it can support a network of ASCII terminals and printers, and character-mode X/terminal windows (Fig. 3.4(a)). This suits it well for departmental computing. Its ability to communicate with other CICS systems means that departmental processors can focus on local processing needs, but can be linked to other processors, small or large, for client/server interchanges.

The architecture of CICS/6000 provides another notable benefit, besides that of distributed processing: it gives significant program-storage isolation. Each program task's data is held in private storage, so cannot be overwritten by other programs. In the past such overwriting has been a problem for the highly-dynamic CICS systems, as will be discussed later, in Chapter 5. At the same time, storage containing system-management information is completely inaccessible to programs most of the time, and any access is strictly through system processes. There are areas of shared storage that can be damaged, but these should be in use only when sharing is a recognized design point for a program. As such, the need for control and care over shared resources should be well understood, and storage violation should be almost impossible.

Open CICS

In producing this UNIX version of CICS, IBM has aimed to provide capacity for growth and evolution, compatibility with and ability to communicate with other systems in IBM's CICS family, and consistency of programming interface. In

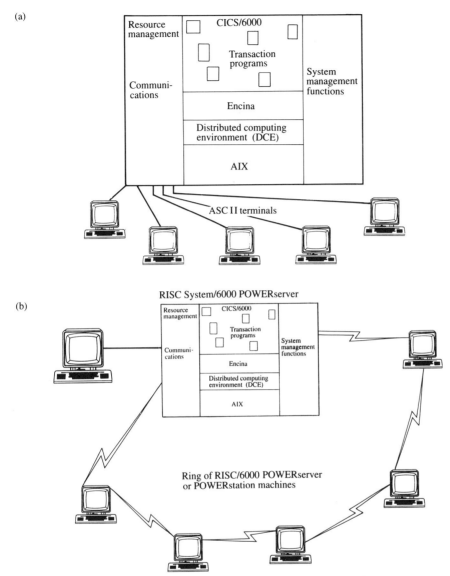

Figure 3.4. CICS/6000 configurations. (a) CICS/6000 and its AIX environment. (b) Token ring.

addition it has used, whenever possible, existing common services of AIX or existing AIX service layers.

CICS/6000 runs on a standard AIX system, and uses the Open Software Foundation's DCE (distributed computing environment) services. In addition, it uses the specialized transaction-processing services layer designed by Transarc, and known as Encina. This provides the special transaction-processing services that do not already appear in the DCE base (Fig. 3.4(a)).

By using the services of existing software layers on top of AIX, IBM ensures that its proprietary CICS software does not have to extend or alter the standard environment. In this way, it ensures that it does not, over time, cause divergence from mainstream AIX (and hence UNIX) development.

Connectivity

CICS/6000 systems can communicate with each other and with CICS systems running on other platforms. CICS/6000 uses TCP/IP protocols to communicate with other CICS/6000 systems. It uses the SNA services of AIX to communicate with CICS/ESA, CICS/MVS, CICS/VSE, CICS OS/2, CICS/400, or with other CICS/6000 systems. In doing so, it uses the LU6.2 protocols of SNA.

Data management

CICS/6000 allows programs to read or update data files, with integrity, using simple programming commands similar to those used in any other CICS system. The file control commands are satisfied by file services simulating those of VSAM on System/370 platforms. The underlying file services are provided by the Structured File Server, which is provided by Encina.

Security facilities

CICS/6000 uses the Open Software Foundation's DCE Security Services to provide authentication, authorization and user account management.

3.7   CICS on non-IBM systems

In 1992, the IBM Corporation and the Hewlett-Packard Company jointly announced new systems, based on CICS, to run on Hewlett-Packard's PA-RISC-based computers. This heralded a new direction for the CICS family, indeed for IBM as a whole: the provision of IBM systems specifically designed to run on non-IBM operating systems.

The Hewlett-Packard systems are designed to run on open-systems computers and workstations. The first announcement promised two products: one to run under the MPE/iX operating system on HP3000 computers, the other to run on the HP-UX operating system on HP9000 machines.

The Hewlett-Packard systems share the CICS/6000 subset of IBM's CICS, including its communications capabilities. Indeed, their emergence owes a lot to the development of CICS/6000. Like CICS/6000, the Hewlett-Packard systems are built for the open-systems environment, as defined by the Open Software Foundation (OSF). They use OSF's distributed computing environment (DCE) and Transarc's Encina.

In June 1993, IBM announced its intention to develop CICS for Windows NT. In its announcement, IBM said that its new CICS offering was expected to reflect CICS OS/2 Version 2, being a client–server offering CICS for Windows NT will be able to work with all other members of the CICS family and will support client systems in the DOS, Microsoft Windows and OS/2 environments.

Provision of the new products shows how readily portable IBM's CICS has become in the open-systems environment, and suggests opportunities for porting to other OSF-compliant environments over time. This portability offers computer users great freedom of choice when designing systems. It enables designers to select from a wider range of hardware and software, confident that application systems will be able to run on any of them.

3.8   CICS systems under VM

IBM first provided a CICS system for VM users in 1987. The system was called CICS/CMS, and was designed to be a simple CICS system for developing and testing CICS programs. Users could code programs and test them under VM's conversational monitoring system (CMS), before recompiling them and migrating them to CICS/OS/VS or CICS/DOS/VS systems for full testing in a production-like environment.

In 1987, IBM announced CICS/VM, a full-scale transaction-processing system for the VM environment. It was designed to provide seamless access to transaction-processing programs from within other programs: a desktop-like system. It was particularly suited to departmental computing, and to the role of business decision support, allowing users to work with PROFS, CICS transactions and other system facilities at the same time. The CICS transactions gave rapid access to shared data in databases or files, and the communication capabilities gave departmental systems access to host-based programs and data.

IBM extended CICS/VM in 1988, when it issued the second release. Among the extensions at that time were program development and testing capabilities, including those previously provided through CICS/CMS. CICS/CMS was thus effectively phased out when CICS/VS Release 2 became available.

Subsequent modifications to the product mostly extended its capacity for communication with other CICS products, particularly CICS OS/2.

Use of the VM-based CICS products has been limited. In many cases, enterprises prefer the System/370 model of CICS transaction processing for business-critical transactions. For smaller distributed systems they preferred to run CICS/DOS/VS. Even within larger systems, they preferred to run CICS/VSE within guest VSE/SP systems under VM/SP. Furthermore, CICS OS/2's emergence (see earlier) has provided an alternative program-development platform and personal-computing environment that is more attractive than the VM option. In particular it offers the same ability to provide a 'desktop' of applications, including CICS business transactions.

IBM announced the withdrawal of CICS/VM and CICS/CMS from the transaction-processing marketplace in September 1992.

3.9   CICS/DPPX

IBM has provided a limited subset of the CICS programming interface for use in programs written to run under DPPX/370. This allows existing System/370 users to make use of existing CICS programming skills to produce simple transactions for DPPX.

CICS/DPPX's value lies in providing a means of developing CICS API-compliant versions of existing programs running on the IBM 8100 system. Many users of this popular (but now old) mid-range system need to migrate to new platforms, but need to find a smooth migration path to a solution with an assured future. Provision of the CICS EXEC interface allows them to convert programs and data to a form that can be migrated to CICS systems on other platforms.

Even as recently as 1992, IBM has continued to extend the capabilities of DPPX/370, providing an intersystem communication capability that makes it possible for CICS systems to share programs and data across a network.

3.10   Summary

The family of CICS products is already large, and promises to grow through the 1990s and into the twenty-first century. With its massive existing program inventory, the CICS family will have instant appeal on a variety of platforms, giving the economies that come with common programs, packages and utilities, and with transferable skills. Already the different CICS products share a broad subset of the CICS programming interface, as you will see in Part II.

Part II
Application programming

4
CICS programs and programmers

IBM's CICS provides the framework for any transaction-processing system you might want to create. It handles the complex control, scheduling and management tasks that are vital to a real-time system. It then provides the programming interfaces that allow you to adapt the system perfectly to your business needs. It enables programmers to design programs that hide system complexity from end-users. At the same time, it protects those programmers from other complexities (Fig. 4.1).

The programming skills needed in the CICS environment are similar to those needed in most other environments. The programming languages are the same: COBOL, PL/I, assembler language, C, RPGII. The need for rigorous specification, design and testing is the same, too. Nevertheless, there are special disciplines and processes that make a CICS transaction designer or programmer special. This chapter and the next two examine the special disciplines and skills.

This chapter looks at the needs of the CICS transaction end-user, and that user's environment, and relates them to the work of the CICS program analyst/designer and programmer. In doing so, it shows why transaction processing places greater demands on the programming team than does conventional processing. It shows what tools CICS provides to help the application programmer to be productive.

4.1 Productivity from CICS services

Whereas batch systems can afford to focus on the needs of hardware or the characteristics of data, online transaction systems have to be designed very carefully to meet the needs of the transaction users. As you will see in this chapter, a transaction-processing system is meant to be a productivity aid and a convenience. If users find transactions either unproductive or inconvenient, the designer has failed, and the value of the system will be diminished.

This has been apparent for years to those responsible for the design and development of CICS systems. It has become similarly apparent in recent years to developers of programs for personal computers and workstations. The windows

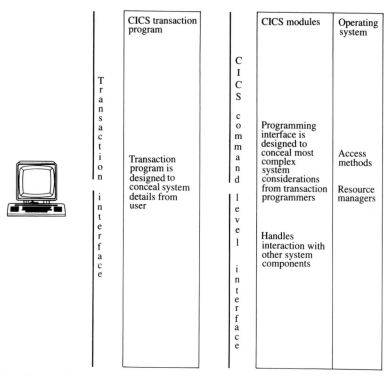

Figure 4.1. Concealing complexity.

technology of today is a graphical equivalent of the mapped screen of the CICS transaction. Other parallels abound: modern workstation programs are often designed to transform the workstation into a platform dedicated to a limited number of programs, concealing system complexities from the user. This is done sometimes by custom-designed front-end interfaces and sometimes by using windows-style or other popular interfaces. For decades, CICS system and application programmers have provided front ends to programs that give each attached terminal the appearance of a dedicated program platform.

4.2   Evolution of the end-user

So, there is nothing very clever or new about designing systems with the end-user in mind. However, 'the end-user' has to be defined, and we need to consider a number of different classes of end-user. It is fair to say that the CICS end-user population has evolved over the years, and is very different from the population of twenty, or even ten, years ago.

The end-user was originally a back-office person, answering telephones, entering customer data, performing customer account queries, entering order information and so on. Such an end-user was often a dedicated terminal operator, maybe simply a data-entry typist with no other responsibilities.

Since those early days, the end-user in the out-of-sight back office has been joined by more visible front-office employees, with transactions that need truly rapid responses, tailored in ways that can satisfy any potential customer need. Typical examples of this occur, for example, in travel agencies and insurance agencies. The operators in such organizations use CICS as a tool to help them in their direct communications with the public. Interaction with CICS forms only a very small part of their responsibilities.

In some industries, for example banking, employees have been bypassed completely for most everyday transactions, with customers communicating directly with transaction-processing systems. The most obvious example of this is the now-commonplace use of bank teller machines.

The next evolution of the user has already started, and promises to be more rapid and varied in outcome than earlier advances. It is driven by user expectations and business competition, but is made possible by advances in communications technology and acceptance of open-systems principles. The transaction-processing end-user of the 1990s expects much greater convenience and flexibility: the ability to carry out transactions at any time; the ability to complete them from home, or the airport, or the car; instant responses. The same users are also less tolerant of seemingly artificial barriers, such as departmental divisions of responsibility or (probably related) the use of multiple, unconnected systems within the same organization. Each business unit within an enterprise is expected to be able to handle queries about the others, or at least to be able to route them quickly and effectively.

The technology exists for CICS users to satisfy these growing customer needs and expectations. Different CICS systems can communicate freely, despite the different systems on which they run. Their programs can therefore be made to appear the same on every platform. At the same time, CICS communication capabilities allow one CICS system to route requests to another without the operator knowing. Furthermore, the front-end programming interface of CICS/ESA allows an enterprise to join together CICS and IMS systems, giving users the impression of a single corporate system.

On top of the CICS system itself, packages such as IBM's CallPath products help to turn the impression of corporate seamlessness into reality. Running on CICS, CallPath directs telephone calls to suitable terminal operators, while simultaneously presenting them with caller-related data from databases or starting transactions in anticipation of enquiries.

4.3 Meeting the needs of end-users

The emergence of new uses for CICS, to meet the needs of new kinds of end-users, makes it more important than ever to research end-user requirements before designing a program. Application programmers are taught to begin design with an understanding of the end-user. In the early days, this used to be a client department, say the sales department or the accounts department. The managers of such a department would raise a requirement for a new transaction system, and a systems analyst would conduct a series of interviews to clarify the details.

The analysts and programmers would then prepare a full specification, probably with prototype code and sample screens. This would give the client department a clearer idea of the concept, and a chance to refine or clarify the requirement, or change or extend it.

Evolving needs

Programming teams usually find that reviews with clients generate significant changes. Many clients do not have a clear idea of their requirements until they have some samples to assess. Even those that thought they had a clear vision can change their minds when confronted with the reality of a prototype. This is especially true of transaction systems, which require logical flow sequences.

A useful follow-on from the review and prototype process is the end-user trial. Despite having already held design reviews with staff from the client department, any systems analyst would be wise to carry out further tests, using typical users of the transaction. Managers and supervisors are not, after all, the people who are going to use the transactions day after day for months at a time.

It is important, though it may seem self-evident, to emphasize that providing online systems will almost certainly change completely the way users do their jobs. Besides the obvious changes that you intended when you decided to commission the system, there will be other changes in work patterns. This in turn will generate new, unexpected demands. It is especially important, therefore, to try to provoke prospective users into anticipating additional needs during the development and review cycle. As with any system development, it becomes progressively more difficult and costly to make radical design changes to real programs as time passes.

Another phenomenon often encountered with real-time programs is that use of a program, if it does its job well, will often exceed expectation. If the program is effective, it will become popular and heavily used. If it saves users effort in doing particular jobs, the users will become more willing to do those jobs. If it makes them more efficient, they may start to do the same job more frequently than before. Suddenly, the historical data on frequency of performance of the job is invalidated. This can be excellent for your business, but may become a nightmare for analysts and designers, who become the victims of their own success. Having failed to predict correctly the dynamics of the workplace, they may be accused of poor capacity planning.

Environmental pressures

In many situations, users of real-time systems need information quickly. They need answers to business questions, seeing the results of transactions but remaining unaware of the underlying programs or systems. They need to get reliable information, to have confidence that updates have been made reliably; they do not want to be left in doubt about the state of the transaction. Some users, for example data-entry personnel who are paid according to the amount of work processed, need to type fast. Other operators, for example those monitoring or controlling a continuous process, need a particularly clear presentation of data. All operators need foolproof handling of errors. We know from experience that terminal operators used to a response within a few seconds will begin repeatedly tapping the ENTER key when the response time rises. An online program should anticipate this sort of behaviour and handle it sympathetically.

When dealing with members of the public, programs have to be particularly foolproof and must inspire confidence. In the early days of bank teller machines, it was instructive to wait in line behind fellow customers using the machines. Despite evident effort by the manufacturers at user-friendly design, the machines confused and frustrated many users. Yet, nowadays, almost all bank customers have come to terms with the technology and would probably accept additional complexity in return for extra services.

The important point with each of these people is that they have no interest in the system or the program. They simply seek the end result of using the machine. Teller-users want money or account information; store assistants want stock data, or prices, or credit authorization. In the more traditional CICS transactions, users want to be able to do their jobs without interruption or confusion. A data-entry operator wants to type without pause and without thinking, getting best productivity to earn the best bonus; office workers need work-related facts and customer data quickly, to keep customers happy; managers need data at their fingertips to help them make decisions; and so the story goes on—warehouse inventory controllers, hospital or hotel registration clerks, police traffic managers. All need to talk to the system as though it is waiting single-mindedly to respond only to their requests.

4.4   User-friendly look and feel

At the user's end of the process, the program designer needs to make best use of all of the facilities of the terminals provided, to give the user the most helpful screens possible. Some users, for example, are paid piece-rate for numbers of keystrokes. These people can type extremely quickly, but resent unnecessary keystrokes, for obvious reasons. Most screens have facilities for faster data entry: autoskip upon filling field, for example. The end-user of this sort of transaction will be helped by autoskip, but only if expecting it, and only if it is used consistently.

Programs have to be designed to have an appearance and 'feel' consistent with the existing user environment (like the modern personal-systems concept of the consistent 'desktop').

4.5   Evolution of transaction processing

The CICS end-user is working in real time, and expects immediate response. Twenty years ago, only data-entry people, programmers and some professionals used computers. To them, the computer teletype offered the fastest means of achieving the results they needed. Response times of seconds or minutes were acceptable, even welcomed, because nothing offered a faster alternative.

In the back office, the computer was competing with the filing cabinet. When it replaced the filing cabinet, it had to offer at least two advantages: faster access to customer records, and access to many more customer records. The end-user perceived only the first of these, and the access-time results had to be good to achieve satisfaction. Only then could the systems be accepted and used properly, so that the second objective could be achieved, allowing massive growth in business.

In the front office, or the service-by-telephone world, the fast response time needs to appear almost instant. If your customers telephone because they want rapid service, you cannot ask them to wait for very long. Queries and responses must appear part of the conversation. In the ideal world, the conversation would flow without any pause. In fact, most organizations currently use technology that makes the reason for pauses appear obvious. The operator usually asks for customer account details, and the caller can usually hear the tapping of keyboard before getting a reply unless there is canned music to conceal the tapping.

In this sort of transaction, you cannot afford to have operators saying 'Sorry, the system has just gone down,' or 'Oh, I seem to have lost your data'. That kind of response is likely to lose business to a more impressive competitor.

When the customer is also the operator, you can afford delays or loss even less. The modern bank teller machine is expected to provide very high levels of service, dispensing money around the clock to very large numbers of customers. The average customer expects easy-to-use systems, rapid response, high availability and accurate counting of money. There is no hot-line to the systems programmer when the transaction goes wrong at the teller machine. Yet the loss of confidence of customers can damage a bank's business: modern customers are more willing than ever before to take their business elsewhere.

Success in all of these transactions depends on good systems analysis and good program design. You also need the good underlying facilities of a transaction-processing system: and as a purpose-made transaction processing system, CICS provides all of them.

Within good program design you need good recovery design. If a transaction goes wrong, or the systems go wrong, or the telephone connection gets cut, you want your end-user to have confidence. You want your telephone operator to be able to answer with confidence when the caller asks whether his order has been accepted or not; you want the teller-machine customer to be confident that the money requested will not suddenly be issued to another customer when the system returns to life.

4.6   Setting expectations

It is worth mentioning in passing one of the lessons often learnt by program designers, and frequently of value in the end-user oriented world of transaction processing.

User perception of a system can be coloured by unreasonable expectations, and these can be fuelled by untypically light workloads early in the life of the system. After manual procedures, a two-second response time can seem miraculous. However, after a month's experience of one-tenth second response times, the same two seconds can seem an age. The wise programmer might find ways of introducing artificial delays into transactions or systems, withdrawing them as the natural load increases. The same 'throttling' action could, contrary to expectation, improve overall user satisfaction by making a system perform as 'badly' during periods of low activity as during the peak periods. This is not to advocate poor service to users when they need better; merely to suggest that you should forestall unwarranted impatience.

4.7   Applications, programs and programmers

A CICS application is just what it says: one particular application, or use, of a CICS. In the same way, a personal-computer application is simply one way of using a personal computer. For example, as I write these words, I am applying my IBM PS/2 notebook computer to word processing; later I may apply it to the task of creating or modifying a data spreadsheet. Each of these applications uses a program that transforms my PS/2 temporarily into a dedicated specialist machine: the first a word-processing machine, the second a sophisticated data-handling and presentation machine. To me (I can be called the application end-user), the PS/2 and its accompanying software temporarily *becomes that application*.

There are countless possible ways of using (applications of) a personal system like the PS/2, and each one can be realized only if you get a programmer to write some special application programs for you. So, by my definition, one or more application programmers worked together to produce the word-processing program that enables me to type this.

In much the same way, a CICS application program is a program (or set of programs) that allows each of tens, hundreds or thousands of end-users at the same time to see an entire multi-million-dollar mainframe computer, and all its peripheral equipment, and its system software (including CICS) as a specialist machine dedicated to a simple task. Such a task will not typically include calculations of the sort performed by a spreadsheet program. Instead, it will usually involve searches for pieces of data, and coordination of changes to one or more of them.

Although I referred to a multi-million-dollar computer, CICS is not limited to such large systems. A CICS system becomes of value as soon as more than a handful of people might want to perform enquiry and updates on the same data at roughly the same time. A CICS system for a small office may run on an OS/2-based network of personal computers or an OS/400 computer. Either can start with only a few terminals, but can expand to meet growing business demands. Other systems will, in years to come, be built from the highly expandable AIX systems, based on low-cost workstations built to conform to an open-systems architecture.

CICS application programs are produced by CICS application programmers, and these people have special skills that have not traditionally been associated with programmers of mainframe batch, or personal-computing, applications. Their skills are made necessary by the nature of transaction processing: the need to give the massively powerful systems the 'look and feel' of personal systems; the shared nature of the environment, both system and data; the unpredictability of real-time use; the importance of protecting extraordinarily valuable corporate data, usually concerning customers.

There is no point in having a transaction-processing system unless you have an application for it, and such an application will be based on one or more specialist programs. You can buy ready-made CICS application programs (just as you can buy spreadsheet programs for your own PS/2), but these will not always match your corporation's exact needs. So you will probably commission some application programs of your own, or get the ready-made ones tailored to your needs. Application analysts or designers will design the programs, and application programmers will 'manufacture' them. So, application programmers are key to the effective use of CICS: vital for your business success. You may employ application analysts, designers or programmers directly. On the other hand, you may subcontract the work to an independent supplier, buying or renting a finished package and related support services. For the purposes of this chapter, we will assume that the programmers work for you, as at least some probably will.

It is worth now looking at application programmers and at their place in the data-processing department. To do their jobs effectively, they have to work closely with other members of your staff, and it can be difficult to separate the individual contributions. Let us look more closely at the application programmer and his or her colleagues.

4.8   The application-development team

We considered the different roles of the application-programming team in Chapter 1. We will now look more closely at the work and roles of these people. We will look at system programmers and others in Part III.

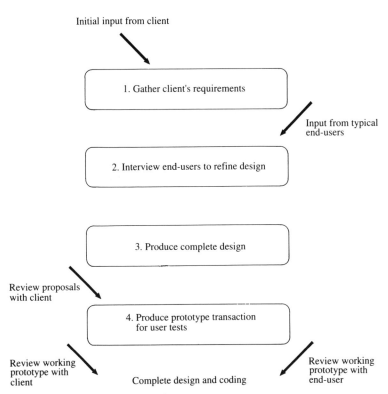

Figure 4.2. Analysing the clients' needs.

Analysts

The word 'analyst' suggests that you consult one of these people whenever you need your head examined. That's not too far from the truth; you call in an application analyst whenever you need advice on a new application. In this case, your time on the 'analyst's couch' is spent explaining your thoughts about business needs, and your visions of how they might be met by a CICS transaction-processing system (Fig. 4.2).

The analyst will dissect your requirements, viewing them in terms of the data that the system will be expected to handle, and the dialogues that it will need to conduct with a typical end-user. Assuming that the system to be built (the application) is a suitable candidate for CICS transaction processing, the analyst will carry out his or her analysis on several different levels, asking a variety of questions.

The first level, and one that the best application-programming teams review continuously, considers the end-user of a proposed system. The analyst needs to understand the end-users, their environments, skills, levels of knowledge, states of mind and many other things. Part of the study of the environment will be the equipment to be used directly by the users: will they use terminals with large or small screens? Cash tills? Teller machines? Printers?

The second level is that of resources and capacity planning. The analyst needs to know the expected level of use of the application. Once a day? Ten times a second? He or she also needs to know what computing power can be applied to the system. Is it to be added to an existing system, or will a new computer be installed to accommodate it? How much money is available?

At a third level, the analyst looks at the data to be processed by the application. Does it already exist? Does it have to be shared with other applications or systems? How valuable is it? How up-to-date must it be?

At a fourth and subsequent levels, the analyst studies the underlying system and the corporate communications networks: availability and skills of programming and operations staff; schedules; and growth predictions.

An analyst for any computer system should consider most of the items at most of these levels. For CICS, and indeed for any sophisticated transaction processor, each level has special considerations. For example, growth predictions can be vital in systems that provide a direct service to customers. A system that begins by giving rapid responses should not be allowed to degrade over time as the volume of transactions grows. Expectations raised early in the life of the service should be maintained, or customers may become disenchanted. You should anticipate early growth and ensure that your systems have capacity for growth. Then, to dampen initial expectations, perhaps dampen system-response time artificially.

The analyst is analogous to an architect, who receives a client's brief, prepares a proposal through consultation, then commissions a building company to carry out the scheme. On a complex project, an analyst will return again and again to clients, end-users and others to review and revise assumptions. Near the end of the process, though, it will be time to engage the services of the application programming team: the builders, using the earlier analogy.

Application programmers

Application programmers combine their detailed knowledge of programming languages and techniques with their CICS knowledge to create programs that meet the analyst's specifications. As you will see throughout the next chapter, having knowledge of CICS means understanding the dynamics and statics of the entire system, not just those of individual application programs.

The programming team designs and codes the programs and associated screen dialogues. It uses special services and facilities provided by CICS to create efficient and viable programs in the very dynamic CICS environment. The special services help programmers to solve the conflicts that are bound to occur when tens or hundreds of users try to use the same programs, the same devices and the same computer storage at roughly the same time. In the next chapter we will look at some of these special services and consider why they are so important. Often, the services are supplied 'invisibly', requiring no specific action by the programmer. However, programmers who understand the environment in which their programs are to operate will certainly be more effective than those that do not.

Programmers who take the trouble to study the way CICS works soon realize that there is a vast difference between the operation of a real-time system and a single-user, personal or batch system. The real-time system seems almost 'alive'. This almost organic nature of a transaction-processing system makes it impossible to predict the exact conditions under which a program will run. Simply recognizing this can be valuable, as it should encourage programmers to appreciate the wider impact of command sequences that they use. In the next chapter we will look at some of the situations in which this appreciation becomes important.

Good application programmers are employed for their language skills, knowledge of techniques and methodologies, and experience. They use these to create elegant and efficient programs. Often they are able to do so because they are freed from the need to understand quirks of the installation process, library structures, job control and so on. Very often, an application-development organization improves the creative environment by providing a team of application-support specialists.

Applications support

In large organizations, application support is usually provided by more experienced CICS application programmers and designers, or perhaps by a separate group of system programmers. Support staff help to improve programming productivity and quality by creating the environment for efficient application development. They set up and maintain useful test systems, enabling application programmers to write and test programs without having to know how to set up and run the underlying systems. The application programmer is thus free to concentrate on the needs of the end-user, the nature of the data to be handled, and the whole range of error situations that could arise in real use.

Applications-support people are typically the first in the application-programming team to see a new release of CICS. They work with the systems-support team to define the test systems needed by the application-programming team. They are first to use the systems, checking that they can create the required application-development environment and run the necessary support programs, for example the compilers, debugging tools, application generators and screen generators. They ensure that the necessary job control exists to allow programmers, for example, access to dump data (for problem resolution) and system startup.

Frequently, applications-support staff are the providers of basic application-programming education, and of additional education on features of new software systems and facilities. They provide a pool of people knowledgeable about both applications and systems matters and also help with debugging, detailed design problems and standards. They provide an interface to the technical-support and system-programming team, which we shall be looking at in Part III.

4.9   Team effort

As I have tried to emphasize, the boundaries between the roles I have described are blurred, and in some cases artificial. There is no reason, except efficiency through specialization, for demarcation. Indeed, in some data-processing organizations, someone will be doing all parts of the job. However, in most organizations, good teamwork will get the best of individual skills: analysts specifying the design and later seeing that applications meet requirements; programmers implementing the design and testing; peer programmers checking conformance to standards; application and system-support people ensuring that an application will not affect the system adversely, either its performance or its resources; operations people ensuring that procedures do not impede efficient operation.

Nevertheless, the true reason for having a transaction-processing system is to run application programs. For this reason, the real deliverers of an end product are the application programmers. It is with them in mind that we will look next at the challenges of programming for a real-time transaction-processing system.

5
Programming for CICS

This chapter describes the challenges set by the coexistence of application programs and the contention between them. It shows how this contention makes design of CICS programs so important. It shows why knowledge of how CICS behaves is important to the development of effective programs, and why cooperation between application programmers and systems-support people is so important.

5.1   Transaction-processing model

To understand the special challenges of programming for transaction-processing programs, we need to look at the model of a typical transaction. First, consider again the user's needs: to look at, and maybe change, a single piece of information within a large collection of data; if changing information, to ensure that all related information also gets updated; to have confidence that the outcome of the transaction is certain—completely successful, or completely unsuccessful, but not half-and-half.

A typical CICS system processes large numbers of transactions every hour of the working day, and the most heavily-used systems regularly handle hundreds of transactions every second, initiated by hundreds or thousands of end-users. So the CICS transaction has to be designed for efficiency, and with special consideration for other users of the system.

A simple CICS enquiry application follows this kind of sequence:

1   First some things that CICS does
    –Receive input from terminal
    –Decide which program should handle it
    –Start the program and give it the input
2   Then things that the application does
    –Check that the data is valid
    –Perform some standard program operations
    –Ask CICS for data from a file or data base

3   Then some things that CICS does
    –Stop the program while getting the data
    –Start another operator's program or relinquish system control to other
     subsystems
    –Get the requested data, restart the application program and pass the data to it
4   Then some more things that the application does
    –Do some more standard operations
    –Send some results to the terminal
    –End
5   Then some things CICS does
    –Pass the results to the terminal for display
    –Remember to watch for more input from the terminal
    –Handle other tasks elsewhere in the system.

This is a somewhat simplified account, as CICS processing involves many more
subprocesses than are identified here. However, it shows that CICS operation and
application execution are totally interwoven. As you can see, CICS is involved
repeatedly throughout the lifetime of the task. Steps 1, 3 and 5 involve CICS. The
program itself is actually running only through steps 2 and 4. In fact, the time that
CICS itself spends running is actually quite small. As soon as it receives a request
for services from the application program, it passes it on to another system that
will satisfy the request (the operating system or database manager, say), then
triggers another task or, if no other task is ready, lets another subsystem fill in the
time between activities.

    In a typical program, steps 2 and 3 would be repeated several times. For each
step 3, the program would go into 'suspended animation' while CICS did some
work on its behalf. Such work need not involve getting data; sometimes it would
be providing some other service, such as finding extra storage for the program to
use to manipulate its data.

    At first sight, it seems that this disjointed progress must be very inefficient and
inelegant. In fact, it works splendidly, as long as programmers cooperate. It is the
key to CICS's effectiveness. A transaction-processing system depends on a good
'community spirit', with each program taking only its share of available time, then
making room for someone else. CICS's underlying design makes it easy for a
program to cooperate, as the program has to go through CICS to get either data or
the use of resources. In doing so, it must suspend activity so that CICS can let
other programs run.

    It is possible to subvert the system by designing programs ill-suited to the CICS
environment. For example, the uninitiated programmer could design a program
that performed extensive calculations, often referred to as 'compute-intensive'.
Such a program would remain running, self-sufficient, for a long time, monopoliz-
ing the processor power, before pausing for input or output. If used significantly in
a production system, its presence would soon be noticed, as the service to users of

other programs would deteriorate. However, before detection, such an application could have an impact on the service to your business. For this sort of reason, skilled application programmers are key to successful transaction-processing design. As nobody is infallible and computer systems are unforgiving, the skilled programmers need the reassurance of support through code inspections.

5.2   The EXEC CICS programming language

As we have seen, CICS coordinates and rations application programs' use of system resources, and appears to the operating system as a single, albeit rather large and busy, application. It can only do this if programs follow the rules of CICS programming, asking CICS for resources and services, not bypassing it to ask for them from the operating system or other subsystems. CICS helps programmers by offering special programming commands, each starting 'EXEC CICS'. Programmers have to use these instead of certain native language commands. So, for example, the command

```
EXEC CICS READ FILE('ACCDATA') INTO(ACCOUNT) END-EXEC
```

might be used by a COBOL program to read a file record. No other file-access commands should be used instead, as they would bypass CICS control and introduce a chance of contention with other programs.

Other commands allow programs to write to files or to send and receive communication data to and from terminals, for example.

Your application programmers have to learn which programming commands are provided by CICS, and which native language commands are replaced and should not be used in CICS programs. They then need to learn the best ways of using the new commands in the new environment. The new CICS/400 and CICS/6000 systems can accept a wider range of the normal commands of the environment, but programmers still need to understand any limitations.

In addition, they need to learn the concept of command translation. They will be used to the idea of compiling program: translation is a similar process that has to precede compilation. In it, the EXEC CICS commands are turned into native language statements that can be compiled along with the rest of the program.

5.3   The good citizen

The use of special commands and the need to translate them before compilation has a useful side-effect. It makes it clear to programmers that programming for CICS is not exactly the same as programming for single-user or batch environments. It should help to remind them of the effects their programs' actions have on other programs. We have seen one example of an effect—the monopolization of the system. Other effects need equally careful attention.

As well as understanding the mechanics of programming languages, CICS commands, translation and compilation, good CICS programmers understand the environment (which we looked at in Part I), end-users, and the typical life cycle of a transaction. The latter is particularly useful when learning about CICS programming for the first time, as it helps to explain some of the new rules of programming needed in the CICS environment. Knowledge of CICS processing and environment can undoubtedly help programmers to produce efficient and reliable programs. Let us see why.

5.4   Life cycle of a transaction

The following is a rather simplistic sketch of the life cycle of a CICS task. Its purpose is not to teach you how CICS works, but to provide a framework of concepts within which you can understand what follows. You should not try to remember the details, as there are better places to read about them. Instead, concentrate on the 'task' nature of the process, note its complexity and try to recognize the implications of there being hundreds of similar processes taking place at one time.

A CICS task starts when an end-user at a terminal sends some input data, including the name of a transaction to be performed. Figure 5.1(a) shows CICS at the instant the data arrives from Terminal T. For clarity, CICS is shown as empty, though of course it would probably already be handling many other tasks.

Figure 5.1(b) shows CICS activity building up during the lifetime of the transaction.

Until the arrival of the message from the terminal, the only evidence of the terminal and its end-user is some identification data held in internal CICS tables. These are enough to provide a link between the terminal and a transaction when it starts to run, but occupy very little storage. As the data arrives, it is stored by CICS (1), which also records on a CICS pending work queue (2) that there is some work to be done on behalf of Terminal T.

Milliseconds later, CICS reaches T's entry in the work queue, and starts to tackle the task. CICS assigns the task some storage (3), and moves the input data to working storage (4) and loads an application program (5) to start processing it. As the program requests customer data, CICS gets a data manager program (DFP in this case) to supply it. When the data has appeared in storage, ready for use, CICS provides access to it, creating either a file area or pointer area (6) in the process. If the program requests other data, CICS contacts DFP again, or perhaps a database manager such as DB2, and creates similar storage areas. The program is free to work, through CICS, on its copy of the data, updating it if necessary.

In processing, the program produces its own working data, for which it needs space. Some of this is already available as preassigned working storage (3). Other

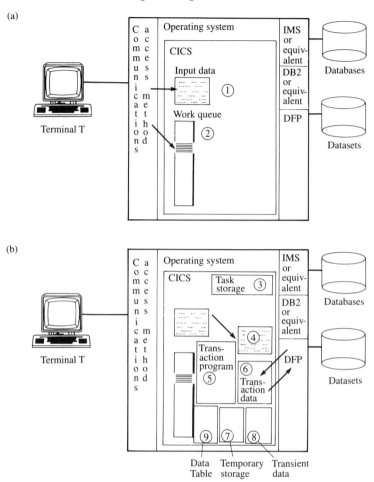

Figure 5.1. The life cycle of a transaction. (a) No task-owned storage or programs exist in the system when terminal input is first received. (b) Programs and data are loaded and storage is acquired throughout the life of the task.

space can be obtained from CICS by asking directly for some main storage, or by asking CICS to put data into temporary storage (7), transient data storage (8) or Data Tables (9).

When the program has finished any processing, it places results and any other necessary information into an output data area, and asks CICS to send it to the terminal, using the services of the VTAM subsystem. It then terminates, leaving CICS to send any updated data back to DFP (or the database manager) to be recorded permanently. Not only does CICS handle the communication of data to both the terminal and the data managers, it also clears up the debris: storage areas, queues and other data areas. At the end of the process, only the data files and databases bear lasting witness to the passage of the task.

As shown by this brief, simplified and deliberately incomplete description, the

CICS environment is very dynamic, even when all tasks except one are hidden from view. Even in the largest computers resources are limited, so are shared between transactions wherever possible. Among the most valuable of resources is computer storage, which as you can see is acquired and released throughout the life of a transaction, being reallocated to other transactions as needed.

5.5   Sharing space

In the CICS environment, where it is possible for hundreds of users to be using the same application program at the same time, you cannot allow everyone to have their own copies of the program. A sophisticated application program can use hundreds of thousands of bytes of storage. If hundreds of users need the application at peak times, the programs alone begin to fill the system storage, and the system is soon spending most of its time finding room to run them, one by one. In between, it has to store them on disk, then restore them.

CICS's solution is to allow all of the tasks that need to use a particular program to share the same copy of that program, but without leaving traces of former occupancy when leaving the program for the next user.[1] To permit normal data handling by every user of the transaction, CICS provides every CICS task with its own storage areas for data, linking the areas to the terminal that started the task. In this way, CICS ensures that each application program addresses only the storage belonging to the task that is being processed at any time.

This has significant implications for the application designer. If used to normal batch programming, he or she will have to learn to do what is known as reentrant programming, learning not to use batch programming language storage declarations. Any working storage needs to be saved by CICS when the user's task is not using it, to be restored later. CICS will keep track of, and protect the contents of, such storage until a program releases it, either explicitly with a program command or implicitly when the program ends. It is therefore relatively easy to produce reentrant programs that can be executed by one or more CICS transactions, forming part of thousands of tasks. Each task and its data will be isolated from other CICS tasks, unless your programmers request otherwise.

5.6   Breaking the isolation

Quite often, analysts or programmers decide that an application will be most effective if it is broken into a series of related transactions. In such a situation, the carefully-provided isolation of one task from another becomes a disadvantage. However, all is not lost: CICS offers yet more facilities designed to get around this problem. Your programming staff need to know about these facilities, which will not have been necessary in single-user systems. They will use each of the facilities in a different situation. We shall look at some of the situations very briefly here, as they illustrate the fascinating range of new challenges in the real-time environment.

First, consider the commonly-encountered situation where one program needs to process data, leaving the results to be processed further by another program. For this situation, CICS provides storage areas called *transaction work areas*, and communication areas called *COMMAREAs*. Each kind of area can be made available to each system task, so is exclusive to that task. Each is invaluable in different circumstances. Your programmers need to learn when to use each kind. They then need to learn when to use another facility instead: *temporary storage*. This is CICS-managed storage that is available for use as a 'scratchpad'. Data placed in this storage can later be retrieved or updated, in any order, by the same program or a different one. If the data is particularly vital, it can be placed on disk instead of in main storage. The same effect can also be achieved, under CICS/ESA and CICS/VSE, using *Data Tables*.

The storage areas for temporary storage are usually referred to as 'queues', because data items are placed in a queue, awaiting processing. However, temporary storage queues and Data Tables are often treated like easy-to-access files. Another CICS facility, *transient data*, is always handled like a queue. Data items sent to a transient-data queue can be retrieved later, one by one, but only sequentially, not randomly. Retrieval of a transient-data entry causes it to be erased, so the queue cannot be viewed as a file in the same way as a temporary storage queue. However, it is ideal for such uses as accumulating lines of data for printing.

The point of describing these facilities is to show you how many choices there are to be made in a real-time system, even for as simple a matter as storing program data. CICS provides the facilities needed to meet any likely situation: your programming staff need to understand the underlying real-time programming concepts before they can make the best design judgements.

5.7   Sharing resources

Another consequence of sharing the same systems, resources and execution time with other transactions is that you have to make sure you do not create problems working on the same pieces of data at the same time. CICS does a lot to prevent problems, but programmers still need to be aware of dangers. In the earlier description of the life cycle of a transaction, data access looked very simple: the program asked CICS for some data, updated it and expected CICS to return it to DFP at the end. Behind the scenes, CICS and DFP will have locked the data to prevent simultaneous access by other programs, releasing the lock only when the task ended. The program gets this protection automatically, even if the programmer is unaware of it. However, to be effective programmers should know something of the underlying process. In more complex situations, ignorance can create problems.

Take, for example, two end-users who start to perform the same transaction at the same time. Each user has set CICS a separate task, consisting of the execution of the same CICS program. This program starts by updating FILE1, then goes on to update FILE2. One of the tasks will be delayed, as the other will have accessed FILE1 first (and hence temporarily prevented access to it by other programs). It will have to wait and try again later, when it too can access first FILE1, then FILE2. The need to wait may delay response to the end-user by a few milliseconds, but is not a problem.

However, two slightly different programs could create a serious problem. Suppose that the same two end-users started to perform two different transactions, so that their CICS tasks involve execution of different programs, but still at the same time. In this case, the first program starts by accessing FILE1, then goes on to open FILE 2. Meanwhile, the second program starts by accessing FILE2 before FILE1. Each program will find its second file locked, so will wait a while before trying again. If both programs are designed to keep retrying indefinitely until the held file is released for use, they will remain locked indefinitely. Such a *deadly embrace* or *deadlock* can be anticipated and avoided by programmers who understand the CICS processes rather than taking them for granted.

The deadly embrace is probably best avoided by installation conventions governing file-opening sequences, methods of handling file_busy situations, and so on. However, other resource-sharing problems can be equally serious but are best solved by educating programmers and conducting code inspections. For example, programs should not be allowed to hold files indefinitely while awaiting operator input. They should be designed to cope with the possibility of a ridiculous delay, say when an operator takes a lunch break midway through a transaction. CICS itself can cancel transactions after an interval, but that may be unacceptably long for others waiting for locked files.

These are just two examples of responsibilities of programmers in a shared real-time environment.

Cleaning up

It has to be emphasized that one of the truly indispensable functions of CICS is the translucent way that it handles the contention for resources between different users and the programs that serve them. It is worth looking briefly at the sorts of things that the system provides.

Note my use of the word 'translucent' rather than 'transparent'. A theme of this part of the book is that your CICS application programmers are a special breed of programmers. Theoretically, they are provided with an *almost* transparent programming interface that turns *almost* ordinary programs into real-time applications. However, if they treat the interface as truly transparent, and do not understand the underlying processes, your systems will work inefficiently and may suffer damaging failures. Knowledge of the basic system processes makes all the difference.

We have seen that CICS will get storage in which to run programs, to hold file data that programs read, to hold programs or screen data, or to provide programs with working 'scratchpads'. It will also release for other use any such storage when a program has finished with it. In the same way, it will release other shared resources when programs finish with them: files that a program has finished reading; communication links that are no longer in use.

The simplest way of getting these resources released is to end the program: on detecting the end of a program, CICS 'cleans up' after it, releasing all borrowed system resources. However, as explained earlier, in a really busy system even this may hold up other users. So CICS programmers learn to be even more frugal with resources, and are offered a way of forcing premature clean-up, part-way through programs. The process is known as 'taking a syncpoint'. By issuing a SYNC-POINT command, a program tells the system to synchronize all changes it has made to the data resources, confirming that they are to be made irrevocable; in other words 'committed'. After this, files and database records can be updated fully, closed and released, even though the program continues to do other work. In CICS parlance, a piece of work that can be isolated from others and committed in this way is called a 'logical unit of work'.

In the same way, a program can explicitly release main storage that it has been using by issuing a FREEMAIN command to the system.

Working in bursts

Of course, the programmer might choose to end the program rather than synchronize everything. Any further processing could then be performed sub-sequently by another program. This would have the advantage of making the program conform more closely to the model of the 'ideal' CICS application: short and concise. However, this would normally give a sequence of operations a very disjointed feel, disturbing application end-users. So CICS offers additional facilities, allowing programmers to perform what is known as 'pseudoconversa-tional' programming. With this technique, a terminal user is able to see a series of programs as though they were a single continuous program. Each program ends with a screen that collects operator input that will start the next one. The system 'remembers' which program to run next to handle the input. So the only detectable delay between programs is due to the operator thinking or typing.

The advantages of this approach are obvious. The system does not have to keep the task's storage during the time it is waiting for input. And if no-one else needs the program, that can be overlaid and its storage reused. Yet the operator is unaware that the program has ended. The operator-to-system communication can continue like a conversation. Technically, it is not quite a true conversation—hence the name.

Programmers designing pseudoconversational programs need to take more care with the design of the 'pieces' of the conversation. If data needs to flow from piece to piece, there has to be a way of passing it. There are several ways of doing this, and the programmer needs to choose the best; all the time, of course, remembering that the program may be used by hundreds of operators at the same time.

5.8   Recovering programs from catastrophe

This mention of the hundreds of users brings me back to the reason why in real-time systems good application programming is so very important. Just as hundreds of users can update the same file every few seconds, they can together do an enormous amount of damage, or lose an enormous amount of input, if anything goes seriously wrong. For this reason, application programmers in the CICS environment are protected by the underlying system from the most basic consequences of failures. In addition, they are offered optional services that can be invoked from within application programs, and others that can be provided by the systems-support team.

We have already looked at the way SYNCPOINTs get the system to confirm all changes so far made by a program. Until this command is issued by a program, all of the changes it makes to system resources (for example, files) are conditional on its successful execution. If the program fails to complete, for any reason, all of the changes it made will be cancelled, and it will be as though it had never existed. This process is known as 'backout'. It is provided without the application programmer having to do anything. However, the systems-support people need to do quite a lot behind the scenes to make it work, as you will see in the next part of the book.

Although application programmers do not have to do anything to make this recovery work, it makes sense for them to know about it. The dialogue seen by users of a CICS application needs to leave the users in no doubt as to the result of their transactions. If backout has occurred, then a user needs to know that the transaction needs to be entered again. If parts of the transaction have been committed because they formed a logical unit of work, they must not be entered again. This, therefore, is another case of the facilities being translucent rather than transparent, demanding careful design.

Designers have to produce transactions in a way that makes it safe for any step to go wrong. They should plan what happens to both customer data (from a file or database) and communications data (messages that were on the wire at the time of failure) in the event of failure. All failures should be fail-safe, with predefined recovery procedures. Part of the initial application brief should consider how critical the data is that the application is going to handle. It should make sure that the systems can afford the recovery processes you design. Application designers have to work with the system-support team to get the right capabilities 'switched on' in the basic system when the application is commissioned. They also have to make sure that the operations staff know the application's requirements too, as they may need to refine their processes to handle the operations of any recovery that is needed for the application.

5.9   Data management

In the last section, we viewed data almost as a liability rather than an asset: what happens if things go wrong, and how it is recovered. Most of the time, however, data comes and goes exactly as requested by CICS programs, needing no recovery or operator intervention. All the same, it still needs special thought by the programmer.

File access

CICS allows programs to handle data from a variety of sources. It has always provided access to ordinary files, and continues to do so through the VSAM access method for CICS/ESA and CICS/VSE. On other CICS systems, such as CICS/6000, CICS/400 or CICS OS/2, CICS emulates VSAM file handling, though uses available native file systems. In each case, the result of the emulation is that application programmers are able to code the same program statements to achieve the same results. So, a statement such as

```
EXEC CICS READ FILE(cust_data) INTO TABLE1 END-EXEC.
```

will have the same effect on each CICS system, and should give the same responses on each if things do not go as expected.

Database access

As well as giving access to files, the CICS programming interface allows simple access to sophisticated database systems. On the mainframe systems, programs can contain commands for accessing hierarchical database-management systems: IMS on MVS systems and DOS DL/I on VSE systems. CICS programs use EXEC DLI commands to access these databases, the commands having something in common with both the EXEC CICS commands and the DL/I data language. For example:

```
EXEC DLI GU SEGMENT(STUDENT) INTO(CLASSLIST)
        WHERE(SUBJECT=MATHS) END-EXEC.
```

Alternatively, programs can contain CALL commands. This older CICS programming interface provides access to a more complete set of DL/I function. However, the EXEC language is simpler to understand and is similar in appearance to the EXEC CICS language. It can also use valuable CICS debugging facilities, EDF and trace, which we will look at again later. A program can contain CALL commands as well as EXEC commands, but there are rules about how and when they can be mixed. The CICS programmers need to understand the rules to be able to write effective programs.

On both mainframe systems and smaller systems, CICS programs can issue EXEC SQL commands to gain access to SQL relational databases. On the largest MVS systems, the SQL requests are serviced by Database 2 (DB2); on VSE systems, by SQL/DS. CICS/400 application programs can use AS/400 SQL, and CICS OS/2 programs can use SQL through the OS/2 Database Manager. CICS/6000 can work with a number of relational database products that conform to the X/Open XA interface.

Once again, the CICS database commands look like both CICS commands and SQL language commands. For example:

```
EXEC SQL
    SELECT CUSTNO, CUSTNAME, TELNO
      FROM ENGLAND.CUS
        WHERE COUNTY='HANTS'
          END-EXEC.
```

EXEC SQL requests in CICS commands can read or modify data, define database objects (such as entire databases or tables within databases), or change what individual users are authorized to do with the database.

Available in all languages

All of these file and database access commands can be imbedded in application programs written in commonly used programming languages such as COBOL or C. The commands continue with standard data-access keywords, so require little special learning for those experienced in use of files or databases.

The special skills needed with data remain those that I have described earlier in this chapter: designing programs to handle data in a socially responsible way—not interlocking many files and databases during long periods of processing or conversation; anticipating problems that could arise in the event of failure.

In addition, there are many minor pieces of knowledge that are essential for good programming. For example, programmers should know that reading data prior to updating it is more costly than simply reading it. Lazy or uninformed use of the wrong kind of reading operation will get the right results, but will waste processor time, sometimes proving very expensive.

5.10   Storage violations

As you have seen, CICS works within the operating system to provide a specialized transaction-processing element. In doing so, it manages an address space on behalf of many application tasks. It loads and executes them within the space it is assigned, but does not police their use of the space, so badly designed and tested programs can cause havoc. Programmers have to be disciplined to design and test programs fully. In particular, they need to check parts of programs designed to follow repetitive processes, gradually stepping through storage, making changes. The stepping process needs to stop when data runs out, or it will overwrite other data or executable code. Similarly, programmers need to check pieces of code that load or move data, ensuring that there is room at the target location for all the data to be moved, without overwriting other data.

Badly designed programs have always been able to write all over parts of storage controlled by CICS, including storage occupied by parts of CICS itself. This has meant that other programs and their data, and CICS and its data, are open to corruption. Such corruption is usually readily detectable, recognized as a 'storage violation', but is often difficult, time-consuming and expensive to diagnose. It can also be difficult and expensive to correct, as the time between the occurrence of a storage violation and its discovery may be enough to allow new transactions to start and complete, processing suspect data.

Every time you discover a rogue program damaging storage, you must wonder whether it has previously caused damage without detection. If so, what did it affect? Application storage? If so, why didn't another application fail? Did the affected code get executed? If so, what did it do? Did data get overwritten? If so, what data? Was it subsequently stored? Or reaccessed? Have you corrupted someone's data undetected?

Preventive medicine

The incidence of storage violations has reduced since the introduction of the command-level programming interface. This and the use of high-level programming languages such as COBOL, rather than assembler language, has reduced the use of high-risk programming techniques. Nevertheless, storage violations are still an occasional cause of CICS problems.[2]

CICS/ESA introduced changes that protect the system itself from violation. Its internal control blocks have been relocated as part of the product's restructure, and are less likely to be overwritten by rogue programs. In addition, Releases 3.3 onwards of CICS/ESA use the MVS/ESA subsystem storage protection capability that can stop programs from altering CICS's storage areas or code. You can switch this protection off for selected programs—but at your own risk.

CICS/ESA therefore protects itself from damage, if you let it. Even if you decide not to use the protection in production systems, it can prove useful in test systems as it will terminate rogue programs. Early users of the facility found a number of previously undetected faults in their existing inventories of programs by this means—the programs terminated on their first execution with protection switched on.

This again highlights a key message for CICS users: CICS programming is special. If a production program unexpectedly accesses system storage, you need to look again at its design and at your coding standards and inspection procedures. Many CICS users almost never experience storage violations, because they have instituted programming standards that prevent the kinds of errors that cause them. At the same time, they impose program design inspections, coding inspections and rigorous testing procedures before accepting programs for production use. Your application-programming staff should be performing checks for storage violations as part of their standard design and code inspections. They should review all program indexing code, and all data sizes and limits. All programs should be subject to inspections and tests, but the online programs for any transaction-programming system, including CICS, need special review against the background of the dynamic environment, rather than the normal static design environment.

First, though, make your programmers aware of the special nature of the CICS environment, so that they can proceed with caution. This brings us to the model process, in the next section.

5.11   Teamwork and process

You will now understand many of the special considerations for those programming for a CICS transaction-processing system. You should begin to understand the reasons why CICS application programmers are often in demand. You should also understand why application programmers function best as part of an overall CICS team, rather than as isolated individuals. The stages of application design require teamwork between the programmers, analysts, application designers, peer programmers, systems specialists and application users. The standard sequence of events (design, inspect, unit test, code inspect, system test, education and training, production) will be augmented in the best-run organizations by regular peer reviews, and by ongoing support of the application-programming staff by other team members.

Teamwork for the programmer

The application-programming team needs to work closely with a variety of other members of the data-processing organization in your enterprise. The section on storage violation should serve as a reminder of how they can benefit from critical inspection of their code. However, even without these interactions, they have many calls on the other team members.

The application-programming team depends upon the teams supplying and supporting the operating systems and communications software. They also depend on database administrators for support of existing databases or provision of new ones in support of new applications. And when the databases and applications exist, they need security administrators (such as the administrators defined for IBM's RACF security package) to provide security controls—both access for authorized users and protection from unauthorized users.

Most of all, though, the CICS application-programming team depends on the CICS systems-programming team: the systems-support people. These will be the subject of the next section of the book.

5.12   Summary

To do their jobs properly, CICS programmers need special insight into the working of the CICS system and the dynamics of the multi-user real-time environment. CICS provides many tools and facilities to make this easier, and it is aided by complementary products of both IBM and other vendors. We will look at some of them in the next chapter before we go on to look at the systems-support team.

Notes

[1] In the earlier description of the life cycle of a transaction, CICS might not have had to load the program to process the input data. It might already have been loaded for use by another task.

[2] Note that the architectures of CICS OS/2, CICS/400 and CICS/6000 practically eliminate storage violations in those systems.

6
CICS application services

Now that we have considered the skills and knowledge that the CICS programmer brings to real-time transaction processing, we shall look at the services and support that CICS provides. Most of the programming challenges described in Chapter 5 are addressed by CICS, through the application-programming interface and related utility programs. The programmer's responsibility is to understand and use what CICS provides. As you will see from this chapter, there is a lot to learn.

6.1 Mapping needs to facilities

CICS is designed to allow your team of programmers to concentrate on developing good transaction programs, focusing on business logic and usability rather than the complexities of the multi-user environment. The application programs that tailor the system to your business needs are written in the languages that are most widely taught to commercial programmers: COBOL, C and PL/I. Assembler-language programs also work, if you have programmers who enjoy writing them, or if you have inherited a lot of existing programs. As a result, it should be possible for you to recruit partly-trained programmers with relative ease.

I use the qualifier 'partly' because, as we saw in the last chapter, CICS programmers need additional skills. As well as having access to normal programming-language facilities, your application-design and programming team has the use of special CICS application-programming commands. These enable the programmer to overcome many of the challenges described in Chapter 5, in the process developing good real-time programs.

The CICS programming commands are straightforward enough to have immediate meaning for the programmer, but different enough for anyone coding them to need to use them carefully. The skilled programmer who is new to CICS needs to learn when to use CICS commands instead of familiar native-language commands. He or she then needs to know which CICS commands correspond to which standard language verbs.

As explained earlier, CICS commands are generally substituted whenever the native language would have requested services from the operating system, or from another subsystem (for example a file manager) by way of the operating system.

This means that the kinds of services requested are:

- File access
- Database access
- Communication with terminals and printers
- Other communication (across systems)
- Storage acquisition
- Queue management
- Program loading and invocation
- Task initiation.

In addition, as we will discuss later, there is a wide range of commands that allow very precise control of system functions, such as system startup or logging of changed data to enable recovery from catastrophic failures or errors. Although these commands are part of the application-programming interface, they are not usually considered appropriate or necessary for everyday programming. They are therefore covered in the system-support section of this book.

To summarize: CICS aims to make it possible to achieve any programming effect in the multi-user transaction-processing environment. Any effect should, preferably, be achieved through the standard programming language (such as COBOL), but whenever a request could result in contention for resources a CICS command is used so that CICS can act as resource scheduler, workload manager and communication director.

6.2   Language products

Language products, such as COBOL or C, are best at providing business-related programming languages and their associated compilers. They have the advantage of being widely taught, ensuring that you have access to a pool of skilled programmers. They also have the stability and portability that comes with compliance with internationally-accepted open standards. CICS does not try to replace them, but complements them by providing special processing commands for the transaction-processing environment.

These commands do not subvert or modify the standard languages. Instead they are typed into the program source as though part of the language, eventually being replaced by standard language sequences before the whole program is compiled and link-edited ready for execution.

CICS provides a translator that turns the coded CICS commands into instruction sequences written in the language of choice. Your programmers run the translator program, then pass the file containing the translated program to a compiler in the normal way. Normally, your system-support team will have written procedures to perform these steps, link-editing the resulting output automatically, so application programmers need not observe the separate processes. They will probably know about the processes, though, as each will produce a report, including error or warning messages if the code seems to contain errors. The translator produces messages that can provide the first layer of defence against program design flaws. Later we will look at other layers in the defence.

6.3   Screens—BMS

One of the first concepts a new CICS programmer will learn is that of basic mapping support, known by its acronym BMS. This is the CICS solution to the problem of how to manage the contents of terminal screen displays. BMS has been around as long as CICS itself, and is still, for many users, the favoured method of defining screens—because it works. At first, it seems complicated, as it involves assembler-language concepts of macros and assembly. However, it provides a reliable and effective mechanism that is easily incorporated in standard procedures. As with many programming processes, it is a natural candidate for the 'reuse' approach to programming: new BMS maps can be created by copying existing ones, modifying them and saving them.

Once the concepts of BMS are understood, maps become one of the most straightforward aspects of CICS programming. They are almost static elements, needing some ergonomic or aesthetic design, but none of the complex real-time analysis.

With the advent of programmable workstations and graphical display techniques, there are now alternatives to the text-based basic mapping support. This is discussed under 'Mapping and programmable terminals', later in this chapter.

Mapping

The need for mapping was recognized early in the life of CICS. CICS was among the first of the programs that needed to communicate using whole screens of data, rather than single lines of teletype text. The principles of CICS mapping are quite easy to understand, as Fig. 6.1 illustrates and the following text explains.

First, it is worth noting the problems solved by mapping. The first is one of variety: data-processing departments are rarely equipped with only one terminal model, and probably buy new models as they emerge. So a programmer can never be sure of the range of screen sizes and shapes that will be used with a particular program. The second problem is that of tedium and cost: any programmer can be trained to build and transmit data streams to control a terminal, but it is inefficient and costly. Mapping saves programmers from having to know in advance what terminals their programs will communicate with. It also saves them from having to devise complex program routines for building data streams for each kind of terminal to be supported.

(a)

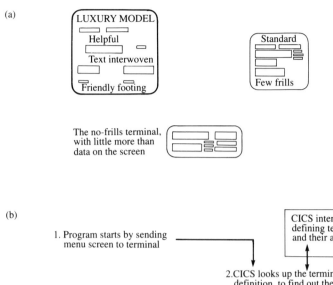

The no-frills terminal, with little more than data on the screen

(b)

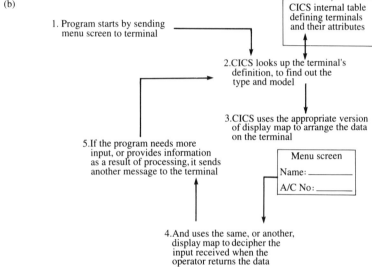

1. Program starts by sending menu screen to terminal

CICS internal table defining terminals and their attributes

2. CICS looks up the terminal's definition, to find out the type and model

3. CICS uses the appropriate version of display map to arrange the data on the terminal

5. If the program needs more input, or provides information as a result of processing, it sends another message to the terminal

Menu screen

Name: _____

A/C No: _____

4. And uses the same, or another, display map to decipher the input received when the operator returns the data

Figure 6.1. Mapping data to different screens. (a) A variety of maps to enable data to fit each available terminal. (b) CICS works out how to display data for a given terminal.

However, programmers do need to understand the concepts of communication with display terminals, and to know something of the way CICS relates input and output requests to fields on the screen, through mapping. This section briefly shows you what is involved.

Maps and fields

A screen on a text terminal, of the sort traditionally used for CICS applications, consists of a matrix of character positions. Internally, an application program holds a 'map' of the screen, so that it can write to, or read from, any character position. The map is written as a series of data statements, just like any other data held by a program. The map makes it possible for a program to associate meaningful names (such as account_name) with fields of data on the screen, so that program commands can refer to pieces of data by name. A different version of the same map is held by the CICS system. CICS uses this to relate the names used in CICS input and output requests to the correct places on the terminal screen. CICS actually holds not just one copy of its map: it holds one copy for every different kind of terminal that might use the application program in your system.

When a program instruction sends a message to (or receives one from) a display terminal, CICS uses the program's internal map to find out what data to transmit, and to which field names. It then uses the appropriate version of its own internal map to decide where the data should be placed on the kind of display screen being used by that particular user (Fig. 6.1). Once it knows all of this information, it uses it to build and transmit a data stream suitable for the kind of terminal.

The beauty of the process is that if you decide to introduce new kinds of terminal, you do not have to rewrite all of your existing programs. You simply create a new version of CICS's maps for each application that will be used from the terminals. This idea is known as 'device independence', meaning that the programs themselves can be kept free of considerations of device characteristics and data streams.

Planning mapping sequences is a bit like using storyboards, a practice used in the film or television industry. A film director will often plan the sequence of shots in a film by creating a set of sketches of the key shots. In the same way, a systems analyst should have worked with client departments to discuss and review the proposed flow of screen dialogue with a new application. Each screen in the dialogue can be represented directly by a map, and can therefore be defined formally both to the application program and the CICS system.

Mapping processes

What does this mean for your programming staff? Well, depending on your organization and local practices, some or all members of your team will be trained in defining and creating the maps to be used by CICS. All application programmers will learn how to imbed internal maps into their programs. Someone will have to maintain records of the various maps that exist, and the versions of each that are created for different terminal types.

You should not underestimate the range of terminal types available nowadays: ordinary non-programmable terminals; personal computers and workstations; industry-specific terminals; teller machines; retail store cash registers.

Of course, you may sometimes need to create your own communications data streams. IBM can deliver only a finite number of different mapping enablers, covering frequently-used terminal models. Often, terminals from other manufacturers have been designed to emulate the ready-supported devices from IBM, so

CICS supports such terminals automatically. However, if you have special or unusual devices, you may need to have communications tailor-made for them.

In this case, either your application programmers need to be versed both in the detailed requirements of the terminal in question and in data-stream building, or you need to enlist the support of the systems-support specialists. I am going to assume the latter, and will handle this subject in Part III.

Mapping and programmable terminals

The vast majority of terminals attached to CICS systems today are simple non-programmable display terminals with keyboards. Their simplicity enables an organization to achieve very high levels of reliability while minimizing the need for support and maintenance. They generally need no reconfiguration, and provide little scope for operator error. Nevertheless, use of programmable workstations with CICS systems continues to grow, as the power of a workstation can offer some advantages.

Where programmable workstations have to be installed for other applications, their ability to run both CICS OS/2 and OS/2 Presentation Manager allows them to use sophisticated graphical displays as user interfaces to CICS transactions. In this way, CICS transactions can be made to blend into the existing user environment. So CICS OS/2 offers an alternative to BMS.

Thanks to the communication capabilities of the CICS family, this alternative is automatically extended to workstation users attached to host CICS systems, by cooperative processing, as shown in Fig. 6.2. The CICS OS/2 system communicates with end-users through Presentation Manager, then passes any transaction requests it cannot handle on the local CICS OS/2 system to a host CICS 'server' system for processing. The end-user continues to work in the familiar graphical mode, unaware that a host-based system, rather than CICS OS/2, is handling the request. The input and output data is handled using Presentation Manager rather than BMS. To the host CICS system, the request is treated as a routine request from a connected terminal.

Users of the CICS/6000 systems that run IBM's AIX operating system have their own substitutes for BMS. They can use X/Windows or Motif facilities to develop transaction-processing dialogues that blend into the existing user environment.

6.4   Screen generators

Both BMS and Presentation Manager require special investment in screen design. Depending on the volume of new screen design, and the skill level of available staff, you may find it advisable to invest in a *screen generator*, a program that enables them to design displays interactively from their own terminals.

A screen generator enables a programmer to look at the layout of a screen as he

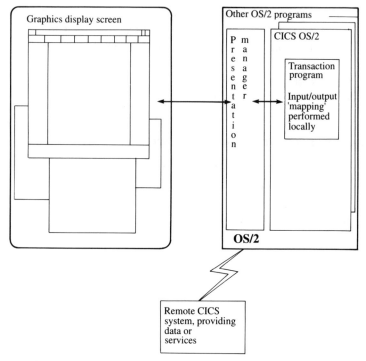

Figure 6.2.   Mapping and programmable terminals.

or she creates it. As assembler-language skills become more scarce, it also frees programmers from the need to code and assemble (and probably debug) BMS macros.

Despite the availability of these productivity aids, many CICS programmers continue to design and produce screen maps in the old way, using macros. To those experienced in the method, screen generators seem to offer little advantage. In many cases, new screens can be created by copying existing ones and modifying them. Your staff may find that this is preferable to learning and maintaining another utility program.

6.5   Application generators

Just as a programming department can increase productivity by using a screen generator to create BMS maps or graphical displays, it can use application generators to create whole programs and suites of programs, sometimes with all related maps as well. The application generator is one solution to the perennial problem of skills shortage. In theory it is possible to employ less-skilled program-mers to write CICS programs if you allow them to use application generators. For this reason, the use of application generators has increased over the last twenty years, as the demand for new CICS applications has caused a growing backlog of work.

An application generator shields programmers from many of the real-time design challenges that we have looked at. The programmer codes at a much higher level, in effect telling the application generator to link ready-made blocks of function to form a program. Error handling or disaster recovery are typically handled within the supplied blocks of code.

This approach to application development increases programmer productivity, and allows data-processing departments to employ programmers with lower skill levels. In some cases, programmers unskilled in the particular application generator can be hired and trained within days.

However, there are costs arising from this approach. Some application generators are in effect interpreter programs. They produce code that has to be interpreted—that is translated—at run time. This can consume a lot of system resource. In effect, in using application generators you are trading a need for programmer skills against a need for processor power. When skilled staff are in short supply, there may be no choice. If skilled staff are readily available, the choice between less-efficient generated programs and programmer-coded programs may be decided purely on cost. In making the decision, you will need to consider whether your programs tend to be simple or complex. Application generators produce very reliable programs for routine operations, but can require specialist coding for more complex programs. If a large proportion of your programs involves such specialist coding, an application generator may provide little benefit.

Nevertheless, the designers of application generators are themselves skilled CICS specialists, and have tailored and tuned their products, as far as is possible, to optimize the code they generate. Consequently, their output is ideal for those who really do have very large application backlogs, or shortages of skilled staff, and for whom the cost of delay in developing systems outweighs the cost of less-than-optimum applications.

6.6   Debugging and testing

CICS, as we have already seen, is like an operating system within the operating system. It schedules and runs programs, providing them with storage and other resources on request. In its turn, the operating system schedules and runs the CICS task, providing it with storage and other resources on request. An application program running within CICS's storage is responsible for the storage it is allocated, and is expected to request and use resources in a responsible way. This, of course, is easier said than done, and is always open to error. At their simplest, badly-written programs will produce incorrect data, sometimes not even affecting the program itself. Beyond that, as we saw in the discussion of storage violations, some errors can damage the application program, causing it to fail. In a way this is better than the first kind of failure—at least it is usually obvious that something has gone wrong. However, in the worst cases, errors can cause damage beyond the data or the program, corrupting other programs' data, other programs, or even CICS or the operating system.

The consequences of severe errors mean that, despite the best reviews and inspections, it is always wise to run extensive tests of a new program against all possible extremes of data input: first stand-alone functional testing; then more rigorous testing within a representative test environment; then testing under conditions of stress. If it passes all such tests, a program is probably fit for real use, in production. Even then, though, it should be monitored during its first months of use, to ensure that it is performing properly in all conditions.

CICS application design and programming needs special skills and training, and CICS programs need additional design and code inspection and testing. A CICS application has to run in real time, and therefore needs to be tested in real time. The program's real-time environment is usually unpredictable, with interaction with other applications inevitable. Interaction may affect both performance and functional behaviour. Your system-support team will know fairly well the sorts of workload the system can expect at different times of day, and on different days of the week. Yet they will not be able to predict the mixture of different applications being used at any given instant, or whether there will be contention over access to a particular file or database at a given instant.

With a real-time system, it is almost impossible to know, and thus impossible to recreate, the full set of circumstances that could exist at any particular instant. It is therefore sometimes impossible to recreate a particular problem. This helps to explain the continued dependence of staff debugging CICS programs and systems on such apparently crude clues as those contained in dumps and traces.

6.7   Prevention before cure

The earlier you detect an error in software the cheaper it is to correct. In addition to unit tests and full application tests on live systems, your application-development team's process should include:

- Inspection of initial designs and specifications
- Inspection of code against standards
- Independent creation of test cases
- Automated checking for prohibited code sequences
- Stress testing.

After that, they will start using some of the testing facilities provided by CICS. The dump and the trace are very powerful debugging tools, and ought to be used as a last resort, not as initial debugging tools. A programmer should begin testing the program by feeding it with representative data, watching the control and flow of the program, and checking the accuracy of the computed results. He or she should then test its response to invalid, out-of-range, data. Competent programmers have always done such testing, and the most effective have simply been the best at recognizing the most complete set of test data. Nevertheless, the CICS environment adds new dimensions to debugging, and calls for extra debugging facilities.

CICS provides tools for testing commands, command sequences, and entire programs and their screen maps. The most important of the tools is called EDF, the execution diagnostic facility. Others are the command interpreter and the transaction dump. As testing and debugging programs is an important part of a programmer's life, the ability to use these tools is an important skill of an experienced CICS programmer.

Execution diagnosis

EDF helps a programmer by allowing her or him to start a CICS program, but to interrupt it whenever it issues a CICS command. At any such interruption point, the programmer can ask to look at parts of storage, to see if they contain the expected data.

As well as intercepting the program at useful points along its way, EDF monitors the progress of the program, waiting for serious errors. If one occurs, EDF again interrupts execution of the program and returns control to the programmer for further investigation.

Command interpretation

The command interpreter is a CICS transaction supplied by IBM. It allows programmers to try out individual CICS programming commands from a display screen. The programmer can select any command keyword from a menu on the screen, then add operands and data values to it, building a complete command before executing it. Commands built in this way can do anything a command within a program can do: read records from files, display screen maps, and so on. The command interpreter therefore makes it possible to check that commands and command sequences have desired results. If a program under test seems to be giving unexpected results, the programmer can test individual commands to see if the result can be recreated, without having repeatedly to create, translate, compile, link-edit and refresh the program under test. Of course, this cannot catch the most stubborn design flaws: those arising from the dynamic aspects of the program and system. The command interpreter checks program elements out of context, and cannot detect complex logic errors that arise from the real-time environment. Nevertheless, it helps to eliminate more mundane errors and answer queries about fine details of execution, so that programmers can focus on overall design.

The testing and debugging industry

The tools I have listed above are those supplied free with CICS. However, the enormous popularity of CICS as a transaction-processing application platform has spawned an entire industry devoted to aiding application development and testing. Some products do very similar jobs to EDF and the command interpreter. Others go further, effectively cocooning the application program and its data within the CICS system, intercepting every program instruction (not only the CICS commands) before it is executed, to ensure it will do no harm, even giving advice on perceived errors. Other products will check older programs for correct operation after changes to the system—ensuring that they still produce the same results for the same data.

These tools can make application programs much more reliable, and many programming departments have become dependent upon them. They often prove a worthwhile investment, as, like systems-support personnel, they allow programmers to concentrate on the job of reducing the backlog of business transactions waiting to be developed for your organization. As before, although the tools simplify part of the programming task, they represent another set of skills to be acquired by the programmer. Your staff need to weigh the cost of acquiring skills in use of new utilities against the traditional experience-derived skills of debugging.

6.8   Dumps and fingerprints

For the uninitiated, a dump is a copy of the contents of all or part of computer storage. It is stored as an enormous mass of hexadecimal numbers, but can be formatted into a form that is very familiar and meaningful to a specialist. A dump is quickly stored by CICS in a safe place (say on magnetic disk) whenever something catastrophic seems to have happened. In effect, the dump is a snapshot of the computer's contents. It seems a featureless sea of numbers to an outsider, but holds hidden meaning for an experienced CICS professional.

Looking through a dump for clues to a system's failure is like searching for fingerprints at the scene of a crime. You need to know the best places to look, and the telltale signs of unauthorized activity. For example, you do not expect to find recognizable names, addresses and telephone numbers in part of CICS's own program code. To find them there would suggest that a program had gone out of control and overwritten the system with application data. The most experienced of your programming staff know the telltale signs of many different sorts of failure, and quickly find both culprits and causes.

Over the years, a number of products have been developed to help your staff to capture and analyse dump data. Many of them have evolved to perform quite a lot of preliminary analysis. As a result, the CICS specialist can expect to be shown where to start looking for the problem. Nevertheless, the human skills of deduction are still needed to pinpoint the cause of a problem. In the dynamic CICS environment, it is possible for a rogue program to have finished execution and disappeared before an error is detected. In such a case, a programmer needs to employ other tactics: reviewing change history, or setting traps. One such trap is possible using traces.

6.9   Traces and footprints

Just as browsing a CICS dump is like looking for fingerprints through a magnifying glass, tracing is like looking for suspicious footprints.

The CICS trace program records significant events in the life of the CICS system. When it is switched on, it watches every CICS-related move made by one or more application programs. Each time one of the elements of CICS starts to execute, or stops executing, the trace program notes the event in a file on disk. CICS's every move is thus catalogued, until a failure occurs. By tracing the sequence of events, a programmer can relate the eventual failure to the events taking place in the program, thereby pinpointing the source of error.

As an alternative, a programmer can imbed special trace commands in programs that are being tested. These commands emit trace entries, so the programmer can confirm the flow of the program under different circumstances.

As you can imagine, tracing the progress of a CICS program can consume quite a lot of CICS 'energy', so it is generally used only when a program is giving problems, or when it is undergoing early testing. Few users can afford to gather trace data continuously, as that would degrade system performance unacceptably.

6.10   Documenting application tests

Having invested in a rigorous testing process, your application-development team should collect comprehensive documentation to support each application in case problems arise once it is in production. For example, they will probably use the trace facilities to produce sample trace data showing the pattern of normal execution, for reference in case of future problems. Similarly, they may produce dumps to show the contents of storage when everything is going well. Placed with design documentation, this can prove very useful in pinpointing the nature of an unexpected failure months or years later.

6.11   System impact — performance

By reviewing the work and tools involved in debugging CICS programs, we have looked briefly at some of the errors that can arise in a CICS application. Good inspection and testing should prevent many hard errors from getting into the production system. Yet once an application program goes into productive use, you can still begin to detect new problems. Very often these concern dynamic effects arising from the characteristics of the system itself, of other applications that share the system, and of data files and databases. Frequently the problems are those of performance—both of individual transactions and of the entire system— rather than complete failure. Performance problems can be difficult for a programmer to predict or resolve without a basic appreciation of the real-time environment.

For example, pieces of a program being used in a busy CICS system will sometimes be temporarily moved from main storage onto disk ('paged out') to make room for other programs to run. Without such paging your system would need massive amounts of real storage to hold all of the running programs. When this paging involves a very large program, only parts of it may be paged out. The pieces chosen will be those that have not been used for a while. When they are next needed, they have to be reloaded from disk before they can be used, causing a small delay and making extra work for the system. Programs designed without due thought can have a significant impact on the amount of paging. For example, a large program that contains long branches backwards and forwards between commonly-used pieces of code is more likely to cause paging than one that keeps related code and subroutines close together, thereby shortening branch paths. Ideally, commonly-executed parts of the program should be kept together. Code that is unlikely to be used, for example error-handling routines, can be placed well away from mainstream code, as this is unlikely to cause paging. A good programmer will learn this and many similar details about CICS.

Choices in CICS programming are invariably in the nature of trade-offs. Few are black-and-white decisions. For example, the choice between using an application generator and coding in a language such as COBOL depends, as we have seen, on several factors. A programmer using an application generator might produce code of the sort that causes a lot of paging. However, the resulting performance overhead may be acceptable if it allows you to get a business system implemented in time. On the other hand, an untrained programmer might produce equally inefficient programs while programming less productively in COBOL. There are dozens of design decisions that can affect performance. These can be decisions about data, about communications, or about your program's use of CICS facilities or resources. Well-trained CICS programmers understand CICS and its environment well enough to anticipate unwanted performance effects. However, the dynamics of the system can make prediction difficult. Even when they understand the principles, your programmers need to test their programs under typical operating conditions, including conditions of high system activity. At times they may need to design and test for a variety of conditions and systems.

6.12   Writing code for many systems

Most of the time, a CICS application programmer can design, code and test programs for a single system. Yet in some circumstances it becomes necessary to take a broader view. Sometimes a program has to be designed to run on several dissimilar platforms; at other times programs need to communicate across platforms.

IBM's CICS products already form a substantial family, and this family continues to grow. One of the greatest strengths of the family is its common set of languages for application programs. Each product in the family uses the EXEC CICS command language to add real-time transaction-processing capability to standard programs. And each product permits use of the languages most appropriate to its environment.

As you would expect, CICS/ESA, CICS/MVS and CICS/VSE support use of the greatest number of programming languages: each allows assembler language, COBOL/VS, VS COBOL II, PL/I and C. In addition, CICS/VSE supports programs written in RPGII. Users of CICS in the other major environments, currently CICS OS/2, CICS/400 and CICS/6000, can write programs in COBOL and C.

Portability

CICS systems on several different platforms can each have a place in a single major enterprise, each meeting a different business need. For example, CICS/MVS, CICS/VSE or CICS/ESA systems are usually to be found at the heart or headquarters of the enterprise. CICS/VSE or CICS OS/2 systems may be commonly found at satellite locations, processing transactions locally but capable of being connected to the central system for some functions. CICS/400 and CICS/6000 are excellent alternative platforms for remote CICS transaction processing, but at a time of 'rightsizing' are also sensible choices for central systems in smaller enterprises. With this range of alternatives, enterprises can choose CICS systems according to the availability of existing hardware and software, human skills and experience, or price and performance.

Often, a system will be chosen because of the packaged software that is available to meet an immediate requirement. After it has been installed, an organization will want to expand its use to include a degree of transaction processing. Generally, if you already have transaction-processing systems in your enterprise, it makes sense to use the associated software inventory and skilled staff. In this situation, the CICS application-programming interface comes into its own, making it possible to write transaction-processing programs that will run on any CICS system; that is, programs that are *portable* across the different systems. Although CICS systems designed for different operating systems cannot execute each others' compiled code, source code of CICS programs can be translated and compiled to be run by each member of the CICS family.

The existence of a common EXEC programming interface across all CICS platforms makes it feasible to design, code and test all CICS programs on a central host system, before installing them and testing them on their intended systems—

say producing and testing programs before installing them for productive use on a remote, unattended OS/400 or VSE/ESA-based departmental computer. Conversely, the common EXEC programming interface also makes it possible to develop and debug programs in the safe environment of a stand-alone CICS OS/2 system, or CICS/6000 system, before transferring them to a multi-user CICS/ESA system for final tests and productive use. The existence of similar debugging aids on each platform makes the transition easier.

Of course, the variety of different CICS systems sets some challenges. There are variations in the CICS EXEC language set supported by members of the CICS family. The CICS programming team needs to ensure that programs that need to be portable are developed using only the EXEC CICS common subset for the systems on which they are to be used. This requires research, education of junior staff, and probably additional inspection stages. It also demands careful design of test cases, to ensure that they cater for language subsets and data and communication facilities in each system. IBM provides information to help create programs that are portable between the different CICS systems.[1]

Communicating

The other major aspect of programming in a multi-system CICS enterprise is CICS intercommunication—the capability of CICS systems to cooperate in executing programs. CICS intercommunication has been possible for 15 years, and has been largely the concern of systems-support personnel and architects of whole systems or networks, but knowledge of it is useful for programmers. Intercommunication is described in Chapter 9.

Use of certain kinds of intercommunication will require programmer participation. A relatively recent development in CICS programming has been the invention of the distributed program link. This is a CICS command that allows one program to 'link to' another program, which may reside on another CICS system. The concept of linking is long-established in programming. In linking to another program, an application program starts the other, waits while it finishes its work, accepts the output it produces, if any, and then recommences its own execution. The distributed program link is new in the way it can pass and receive control across system boundaries, where the systems can be separated by inches— or by oceans. The command has made client/server programming more accessible to the application programmer.

Cross-system communication is not new for CICS, of course. The kind that could for years have involved your CICS application-programming staff is called distributed transaction processing. Of all the kinds of communication, this is the most sophisticated. It involves two (or more) programs working together cooperatively. In effect, the programs have a dialogue, taking it in turns to speak. The processing in each program depends on the last message from the other. Distributed transaction processing requires careful design, to ensure that the effecti... ... ... that changes are properly synchronized and rrors are handled effectively. At this point, of programming starts to merge with that of ogrammer.

programming

etained its ability to isolate end-users from isiderations. Similarly, it has managed to natters from the application-programming las freed application programmers to con- tion needs. However, it has placed special responsible for CICS. Now that we have imer's world, at one of the points where it imer, it is time to turn to look at the work of

operative processing, application program- grammers in a number of areas. Prudent interest in all aspects of the application- anything can affect the system as a whole. In nay supplement or underpin application and customized system code. However, the most affect application programmers are ipport—the day-to-day activities that keep available for application developers and irst chapter of Part III.

7, IBM Corporation.

Part III
Technical support

7
System support

The purpose of a CICS system is to provide an effective service for end-users, who form the CICS 'audience'. We have seen how CICS helps programmers to provide effective transaction programs for a complex real-time environment. However, this is only part of the story. In this section, we will look at what goes on behind the scenes to make programming a viable proposition in the real-time CICS environment, and to make the environment itself reliable and effective. We will look at the work of the system-programming team, at the services the team provides for programmers and end-users, and at the tools CICS provides for the team.

CICS system programmers are the members of the CICS user community most closely associated with CICS, most preoccupied with it, and most knowledgeable about it. As you will see in this and the next three chapters, their work brings them into contact with all classes of user, and with most of the software systems and packages in your installation. This first chapter of Part III describes bread-and-butter activities that have to be performed in all installations. The next one describes the more challenging system-programming activities undertaken by more experienced staff when given time and resources. In completing these activities, CICS staff add value to the system, and provide additional and better services.

Throughout Part III, I describe activities in terms of the users that perform them. For some installations this is a true reflection of how, and by whom, things are done. However, many organizations do things quite differently, with individual system programmers accepting responsibility for all of the things described in this section, doing most of them, to some extent, all of the time. The chapter boundaries are therefore somewhat artificial, but help to clarify a complex set of overlapping activities.

In this first chapter we will look at routine system-support work of the kind involved in the day-to-day operation of a CICS system. The aim of support staff in doing this work is to keep an existing CICS system both running and effective, and thereby to keep programs and data accessible during normal working hours, in support of a company's business.

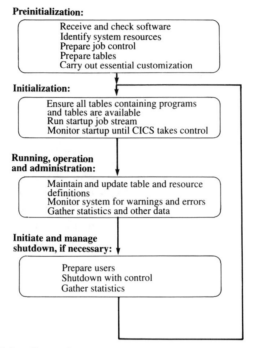

Figure 7.1. General support tasks.

7.1 General support

As Parts I and II have shown, CICS is an application enabler. Without the business applications it supports it has no purpose. Consequently, almost all bread-and-butter support activity relates directly to the application program:

- Providing an environment in which it can be developed
- Providing facilities for testing it
- Handling its transfer to productive use
- Keeping it running reliably when in day-to-day use.

This generates a steady workload for system-support staff: producing systems, transferring them to the operations team, then providing routine administrative and maintenance support. In this chapter, we will step through the elements of this job.

Briefly, the systems support process has the following stages (shown in Fig. 7.1).

- *Preinitialization* Preparing the basic system to receive CICS, preparing the installation-unique elements of the system, and writing job-control routines that will hold everything together.
- *Initialization* Starting the system and checking that it is complete and that it operates properly.

- *Operation* Running the system, monitoring its performance and behaviour. Responding to events, solving problems and adjusting for best results. Administering the system, adding and changing elements dynamically.
- *Shutdown and maintenance* Stopping the system, applying maintenance, restarting the system.

We shall look at each of these, but will start with initialization, leaving the subject of preinitialization until later.

7.2   CICS system initialization and operation

By the time of system initialization, the system programmer should have completed a large part of his or her system-support work. It is useful to start viewing the work from the point of system initialization, however, because that is where most of the CICS system-support processes comes together: where preparatory activities end and production work begins. It is also the part of the process that most resembles installation for other, simpler systems.

System initialization is a long-winded way of saying 'startup'. Ideally, your CICS systems should remain running uninterrupted while your business needs them, continuously available to end-users during their normal working hours. For most organizations this implies ten to twelve hours availability, but for some CICS users all-year-round continuous availability is essential. For example, companies using continuous processes, or multinational corporations with worldwide networks, need round-the-clock access to systems and the data they hold.

Although some organizations maintain a truly continuous service with their CICS systems, most start and stop them routinely. In most cases they keep to a timetable of startups and shutdowns, scheduling routine maintenance to fit the timetable.

In the traditional CICS world of the System/370 user, CICS startup and shutdown is usually a standard procedure for the operations staff. CICS is merely a long-running program that has to be started using a predefined procedure. Operators will perform this procedure at the beginning of the day, taking other action only if instructed by system-support staff or prompted by the system itself. The startup procedure will have been designed and programmed by system-support staff during the preinitialization stage.

In more sophisticated installations, CICS system startup will be automated, with the startup procedure being triggered without operator involvement. As you will see in Chapter 9, many of these sophisticated CICS systems are formed by connecting two or more CICSs together in the same machine. In such a configuration, continuous availability can be achieved by stopping and starting only some of the systems at any one time, leaving the rest to handle any ongoing work. When the number of such connected systems becomes large, the attraction of starting and stopping them automatically becomes obvious; proven automated procedures are more reliable, and punctual, than human operators.

System-initialization program

For CICS, startup is achieved by running a CICS system-initialization program. This negotiates with the operating system to get the resources CICS needs to run. It then loads the programs that comprise CICS, and sets CICS running. Throughout the initialization process, the system operator receives strings of messages, mostly reassuring but occasionally requiring action. As you will see later, support staff design the original startup procedures and test them before they are used by operators of production systems. Support personnel are usually responsible for documenting the procedures for operations staff, and for giving any associated education and training. Their aim should be to minimize the need for operator intervention, especially during initialization.

The system-support team normally becomes involved in day-to-day system initialization only when introducing changes, or when something goes wrong. After hand-over of a new system, they will probably monitor progress for a few days to check that all is well, particularly at times of higher operation activity, such as startup and shutdown.

System-initialization process

As well as loading and running the programs that make up CICS, the system-initialization process brings together all of the elements that make the final system unique to your installation (Fig. 7.2). The greater part of the system-programming effort will have gone into creating and defining those elements, yet the startup procedure is the only really visible result.

System initialization is controlled by the startup job stream, with input from a pregenerated system-initialization table, through which the system programmer can alter the composition and attributes of the finished system. This gives your system-support staff an opportunity to change attributes of the system from one startup to the next. Installations that start CICS afresh every day can make quite significant changes on different days, perhaps making different applications available or attaching different groups of terminals, databases or other resources.

It is rare nowadays for a system programmer to have to create a job stream from nothing. Most installations already use CICS and so produce a new job stream by updating an old one. In any case, IBM provides ready-made sample job streams that can be modified to meet any needs.

Initialization of a production system probably marks the end of a discrete system-programming project. Subsequent support will consist mainly of creating and defining new resources, though this may also mean adjusting the system-initialization job stream and table. Later, we will look at the definition and

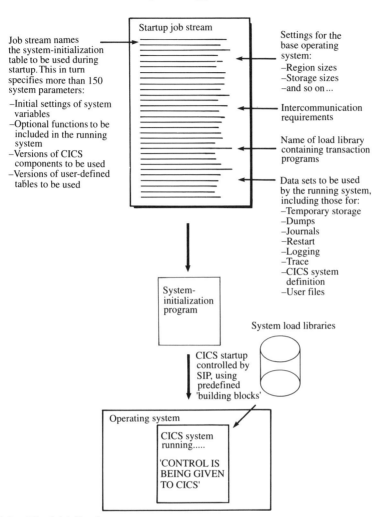

Figure 7.2. The initialization process.

creation of resources. After that, we will return to look again at system initialization, when we consider how the CICS system is first installed.

Day-to-day operation

I have described the CICS startup job stream and system-initialization table. When a new system has been tested properly, and can be trusted to process real work, startup and shutdown become routine processes. Startup is initiated by simple, routine system-operator command sequences (provided the preinitialization work has been done well). Variations from run to run can be made quite simply by using different predefined system job streams; naming a replacement table, perhaps. Predictable changes can be scheduled, say by having different job streams defined for different days.

Clearly this permits a degree of automation during startup, or at least the use of less-skilled staff for day-to-day operation. In fact, CICS startup is usually part of the general system operation task, carried out by system operators. This is an important point, as you need to remember that your running CICS systems are left in the hands of people with very little CICS-specific knowledge. This being so, the reliability of the systems and processes will depend on effective preparation by system-support staff.

Relationships

System-support personnel are highly-qualified CICS system programmers, and usually have a detailed knowledge of CICS, systems in general, assembler-language programming and a variety of subsystems. As the first people to install, tailor and run a new CICS system, they tend to know more than anyone about that system. They are usually responsible almost exclusively for CICS, though they often have to carry out work that involves the operating system and subsystems such as IMS/VS or VTAM.

Operations staff are usually less qualified, with a general knowledge of routine tasks for the entire system. They respond to messages and follow predefined procedures, but are not expected, indeed are often forbidden, to show initiative. They handle all systems, and often know no more about CICS than they do about any other systems in their charge. In many installations, with systems running round the clock, operations staff work overlapping shifts. They need precise, comprehensive procedures and instructions to ensure that they react appropriately to any events.

The largest modern CICS systems are designed for minimal operator intervention. With breathtaking transaction volumes now commonplace, a system cannot afford to wait even seconds for an operator response. Messages that once would have required individual responses from an operator at a keyboard now have to be intercepted, interpreted and handled by programs. Operations staff monitor systems for potential, but rare, disasters, and perform routine tasks and gather trend data from statistics.

Consequently, you can view operations staff as deputies to system-support personnel. They take over day-to-day operation of systems as soon as the systems are stable enough to be used in production, but are expected to call for help when anything unusual happens. For this reason, many system-support groups have continuous support programmes, with individual staff on 24-hour standby in case of emergency. Some are fortunate enough to have home terminals; most simply have pagers, telephones and piles of manuals.

For the purpose of this book, we will assume that operating CICS is part of the system-support task, even though the day-to-day activity is usually delegated completely to operators.

Many CICS users now aim for almost continuous operation, though most systems are shut down and restarted as a matter of routine, as part of their installations' cycles of administration and preventive maintenance. Hopefully, shutdown should be fairly uneventful. It is possible to shut the system down very rapidly in an emergency, but this is best avoided. An operations team will usually be instructed to initiate an orderly shutdown, preventing users from starting new transactions on the system but allowing existing transactions to complete tidily. As the system finally shuts down, it can generate a series of statistics, allowing system-support staff to analyse significant patterns of use of the system or its resources.

7.3   System administration

In between startup and shutdown, most CICS systems run quite successfully without need for radical action. However, every system needs to be watched in case problems arise or support is needed. In a lightly-loaded system, or one subject to few changes, the level of operation activity is likely to be fairly low. However, a system with a heavy workload or one that needs regular changes to applications or to the user population can need frequent intervention. This section looks briefly at the sort of operational tasks performed regularly by your team.

Controlling and checking the system

CICS provides a selection of ready-made programs for managing the system while it is running. Users run these as normal system transactions from CICS terminals.

Master terminal

Probably the most important of these transactions is the master terminal trans-action, known by the acronym 'CEMT'. This allows authorized personnel to control most parts of the CICS system, including resources. It is an extremely powerful tool, potentially dangerous in production systems, so its use is generally restricted to a handful of people.

A system-support team will often permit the use of only one or two of the master-terminal functions: for example, permitting system operators to enquire about the status of particular terminals or tasks, or perhaps to cancel tasks that are causing problems. In the past, limiting the use of the transactions was achieved merely by documenting only permitted operations, and not telling operators about additional function. CICS/ESA now provides such an extensive range of programming commands for requesting master-terminal functions that system programmers can design their own limited-function master-terminal transactions, thereby actively limiting use of restricted operations. You will read more about this in Chapter 8. Nevertheless, the operations team will need access to the full range of operations for use in emergencies, under guidance from system-support specialists.

The range of things that you can do with the master-terminal transaction is enormous. Basically, you can use it to control or adjust almost anything within the system. You can use it to 'switch on' (or off) system functions such as the gathering of statistics, or to adjust system settings such as the number of tasks that are allowed to run concurrently. You can use it to open files so that they can be read by programs, or close them so that they cannot. You can take a terminal out of service temporarily. As well as controlling things in this way, you can enquire about parts of the system to find out which files are currently closed, which tasks are suspended, what values have been set for a wide range of basic system limits, and many other things.

From this list, you can see how very valuable this facility can be. These are the sorts of things you would want system operators to perform routinely. On the other hand, there are some operations you would never want them to perform: shutting down the CICS system immediately, without warning; taking all terminals out of service at once; disabling all data files. In between these two extremes, there will be different subsets of operations that you will want to make available to different classes of operator.

Adding resources dynamically

The CEDA transaction, which allows you to add definitions of things to CICS resource tables, is almost as important as CEMT in the daily management of a CICS system. It is also the link between CICS's long history as a 'table-driven system' and its current role as a non-stop transaction-processing system.

One of the first things you learn when you come into contact with CICS is that it has a lot to do with tables. There are tables everywhere, and for everything. Before CICS will work with almost anyone, or anything, it needs to have them listed somewhere in a table. This sounds inflexible, but it is really one of the magic ingredients that has made CICS such an effective and flexible real-time system. In effect, the table system works like a telephone directory: each resource is listed by name in a table, and the table contains detailed information to help locate the resource. The table usually lists many more resources than would be in use at one time, and provides an efficient way of finding and addressing each resource.

Throughout CICS's early life, all tables had to be precoded, using assembler-language macros, before the CICS system could be started. Once the system was running, changes to its tables had to be saved up until the next time it stopped. This often proved frustrating, as the things that have to be defined include all terminals, all programs and all data files. So you could not introduce a new program to the system, or add a new terminal, without stopping CICS and restarting it with a replacement table.

There are still CICS tables that cannot be changed in mid-flight (and you will read briefly about them later), but in recent years the most heavily-changed tables have been redesigned so that they can be updated dynamically. The system resources that they defined are now identified individually to CICS, through unique definitions. The process of defining these things is known as 'resource definition'. In most organizations this is done by system-support personnel.

If your system is subject to significant change, a major responsibility of someone on your CICS support organization will be the administrative task of maintaining the definitions of resources available to the system. New definitions can be made, or old ones updated, at any time, though many users prefer to save them up to be made or updated in batches at discrete intervals. This batching makes the process more controllable and auditable, but it can always be circumvented to make urgent changes without delay.

As shown in Fig. 7.3, the resource-definition process involves a number of stages, all of which are usually performed by system-support staff. The first stage does nothing to change the running CICS system, but creates a definition for later use, storing it in the CICS system definition dataset. So, for example, it may create the definition of a program: its name, its language and so on. The second stage actually installs the definition, placing it into virtual storage, where the running CICS system can use it. Continuing our example, the definition of a program is physically placed in active system storage, making it possible for CICS to identify and start a program that is needed to perform a transaction. Your system-support staff may use the CEDA transaction, from a CICS terminal, to create a definition and install it for the first time. On the other hand, they may prefer to use a more formal, auditable process, in which case they will use a special offline utility program, supplied with CICS, that they can drive from programs of their own.

We will look in more detail at the resources that have to be defined in the section on Resources and Resource Management.

Defining resources with macros

As mentioned earlier, some kinds of resources have to be defined in tables before CICS is initialized. The contents of the tables then remain fixed while CICS is running, and cannot be changed until it is shut down and restarted. The tables appear in Fig. 7.3, their dark borders symbolizing their fixed nature.

The tables are created by coding macros (a bit like programming) and then assembling them. Referring back to the description of system initialization, you will see that the system-initialization process pulls together the elements that go to make up the running system. Tables are among the elements that make up the system, so the system-initialization table will identify any resource definition

(a)

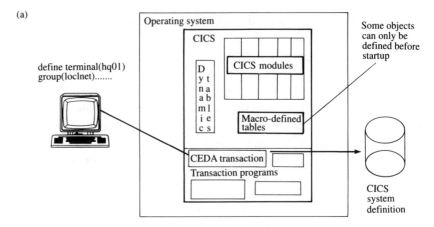

(b)

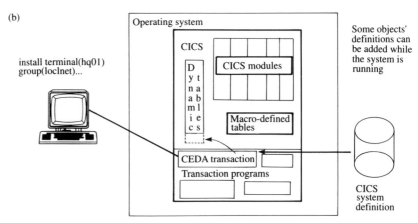

Figure 7.3. Resource definition. (a) Online CEDA transaction is used to define objects such as terminals, programs and files. (b) The object definitions do not take effect until installed onto the running system.

tables that you have created using macros, incorporating them into the system at startup.

Examples of things that still have to be defined in advance with macros are: transient-data queues, journal files, monitoring facilities, and customized startup routines.

Other administrative transactions

CEMT and CEDA are the most commonly used of the system-support transactions supplied with CICS, but others are commonly used too.

The command interpreter transaction, CECI, allows programmers to check the syntax of EXEC CICS application-programming commands from a terminal. It should be of most use to application programmers, but can often be helpful to system-support staff when trying to solve problems in programs. It will allow its users to execute commands, as well as checking their syntax, so you need to control its use very carefully. This ability to execute commands directly can sometimes be a life-saver, though. System-support personnel have been known, for example, to repair corrupted records in files by reading and rewriting them individually from a terminal, using CECI. Obviously, this facility needs to be controlled!

The routing transaction, CRTE, makes it possible for an operator working on one CICS system to ask to be transferred temporarily to another, connected, CICS system. Once transferred, the operator can start transactions with the other system. This can be very useful to system-support personnel responsible for several systems at once; they can, for example, ask to be routed to a second system to carry out system-control operations using the master-terminal transaction.

You will read more about the subject of communicating across systems in Chapter 8.

Yet other transactions allow staff to:

- Switch on *tracing*, which records system activity in great detail, making it possible to discover the reasons for intermittent faults (CETR transaction).
- Broadcast messages to individual users of the system, or entire groups of users, or all users (CMSG transaction).
- Send messages to the operating system's console (CWTO transaction).
- Debug transactions interactively (CEDF transaction). This is primarily an application-programmer's utility, but may often be used by system-support personnel in the application-programmer support role.

Resources and resource management

Having looked at the subject of application programming, and heard about the transactions that define resources to CICS and control its operations, it is now time to consider the resources themselves and their individual definitions. That should complete the picture of the basic CICS system, and explain how it hangs together. It will also show the scope of responsibility of system-support staff, who need to be familiar with, define and maintain the full range of resources in your installation.

We will not consider all resources here, but will concentrate on the main program-related ones, as their maintenance forms the bulk of the system-support activity.

Program-specific resources

The online transaction program is, as we know, the reason for having a CICS system. Under CICS, an online program is started when an end-user selects a

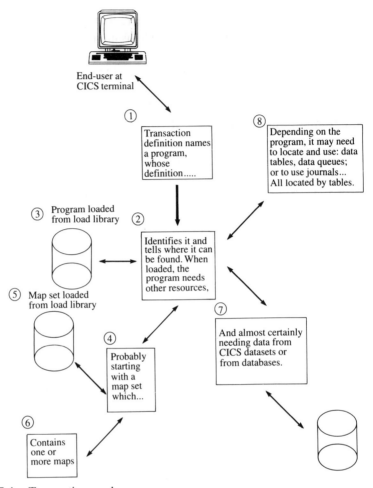

Figure 7.4. Transactions and resources.

transaction to be performed. Figure 7.4 shows how the initial act of a terminal communicating with CICS to start a transaction rapidly involves many different kinds of resource, starting with a program.

To ensure that the right program is started, your support staff need to define (a) the transaction and (b) the program. They need to install the definitions onto the running system. They also have to ensure that the program actually exists and is available for use.

Both the transaction and the program are defined using the CEDA transaction. The program must exist in a form ready to load and execute. This means that it must have been translated (to interpret the EXEC CICS commands), compiled, link-edited and then stored in a load library, ready for use. The load library, by the way, must already have been identified in the system-initialization table (which we discussed earlier) before startup.

Application-support resources

As the program begins to run, it will begin to make requests for services that use other resources. If you recall the discussion in Chapter 5 of the life of a transaction, you will remember that a program will almost certainly want access to a data file. It may also want to write to, or read, temporary storage or transient-data queues, send screen maps to terminal displays, or do a number of other things.

At the time the program makes a request, any resource that it uses must already:

- Exist
- Be defined to CICS
- Be ready for use.

For example, a screen map must be ready to use. A screen map is very similar to a program, and to be ready to use it must be coded as part of a map set, which in turn must be assembled, link-edited and stored in a load library, like the application programs.

Similarly, for CICS to be able to get data from a file, the file must already:

- Be defined and installed using the CEDA transaction
- Be related to a real data set by one of a number of methods.

System-support staff need to understand these things and make informed decisions about which to use. If necessary, the staff need to create the underlying data set. Alternatively, they need to negotiate with system programmers responsible for creating files. The same sort of negotiation will also be necessary when preparing to use other kinds of resources: negotiations with VTAM system programmers for communications-related help; with database administrators for help setting up IMS/VS or DB2 database connections; and so on.

Although the CICS resource-definition structure seems very tangled, the relationships can be seen to be quite logical when you are familiar with them. The layers of definitions allow your support team to keep the system as a whole very flexible and dynamic while giving your application programs an impression of great stability. So, for example, a program can continue to refer to a particular file by the familiar name in its CICS definition, yet the underlying data set may be replaced by a new one. Similarly, a program can refer to a screen map, using it to send or receive data, yet can do so without realizing that a more up-to-date version of the map has been created, or that an additional version can now be invoked selectively, for example to cope with the language needs of terminal operators in a different country or to make use of a new kind of terminal.

This goes some way towards explaining CICS's versatility and universal popularity. Given this flexibility, and independence of data format and screen format, the CICS applications tend to be very stable, and can prove highly portable from one part of your organization to another, to and from subsidiaries and from application vendors.

System-support resources

All of the above-mentioned resources concern applications. The CICS system has other resources at its disposal, most concerned with controlling and monitoring itself, or with communication or working with other systems. Some of these resources are optional, but desirable, while others are mandatory. Any that are used in your system have to be defined by system-support staff. Your system will certainly need a file to hold the definitions of all the resources in your system. This file, called the CSD, needs to be created, made available to CICS, and identified in the system-initialization table.

In addition, your system-support team will almost certainly wish to define data sets for optional, but desirable purposes. For example, data sets to be used to hold information gathered while monitoring the system and gathering statistics; data sets for logging changes so that the state of the system and its data can be recreated in the event of a catastrophe; data sets for capturing 'snapshots' of storage in case of severe errors, to help with trouble-shooting.

The number of data sets that you should have defined, for maximum integrity, is considerable. Your system-support staff have to create and maintain all of these.

Package-support resources

Your system-support staff also need to provide definitions for application packages, for example utilities or programming-support products. For example, users may choose to install a variety of non-IBM monitoring, debugging and other products to help with systems administration, application development and application testing and debugging. These need multiple resource definitions before they will run. Fortunately, package vendors usually supply or document the required definitions, so your team should in most cases simply need to install them and maintain them.

7.4   Performance planning and tuning

Performance management is one of the ongoing responsibilities of a system-support team. Besides carrying out administrative and trouble-shooting tasks already outlined, cautious teams take steps to detect problems before they become serious. Performance problems can be detected early by gathering data and looking for trends.

Statistics

CICS can gather statistics on the number of times certain limits are reached during a given measurement period. For example, it can record how often the system contained the maximum permitted number of concurrent CICS tasks. It can also record the number of times particular events occur: the number of times a particular program was used, for example. CICS provides a utility program to print this data, and in its raw form your staff can certainly examine the output for trends, sudden surges of activity, and other points of interest. Your team has to define data sets and set special system parameters before CICS will provide suitable statistics. It also has to be prepared to analyse the data that is generated.

Performance tools

Most CICS support teams nowadays use specialized performance tools to help to gather and interpret their performance data. Such tools are available for both MVS-based and VSE-based CICS systems. They vary greatly in sophistication, some providing real-time display of performance data and raising alarms if thresholds are exceeded, others simply providing more elegant reports of the statistics data. Your staff may find it easier, and more productive, to use these kinds of tools rather than trying to analyse the raw data. Even so, evaluating the tools, installing them and learning to use them effectively is yet another system-support activity.

Objectives and remedies

Your team has to decide on its objectives in taking action on performance and tuning. If your CICS system has very low transaction rates and rarely approaches thresholds, let alone exceeds them, they probably should not waste time doing more than reviewing the shutdown statistics at the end of the day. On the other hand, if your installation is growing rapidly, or is introducing new applications, or is known to be heavily laden, it will probably benefit from accurate monitoring and reporting.

In times of growth, your system-support team needs warning of the need for increased capacity. This will help them either to plan the next hardware upgrade or, if your budget will not stand that, prepare cost-saving strategies. Exactly that choice faced a number of CICS users at the time that a Data Tables feature was announced for CICS/MVS. With no immediate funding to solve a capacity crisis, the feature proved to be exactly what some users needed, in some cases giving 20 per cent improvement in throughput of work with the same hardware.

More modest savings can usually be made by system-support tuning actions, though these have to be approached with care as wrong decisions can make matters worse. Nevertheless, your experienced staff know the system and its applications. They are probably best placed to recognize the reasons for sudden loss of performance. They should look for remedies in both the system itself, in the choices of system parameter values, and in its applications. Badly-written application programs can waste processing cycles more than anything else.

7.5   Recovery

We will look in detail at recovery concepts in the next chapter, so will look at the issues only briefly here. As with performance, the importance of this subject to your installation depends largely on the nature of your system and applications. Some CICS users do not consider recovery important enough to warrant even planning effort; others consider recoverability to be a mission-critical issue for their corporations.

Certainly your system-support team, in combination with your operations team, should have considered:

- Whether to plan against total destruction of systems and data
- Whether to protect against damage to individual disk packs
- What to do about system crashes.

They should have prepared a policy, and should have documented procedures to be followed in any situation.

Of the three situations, the last is the easiest to deal with, as CICS itself provides all you need in order to protect against either failure of an individual transaction or failure of the system while transactions are busy. Your system-support team needs to prepare the necessary journal data sets and resource definitions to allow CICS to handle recovery from such failures. They then need to document accompanying processes for the operations team, so must understand the concepts of CICS recovery and the facilities provided.

For the other situations, you will need to invest both money and time: acquiring additional hardware and software, or freeing system-support staff for design studies and projects to implement new functions or processes. We will look at some of the considerations in Chapter 8.

7.6   Problem analysis

I have already said that trouble-shooting is a key task for CICS system support. In fact in some installations, this sometimes seems to be the only task! As CICS plays such a central part in the system, using the resources of most other subsystems, it is often implicated in any problem. Certainly, the trickiest problems often manifest themselves first in CICS, even when they were caused elsewhere.

CICS itself, being such a dynamic system, is fertile ground for challenging problems. Poor application design, as we have already seen, can cause serious problems. In fact, the large majority of CICS problems are caused by application-programming errors. As these usually have an immediate effect on the CICS system itself, system support will be the first group to get involved in solving a problem, usually called in by the operations team, probably as a result of complaints from end-users.

Successful debugging depends very much on experience. Experienced CICS system-support people will usually pinpoint the culprit fairly quickly. Probably they first ask whether any significant changes have been made to the system recently. Very often, if the system has been stable for weeks or months, errors will stand out as having been caused by new or changed programs, or data sets, or tables.

Chapter 5 described some of the nastier application-programming problems that occur in CICS because of its dynamic nature: deadly-embrace deadlocks and storage violations. CICS is also vulnerable, like most systems, to looping code. It can detect many loop conditions, but there are some that defy automatic detection by calling CICS from within the looping code.

CICS system-support teams have to handle all of these conditions, should they arise. The tools that are available to help them are storage dumps, traces and perhaps debugging programs, which help to analyse the error data that CICS produces.

Another class of problem that commonly provides a real challenge for CICS specialists is that involving cross-product interfaces. As CICS plays such a central role, using the services of the operating system, communications subsystems, data management subsystems, security systems and so on, it can get drawn into the debugging process for any of them. Similarly, if a CICS utility, such as a monitoring package or debugging aid, or application generator, fails, the debugging process often involves CICS. Consequently, CICS system-support specialists often grow to be familiar with related products and their external interfaces: VTAM, VSAM, DB2 or SQL/DS, IMS/VS or DL/I DOS/VS.

Debugging brings system-support personnel into contact with other groups. It renews the contacts, originally established during system definition and set-up, with operating-system groups, communication specialists, database administrators, security administrators and so on. This key debugging role of the CICS specialist, if not of the CICS team as a whole, is rewarding and enriching for the staff. However, it can also be somewhat demoralizing, as it is sometimes assumed that CICS, or the CICS team, causes many problems. The application systems based on CICS tend to be labelled 'the CICS systems'. When any component fails, 'the CICS system' is said to have failed. In other words, everyone's problem becomes CICS's problem. This is true at the user interface too. If the company's customer account system 'goes down', it is the system that gets blamed; in the daily or weekly report, it will be 'CICS' that is reported as down, regardless of reason—hardware, operating system, communications, database, power supply, software package, application package.

7.7   Preinitialization

We started this chapter at the point when the system-support staff were providing a startup job stream and system-initialization process, ready for the operations group to bring up a production system. The sequence allowed us to relate the operations and system-management processes to the preceding application-development process. In doing this, we broke the chronological order of events and bypassed a major part of the basic CICS system-support task: installing, testing and maintaining the system. In this section, we will backtrack to review briefly this part of the system-support job.

In places, this section becomes quite fragmented, as it has to talk about several different systems. Each has its own very different environment, packaging conventions and established practices. Rather than describe each, I shall try to convey the differences in broad terms.

Installation

IBM supplies System/370 CICS systems on tape, along with a pile of publications. Nowadays, it also provides the publications in soft-copy form, on tape and CD-ROM, so that you can view and search them online. For the non-System/370 systems, it provides CICS in much the same way, except that the pile of books is smaller in each case. Future CICS OS/2 systems are likely to be distributed on diskette. Beyond that, CD-ROM offers a compact way of distributing product code and books together.

Planning

Regardless of the platform on which you plan to use CICS, your staff need to do some planning before you begin to use it seriously. You saw in Chapter 2 the extent to which CICS subcontracts much of its services to specialist subsystems. One consequence of this is that it has to be integrated with each of those before it can work properly. Ideally, therefore, you should already have installed each of the required subsystems before you start the CICS installation process.

Integration for VSE

For the VSE platforms, CICS is supplied as part of the system package, so much of the integration has been done for you and it is possible to use CICS/VSE immediately you have finished installing the system package. However, being able to use the system and having it ready for productive use are two different matters. You need to prepare your CICS resource definition tables, application resources and operator procedures. In a simple CICS/VSE system, running only vendor-supplied application packages, this will take very little time. For a more sophisticated system, the process is much more significant, especially if you are migrating from an earlier release. In this case, you need to migrate your existing resource definitions, application components and data, testing them in the new environment.

Integration for MVS

You use a program called SMP/E to install CICS for the MVS platforms. Installing in this case simply means moving the supplied code from tape into libraries on disk, then running supplied procedures to check that everything works correctly. At about the same time, you contact IBM to see if any important or vital changes have been made to the product since it was manufactured. If so, you order copies of the changes and use SMP/E to apply them before proceeding.

For CICS on an MVS platform, the process thus far will have taken one or two days' work—if things go well, half a day's work. Now the real work begins: creating job streams, data sets and tables; testing all of them; establishing and testing interproduct connections; testing applications. This part of the process may take three to six months—a full-time project for one or two system programmers.

The effort will be at least as great for someone who already uses CICS. Although they will already have procedures that can be copied, and will understand what they are doing right away, they will have to check for compatibility between systems, ensuring that it is safe to risk their fully developed production systems on a new version or release of CICS. Such established users have to test the new system against their application programs, data files and databases, utilities, operator procedures and vendor packages before they can proceed with confidence.

In the large MVS-based installations, it will be necessary for the CICS team to work closely with other system-programming teams: telecommunications programmers, responsible for VTAM; MVS system programmers, responsible for keeping the base operating system running; security administrators; database administrators.

Testing

In a large organization, initial installation of a CICS system is often seen as a one-person project. For up to a month, a system programmer will install the CICS code from tape into libraries on disk, create initial tables and job streams, then bring up and test a whole system in a variety of configurations.

In a smaller organization, a dedicated system programmer with time to experiment will be seen as an impossible luxury. One (maybe the only) system programmer will find time to complete the same process in bursts, probably over a period of months.

When the system itself seems relatively stable, the system programmer will start to check its function by installing and running one or more application packages as CICS transactions against copies of production data sets. If you already have a CICS system, this will be a fairly realistic test, as you will have confidence in the basic application and will be familiar with its normal operation. If this is your first CICS system, your system programmer will have to use installation verification programs, or CICS-supplied sample applications, to test the system until an application can be developed or an application package obtained.

Test systems

When the system programmer who installs the system is happy that it is relatively stable, colleagues will start to experiment with it. If the system is a follow-on release, they will check installation-specific modifications, test specially-developed code such as user-exit programs or utilities, and check proper operation of monitoring, recovery, security and other processes. They will then check application-support facilities, such as CICS's own EDF and CECI, and IBM and non-IBM application generators, application test utilities and debugging aids.

When all of these facilities have been shown to work, the system-support team will usually be able to persuade application-programming teams to migrate to a copy of the new system running in an application-development test region, to continue application development and testing. This helps to provide more extensive testing, with a greater, yet more random, workload. It also exercises the error-handling facilities of the new release!

The final phases of testing the new system involve migrating a production application, with a copy of its data files and databases to a test region containing the new system, and running it in parallel with the true production system, to develop confidence in its operation.

Cutover

When the test region is seen to be performing reliably, it becomes the production system, and the old production system is shut down (though is held ready for restart, in case hidden problems emerge within a short time).

With the first application 'live', the support team returns to the test system and begins migration of the next application; the cycle repeats itself until the entire application inventory is migrated. Your team is then free to plan the next migration . . . .

Migration effort

We saw earlier that it can often take longer to migrate from one release of a product to the next than to install a new system for the first time. At first this may seem strange, as many of the procedures and programs already exist and simply need to be updated, but anyone with an existing investment in systems will understand the reasons. The systems exist to support your business, so any changes to them should be made with minimum disruption to that business. So, a system-programming team planning a migration must follow steps similar to those above, testing rigorously at every step.

When you have had a system like CICS in productive use for a year or two, you will have tailored and tuned it to your own circumstances. In part, this will have been achieved by minor modifications, customization and choice of support packages. Both your support staff and your end-users will have become used to the way the total system appears and behaves. It can therefore be quite disruptive to make radical changes that affect your staff. The system-programming team should be best able to cope, but your business will suffer if the transition cannot be made almost invisible to end-users. Ideally, such users should go home at the weekend, returning to work on an upgraded system without realizing. Achieving this neat transition is what makes migration take so much time and effort.

In the next chapter, you will read about system programming initiatives that multiply the power and value of the basic system. As well as enhancing your systems, such initiatives ensure that they diverge from the standard as-supplied product. Each divergent step adds an item to your 'migration checklist' of things needing special consideration during future migration. In the last decade, CICS products have evolved in ways designed to relieve this problem, providing more 'official' facilities and interfaces to make it easier to tailor CICS to meet individual business needs. However, there is a long tradition of modification of CICS, and it will take years for all modifications to disappear. Until then, support staff will continue to bear the burden of additional migration steps, as they aim to give end-users transparent migrations.

Educating staff

Ideally, the migration between releases should be transparent for everyone. As we have seen, though, the closer you tailor a system to your business, the more difficult it is to migrate transparently. Any lack of transparency should be kept as far from the end-user as possible. Clearly, system-support staff will see every change and incompatibility. They should try to find ways of concealing as much as possible from the application-programming and operations team, as well as from end-users.

Whenever changes cannot be concealed, the system-support staff need to educate their colleagues, warning of the changes and providing new procedures and documentation. This education on new releases is a normal responsibility for system-support teams, and is usually undertaken by the system programmer most involved in the migration work. It provides an opportunity to teach staff about new facilities and improvements, as well as incompatibilities.

7.8   Maintenance

Looking in chronological order through the work of the system-support team that we have reviewed so far, we see:

1   Unpack and install the new product or release
2   Integrate the product with related products
3   Reapply required local modifications (if any)
4   Test installed system
5   Install and test utility packages
6   Migrate application staff to new test systems
7   Install or migrate the first real application
8   Test real application
9   Prepare operator procedures and educate other staff
10   Initialize production system, with application
11   Provide administrative updates (such as new resources)
12   Perform trouble-shooting tasks.

The list omits one notable and very important part of the work of the system-support team: maintenance. The omission is deliberate, as the maintenance process is effectively a miniaturized version of the entire list. Being a universally used, heavily modified and dynamic system, CICS is subjected to intense, continuous worldwide testing in everyday use. Almost every installation finds ways that the product does not quite fit its environment, or does not behave as expected. IBM provides corrective code to meet many situations, supplying it immediately to the users that have problems and holding it in case other users have them later. From time to time, IBM produces a new tape containing all known corrections and makes it available to users.

This maintenance process poses a dilemma for all system-support people. Despite the obvious benefits to be gained from worldwide input to the product, every change should be treated as a miniature product update. It should be tested before being applied and used in production, and its effects may have to be communicated to operations and programming staff. As a result, many installations deliberately delay application of maintenance tapes, often waiting until two or more are available, treating the upgrade process as a more major project. Apart from anything else, they feel that this gives the changes time to prove themselves on other systems.

However, the opposing pressure, to apply update tapes as they are delivered, arises from the maintenance process itself. If your installation discovers a serious problem of its own, and IBM decides that the solution is to apply a change to CICS, it may have to design the change to fit on top of a fully-maintained system. This may mean that the change that your system needs depends on other, earlier changes. Suddenly, what started as a minor change can precipitate a full update. Clearly, in this situation, you would prefer to have been up to date already.

Yet again, being up to date brings dangers: some changes prove unacceptable to certain installations. Occasionally, because of minor differences in the way they have set up their systems, two CICS users will need entirely incompatible designs for the same change. If the change is introduced in response to a problem reported by the first user, it will almost certainly create a new problem for the second user. And this problem will have been encountered only *because of* the corrective code.

Clearly, a system-support team needs to develop a maintenance philosophy. This will probably be dictated by considerations of cost and availability of staff. In addition, it will be influenced by the history of problems in an installation. If you have a tradition of stability and reliability, and do not undertake ambitious technical projects, you probably don't encounter many problems. In that case, you will probably apply maintenance in a leisurely fashion, say every six months. If, on the other hand, your team is constantly pushing forward the boundaries of technology, they may be best advised to apply maintenance more often.

7.9   Team work

You should now appreciate the enormous range of routine tasks normally undertaken by the system-support team. Relating it to your organization, you should also be able to understand how the work is shared. If you have a small organization, one person may be doing all of the CICS administration. If you have a very small organization, he or she may be doing all of the administration for all systems: a team of one.

As use of a system grows, so do the demands for reliability, power, security, complex networking and so on. As the system becomes indispensable, it creates a demand for continuous availability and emergency backup. These demands can be met using existing CICS services, but rarely with a team of one. Most require a degree of specialist knowledge and training, or at least freedom to devote time to a single development project. A dynamic CICS system-support organization therefore usually has several CICS system programmers, and can depend on networking specialists, database administrators and so on to provide specialist support on other products.

Given that sort of organization, offering relief from routine chores as well as intellectual stimulation, members of your team can start to look at the kinds of development projects described in the next chapter—the sorts of projects that give them scope for technical development while offering your enterprise an opportunity for commercial advantage.

8
System design and management

If CICS system programming involved nothing more than routine system support, it would be like any other system-programming job and there would be little need for this book. The CICS system-programming community contains many system programmers with fifteen to twenty years' experience. They display continued enthusiasm and devotion beyond that which could be generated by routine system-support work. The intellectual challenges presented by CICS give much more scope than you would at first believe. Yet there are always vacancies for experienced CICS system programmers, and opportunities for newcomers.

System support of the kind described in Chapter 7 is an ideal training ground for staff doing this kind of work. Day-to-day system maintenance, trouble-shooting and user support provide an excellent apprenticeship for more detailed and structured tactical research and development. This chapter describes the kinds of system-programming work that stretches CICS staff while adding value to the systems they support. Having developed reliable systems and established suitable supporting processes, a system-programming team can undertake projects that will help to improve the competitiveness of an enterprise. Very often such projects are more challenging and satisfying for system programmers than the routine work, and help to maintain interest and sustain technical vitality within a team.

We cannot discuss everything that a system programmer does, but we will look at a range of typical activities:

- Customizing the system
- Automating operational activities
- Designing for recovery
- Managing performance
- General consultancy
- Total system planning.

8.1   Customization

A system programmer usually knows his or her system better than do IBM staff. Often the reason is that the system is customized—adapted to meet the special needs of that particular installation. CICS has always offered great scope for customization, and this has undoubtedly been one reason for its success over the years. It has brought disadvantages too, as we will see, but they are doubtless outweighed by the advantages.

Many programming and system-programming activities in CICS could be considered 'customization' in the broadest sense of the word. For example, providing your own suite of applications, using your own choice of utility packages and tuning the system by changing parameters is a form of customization. Each of these turns the deliberately general CICS system provided by IBM into a system specifically designed for your business—that is, a customized system. As we saw in Chapter 7, installation-specific tables and job streams are tailored before being selected during CICS startup: this is also a form of customization. However, for CICS, the term customization is reserved for changes to the product's code; true CICS customization involves writing replacement or supplementary code to run as though it is part of CICS. This is what we will consider in this section.

In its early years, CICS was often modified directly by customers. Many of the code modules that comprised the product were originally supplied in assembler language, which could be changed quite readily and then reassembled to produce unique versions of CICS programs. This helped users to make the systems do exactly what they wanted, but over time has proved impossible for IBM to maintain. With effectively infinite scope for modification, it is impossible to be sure that every system will behave similarly, and therefore to analyse problems if they occur as a result of modifications. It also makes it difficult to ensure that application programs will be portable from one system to another. It also becomes very much more difficult for users to migrate to new releases to get access to the latest technology. Coming to depend on particular modifications, users are torn between the cost of falling behind technologically and the self-inflated cost of transferring to a new release of CICS.

In recent years, users have grown used to having fewer opportunities to modify CICS. Parts of Version 1 Release 7 were supplied as object code only (that is, only as code that has been assembled or compiled into executable form that cannot sensibly be modified). This trend has continued through CICS/ESA Versions 2 and 3. All new CICS code is supplied only in object form, so is extremely difficult to modify. This makes it more difficult to inflict self-damage, but limits the scope for tailoring the system. IBM has therefore found ways to permit modification in a controlled fashion. It provides official, documented customization facilities, but with the warning that they cannot be guaranteed to remain unchanged from release to release in the same way as other programming interfaces.

CICS customization should not be undertaken lightly. It requires a thorough understanding of CICS operation in the area being modified. It also requires assembler-language programming skills. However, these are the sorts of knowledge and skills that experienced CICS system-support people tend to have, and tend to enjoy exercising. A couple of examples of customization facilities should

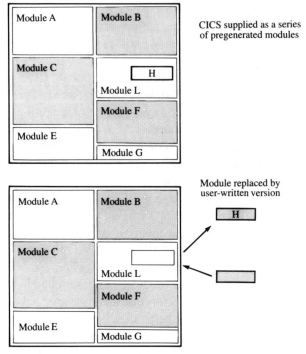

Figure 8.1. Replacing CICS modules.

help you to understand the nature of the work. However, you need to look deeper than this to understand the value of much customization. Good customization can mould the system to your organization, making it more user-friendly, perhaps less costly, or more efficient. Conversely, poor customization can be error-prone, costly to maintain and may inhibit the ability of the system to grow or adapt to change.

We will look at some of the forms of customization that your system-support team may undertake.

Replacing CICS modules

CICS still allows, even encourages, direct modification of certain modules, called user-replaceable modules. These exist in parts of CICS where it is known that requirements will vary radically from one user to another. IBM supplies working modules, and includes comments to explain the modules' designs. CICS users are then free to rewrite the modules to their requirements, within specified limits (Fig. 8.1).

An example of a user-replaceable module is the one supplied for use with CICS's autoinstall facility. This module allows VTAM terminal users to logon to CICS without having previously been defined explicitly in a CICS resource

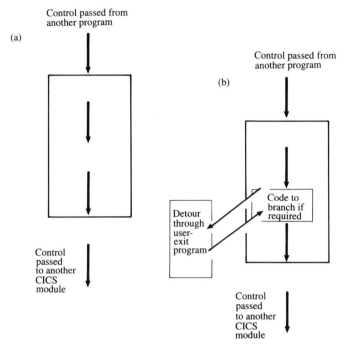

Figure 8.2. User exits. (a) Normal flow of program instructions. (b) Flow with user-exit program in place.

definition table. The user-replaceable module allows individual installations to control exactly how terminals are to be treated when they begin unplanned communication with CICS. Influencing treatment in this way can be vital because CICS supports so many different types of terminal, only a fraction of them being IBM-supplied devices.

Creating user-exit programs

Another way of modifying CICS is to write user-exit programs. These are also user-written programs, but, instead of replacing CICS modules, they work alongside them. The CICS modules are provided in a form that cannot be modified directly, but the IBM developers intentionally provide places for users to attach their own code. These places are called *user exits*, and act like exits on a motorway: they are always there, but you do not have to use them. If you decide to use them, however, you can enable and disable them individually, or even replace them completely from time to time, to meet different needs.

User exits exist wherever IBM's CICS code designers believe that CICS customers may wish to influence the outcome of a system action, or to gather specific and detailed information (Fig. 8.2). Exits often appear in parts of CICS code that interact with the operating system or with other subsystems. For example, there are exits in communications-related modules because many users wish to intercept data streams before transmission, perhaps to compress data and save transmission costs. Similarly, there are user exits within the parts of CICS that generate messages to operators. These allow CICS to intercept messages and reroute, discard or respond to them automatically according to installation-defined criteria. This offers opportunities for automating some parts of system operation, and saves operators from being swamped by messages.

There are also more sophisticated forms of exit within CICS. These are known as task-related user exits, or TRUEs for short. They are really intended only for those developing system-scale programs, such as database managers or system-monitoring programs. They allow exit programs to register an interest in a variety of events in the life of any CICS task: for example when a task requests synchronization of all changes it has made to databases. Their use requires a deep understanding of CICS system events and processes, of recovery principles, and of other matters. As a result, most users wisely avoid using them. If your organization uses them, the programs will probably be written by system-support staff, not by application programmers. Even if they don't write TRUE programs themselves, your system-support staff may need to understand the principles behind them, because many sophisticated subsystems, particularly monitors and database managers, use TRUEs. It is often useful to be able to recognize the processes being performed by such subsystems, particularly those processes that involve CICS. A good understanding can make it easier to operate, tune the subsystems and diagnose problems that arise during the subsystems' interaction with CICS.

Writing utilities as CICS transactions

User exits provide an opportunity for system programmers to design and write programs, but user-exit programs are far removed from application programming, however, being written in assembler and usually involving no human interaction. There are opportunities for system-support staff to write more human programs. To help them to respond with effective, reliable programs, the EXEC CICS programming language has been extended over the years, so that programmers can write utility programs in the standard high-level programming languages, PLI, COBOL and C, as well as assembler language.

For many users, the most important benefit is the ability to create replacements for CICS's CEMT transaction. As you have seen in Chapter 7, CEMT—the master-terminal transaction—is a very powerful transaction. In the wrong hands it can do untold damage to systems, yet without some of its facilities operators and applications staff can become almost helpless. Therefore, although some users seem happy to allow operators almost unlimited access to master-terminal function, others think this is too dangerous and allow only one or two people to have full access.

In order to allow others to have access to a limited number of vital options, some system-support groups write their own subset versions of the master-terminal transaction, using the EXEC CICS commands designed for it. As the commands are essentially ordinary CICS commands, they can be mixed with other commands in ordinary CICS programs. Consequently, transactions can have any desired appearance, fitting in with any installation standards for screen layout and other human factors.

As a result, operators can be given access to a series of ready-made, limited-function transactions. Each transaction can be designed for particular circumstances, accompanied by explicit instructions on use, and with installation-specific online help as backup.

Every organization has a different attitude to use of the CEMT transaction, but two extremes are common: one, that the users must on no account be allowed to use it; the other that users should be allowed to use it, but be warned to take care. The EXEC CICS commands permit your system-support staff to exert as much control as is needed: allowing users to perform one or more of the CEMT functions at a time, but not the rest.

Initialization and termination design

As CICS is such a dynamic real-time system, handling critical business data and services, it is usually necessary to carry out a number of administrative tasks before and after end-users start transactions, for example preparing user-exit programs so that they can be ready for use for the first transaction of the day or running special programs to prepare data sets for use.

CICS can pause during its initialization and shutdown sequences to trigger such programs. Some of them may have been written by your system-support staff. Others may have been supplied with vendor-written application packages or utilities. All will need to be defined to the system before startup, in the CICS program list table. Your system-support staff will need to be aware of the rules governing use of startup and shutdown programs, and will need to review their operation carefully when migrating to a new release of CICS.

In effect, these programs are a form of user-exit programs, though they modify the course of events during startup rather than within the running system.

8.2   Automation

Customization facilities will probably play a major part in any automation your organization decides to do. We saw in the last chapter that although there are very many things to consider before initializing your first CICS systems, it is relatively straightforward to keep them going once they are in production. It is usually safe to leave system operation and control in the hands of relatively low-skilled operations staff, suitably briefed and with written procedures. Nevertheless, most system-support staff know that they can improve efficiency and reliability by minimizing the involvement of operations staff. As you will see in the next chapter, CICS environments can become too complex for ordinary operational procedures. Human intervention can be the most inefficient way of handling a situation in real time, so the largest CICS users have introduced significant amounts of automation.

Startup and shutdown jobs can already be submitted automatically, and many users have established automatic recovery procedures to restart CICS systems after a failure. CICS's provision of extended recovery facilities in Version 2 and Version 3 makes it possible for any user to achieve relatively rapid restarts for a small investment of design resource.

These and many other examples show what can be achieved if you invest in design and coding time for experienced CICS system specialists. As usual, the cost/benefit analysis is yours to make. If your plans for transaction processing are unambitious, you may be able to continue without further investment. However, if your operations are at all complex, or if reliability, availability or round-the-clock operation are becoming vital to your business, it may pay you to invest in customization that will reduce the need for staff or the likelihood of operator error.

Despite the obvious savings this can bring, there can be other important reasons for automating operations, besides the need to protect against operator error. As you will see in Chapter 9, many CICS systems are in fact clusters of systems, often interconnected. In some cases, they will involve different kinds of CICS system: CICS/ESA systems mixed with CICS/400 systems, for example. They may all handle many thousands of transactions every hour.

In such an environment, an operator cannot respond quickly enough to individual messages, let alone to complex problems. In fact, with some of the most active modern CICS/ESA systems, messages may appear at the system console in such numbers that they cannot be read by a human operator before they scroll out of sight. As even seconds of lost system time can be critical at peak business hours, automation is vital to some enterprises. So, as you have already seen in the section on customization, your system-support staff can write exit programs to filter and route messages. Likewise, they can write programs to respond appropriately to selected messages, process system data sets when they are full, or even issue master-terminal commands automatically in response to events.

8.3   Designing for recovery

Just as typical volumes of CICS messages make it impossible to handle operational processes manually, so the mixture and volumes of concurrent CICS transactions make it impossible to unravel unfinished work after hardware or software failures. CICS provides special services to help system-support staff to recover, quickly and securely, from potentially catastrophic failures.

In a real-time system such as CICS, failures of applications or whole systems pose more complex problems than in batch systems. In a batch system, where updates are handled sequentially, a serious failure can be rectified by returning to the system state at the start and applying all updates since the previous reliable backup. For a transaction-processing system, though, things are not so simple. Data-update requests are not fed to the system in a neat, ordered stream. They are submitted at an unpredictable rate, from all sources. Although modern hardware and power-supply failures are rare, both they and application programs themselves can fail midway through a transaction, leaving some work finished, some unfinished. This situation is usually wholly unacceptable. For example, an order may be approved, but associated billing details may have been lost. Or a customer may have been billed, but the shipping details may have been lost. Either sort of failure is unacceptable to a well-run business.

CICS files are typically so heavily used that you cannot afford to take them offline for any but the shortest periods. At the same time, your staff should be too busy to sit around waiting for such failures so that they can repair them. Yet you cannot afford to have each CICS application complicated by having to design recovery routines into it. So CICS transparently provides routines to ensure that each program either completes all related updates or ends without completing any. It is accepted that failure of an application program should not compromise data integrity. Looking at Fig. 8.3, therefore, you can see the process of *backout* for a single CICS transaction. The transaction starts at point 1 and updates a file at point 2. Both events are recorded by CICS in a special file called a CICS journal. In fact, the journal also records details of the data change, including the contents of the file before the change. At point 3, the transaction updates a second file, and CICS again records details of the change. At this point, the transaction (maybe the whole system) fails, so that the transaction cannot complete successfully. CICS's recovery program now springs into action. It can recognize transactions that have started (point 1) but have no recorded completion point (point 4). It searches each task's dynamic log for details of data updates that need to be reversed, carrying out the reversal. It does this for all transactions that were incomplete and involved in a system failure. Very often the failure will be limited to one or two transactions, caused by operator error or program failures. However, in the worst cases, thousands of transactions can be involved.

System-support staff do not need to intervene in the transaction backout process, but they need to set the system up initially so that it can manage the process itself. They need to ensure that the recovery utilities are operating, and to prepare and identify the journals, and to ensure operating procedures keep recycling the journals effectively.

As an extension of this protection against system and application failure, CICS and related products also help your staff to recover from more catastrophic situations. From time to time, a magnetic disk drive will suffer disastrous failure, for example destruction of the disk surface, losing millions of data records.

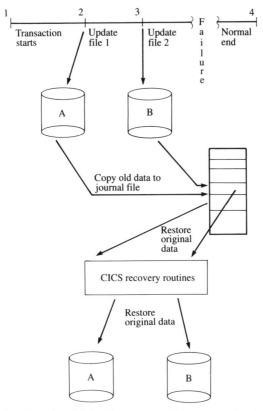

Figure 8.3. Data invalidated by program failure is restored during backout.

Provided the disk was copied (backed-up) recently, you may think that you can recover. However, once again, transaction processing sets new challenges. With very high levels of online access to data, you can have many millions of changes to data in a day. Many will overlap, and will be related to changes on other disks, as shown in Fig. 8.4 (an inventory file on one disk, for example, having been updated repeatedly in conjunction with the shipping data files and billing data files on other disks).

CICS helps to protect you from the consequences of such physical damage to disks. It records the changes you make to the contents of your files, as described earlier in the description of backout, so that you can go back and recreate the files in a process called forward recovery (Fig. 8.5). In performing forward recovery, your system-programming team, or the operations team, takes the latest backup copies of your data files. To this, they reapply all the changes recorded on the CICS journals. The process is similar to that described earlier for backup. However, in the case of forward recovery, CICS needs *all* changes since the backup to be reapplied to the damaged files. The changes will be applied, not reversed as in the case of backout. However, at the end of the forward-recovery

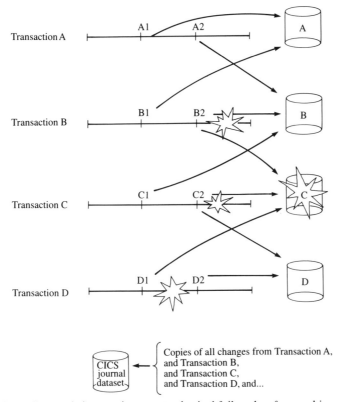

Figure 8.4. In a real-time environment, physical failure has far-reaching consequences.

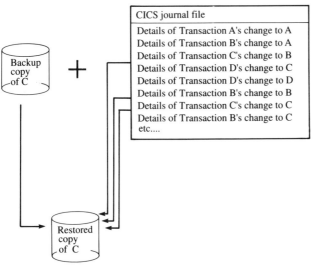

Figure 8.5. Forward recovery recreates a damaged data set from journal and backup files.

process, CICS starts backout. This is because catastrophic failure is likely to occur during a period of CICS activity, and therefore some transactions will have been incomplete when the failure occurred. Having recovered the contents of the disk successfully, CICS will reverse all unfinished transactions, and operators will have to start them again.

Forward recovery involves a lot of planning by CICS system-support staff. CICS itself does not carry out any forward-recovery operations: it merely gathers the journal data that makes recovery possible. System-support staff need to assess and select a suitable forward-recovery program (for example, IBM's CICSVR product), then ensure that it is integrated effectively with the basic system. They need to document the procedures to be followed in the event of failures, including special considerations where a variety of resource managers, such as database managers as well as file managers, are updating data for the transaction in a synchronized manner. Effective procedures will be particularly important in this kind of situation, as it is likely to occur very infrequently, if at all. Many CICS users ignore the need for forward recovery, judging that the cost of implementing it is not justified by the risk of failure. Others see forward recovery as an essential insurance policy, as loss of business data would be unacceptable.

8.4   Managing performance

In Chapter 7 we saw that routine system support includes an element of performance monitoring and trouble-shooting. Given time to do additional work, system-support personnel can make a much greater contribution by focusing on matters of performance.

A key activity, which should be maintained constantly, is detailed analysis of performance and capacity data. This can help to show trends for the system as a whole and for individual applications. This can warn of the need for system upgrades, or for extra storage or communications capacity. It can also help to identify performance bottlenecks worth special focus from system designers.

In highly tailorable real-time systems like CICS, there can never be absolute rules about optimizing performance. As with natural systems, such as weather forecasting, there are too many variables to allow any feeling of certainty. However, as with such systems, historical data and trend analysis allow reasonable short-term forecasts, and experience can suggest the best way to cope with particular sets of circumstances. In most cases, tuning is a trade-off rather than an independent choice: reallocating storage at the expense of other subsystems, for example, or using more main storage to save processor cycles or data input and output traffic.

The trade-offs to be employed will vary from time to time as work patterns, business patterns and application usage changes. In fact, the trade-offs may change from one time of the day to another, and from one day of the week to the next. For example, on particular days your system-support team may give preferential treatment to one class of end-user at the expense of others; say to payroll staff during the period leading up to pay day, or to customer-support staff during known hours of peak telephone activity.

Experienced CICS system-support staff can transform the performance of a heavily used system. They combine their knowledge of your system, its applications and its user population with an understanding of the principles of CICS operation. These principles include high-level architectural considerations. They also include many points of detail, often relating to design of application programs and CICS's interactions with other subsystems.

There are performance analysis programs to help your staff, and they can call on independent external consultants to provide fresh ideas and recommendations. However, your own staff are very often the people best equipped to identify problems and their solutions. Their intimate knowledge of your systems, applications and data allow them to turn general recommendations into appropriate actions.

As well as monitoring performance in your existing system, your specialists also perform a valuable service in evaluating new functions and products. They can assess the impact of new function by modelling them or by developing prototype systems. They can then prepare growth forecasts and cost estimates, to show the overall effect on the system.

In a busy CICS environment, careful performance planning and management can be invaluable. On the positive side, effective management can delay the need for hardware upgrades, or give advanced warning of workload growth. On the negative side, failure to plan can cause performance problems that are as serious as software failures, affecting the productivity of every system user. A serious performance bottleneck in a real-time system can cause such backlogs of work that the entire system, or network of systems, grinds to a halt. An experienced (and properly funded) team of CICS specialists rarely has this kind of experience, as it maintains ongoing records of performance and capacity data. Its members review new proposals from both a technical and performance standpoint, so should be able to identify sources of potential performance problems. As even the best-run projects can spring surprises, it is important to monitor them as they are put to productive use.

8.5   General consultancy

This is an extension of the work that we discussed in the last chapter—but with a difference. It is not a break from the routine work, but an opportunity to do it more effectively and with lasting effect.

Application debugging and design

System-support people expect to be called upon routinely to help debug application programs. Given more time, however, system programmers in many organizations spend time training programmers to be more self-sufficient, by giving formal education on application debugging and design.

Much of CICS debugging revolves around the reading of storage dump data or, if dump analysis programs are available, interpretation of dump analysis reports. Application programmers benefit from both demonstrations and classroom-style lessons on the principles of CICS debugging. The same subject is taught by IBM Education and a variety of independent education vendors. Many system programmers attend such classes, but few organizations can afford to send all application programmers. So this kind of education is often developed and taught internally by system-support personnel.

Similarly, there are courses on application design. These, and a growing number of books on the same subject, provide good source material for internally-provided application-programming courses. Such courses can be doubly valuable, as they can provide a means of establishing and propagating in-house programming standards. Many installations have documented sets of standards, though not all take the trouble to teach them formally. System-support personnel can help to develop application-design classes, able to offer special insight into the effects of poor programming on heavily used CICS systems.

Application-design classes also give an opportunity for presenting good programming techniques, particularly important in the CICS environment. There is plenty of written guidance on this subject for CICS, but a focus on it within an installation adds emphasis. Classes also allow you to provide education on more advanced topics, such as designing applications for recovery, or programming for distributed transaction processing or distributed program link (see the next chapter for more on these).

Evaluating new products

CICS system-support personnel often become involved in assessing and testing new products, both hardware and software. The tests can range from the informal free trials of new software utilities, such as screen painters, application generators or performance monitors, through to full 'beta' tests of major hardware and software products. If you can afford to maintain enough staff to undertake this kind of exercise, you will almost certainly benefit from the investment. Apart from providing staff with rewarding and satisfying challenges, you can benefit by being in touch with the latest technology—probably also being among the first to gain competitive advantage from it.

For CICS users, there is occasionally an opportunity to be part of an early support program. In such a program, you agree to be one of a handful of users to get a new level of the product early. You agree to install the product and get it into productive use within a particular period, usually one of between six months and a year. Although this means that you are first to try everything, and therefore stand more chance of finding problems, you are also one of the few users of the new release needing support from IBM, so you can get special attention. On balance, participation in an early support program is seen as a rewarding experience, and participants often volunteer for additional programmes.

CICS system reviews

Given time from normal work, system-support personnel are ideally placed to perform reviews of processes, standards, applications and system structures. From their everyday work, they have such a broad view of your CICS system, its relationships with other subsystems and its applications that they are well qualified to assess your existing CICS systems and recommend improvements.

The spheres in which such reviews could have value are numerous. Most aspects of CICS systems and application design would benefit from considered thought ranging over all aspects of the system. For example, it might be useful to consider ways of improving CICS performance, such as optimizing the placement of application files on disks, or selecting the best candidate files for use with a new CICS feature, such as Shared Data Tables. It would also be sensible, from time to time, to review your installation's preparedness to handle major loss of data through physical damage. We will look more at this topic later.

Cross-product reviews

As you know, CICS is dependent on many other products for its services. Often these products are administered by separate people or groups, apart from the CICS specialists, who are very knowledgeable about the products for which they are directly responsible but do not understand CICS very well. This sometimes means that interfaces between CICS and other products are not set up optimally. Your CICS system can benefit from a review of its use of such interfaces, for example those that CICS has with VTAM or VSAM.

Good documentation on how to combine use of multiple products is usually scarce. This is partly because advice tends to be either too general to be helpful or too specific to a particular test configuration to relate closely to individual systems. IBM publishes both the more general reference manuals and the more specific system centre bulletins. These provide pointers on where to focus attention when performing cross-product reviews. However, your particular installation will benefit most from a well-funded view of its own. This can prove a fascinating project for one or more system programmers, perhaps with input from an outside consultant.

External contacts

Working with consultants is just one example of an external contact that can enrich the system-support team. As any such team is staffed by highly-qualified professionals, there is a lot to be gained by meeting peers in other organizations. Your staff should, and probably do, attend major CICS events such as user-group meetings, seminars, technical update sessions and technical conferences. Like any other professional group, they benefit from contacts with others doing the same kind of work. At the same time, they can hear reports of projects, tests and studies undertaken by leading-edge CICS users.

Staff members who carry out significant projects and studies, as suggested throughout this chapter, may benefit from the experience of presenting papers at such conferences. Very often the approval of peers at such a conference can give as much satisfaction as in-house recognition.

8.6   Total system planning

So far in this chapter, we have looked at system-support activity as a series of discrete projects. However, much of the value-added work of experienced system-support staff involves standing back to take a broader view of the system. It is such activity that ensures the vitality of major systems.

System-support planners try to anticipate the future transaction-processing needs of their organization, in a variety of spheres. Most obviously, perhaps, they try to understand the likely growth in workload and performance: in the numbers of end-users; in the level of use of particular transactions by existing users; in the number of applications to be supported by the entire system. In addition, they need to consider changes in expectation of users and their departments and auditors: changes in required response time, security, data integrity and re-liability.

They combine an understanding of these needs with a knowledge of the policies of the parent organization: whether it is seeking economies or growth, for example. They can then identify possible ways forward (Fig. 8.6), selecting and recommending the best to senior management. This activity generates several subtasks, most which we will look at briefly:

- *Business analysis*   Determining the needs of client departments and end-users.
- *Forecasting*   Predicting future workloads, using both input from client departments and historical and trend data.
- *Technological assessment*   Monitoring and reviewing advances in CICS and other data-processing technology, anticipating possible uses.
- *Inventory assessment* Reviewing existing hardware and software and application-program inventories to see if they remain viable.

STRATEGY FOR THE PLANNING PERIOD?

New processors
(for growth)

New applications
needing more
power and more
function

New releases of
CICS, positioning
for future growth

Additional CICS
products, to
permit flexible
growth to meet
the needs of the
organization,
leading to...

New releases of
CICS, to provide
specific function

Figure 8.6.   Planning the way forward.

- *Cost benefit analysis*   Review alternative strategies, costing them before submitting them to management.
- *Roll-out* Preparing a roll-out plan when the proposals are approved.

Business analysis

We have already looked at this activity as part of the application-programming process: analysing the needs of clients before and during transaction design. For system support the analysis is somewhat different, focusing mainly on the underlying resource requirements. New programs can prove unexpectedly popular, generating excessive use and requiring more than the scheduled resources. The system planners need to understand the new applications and plan growth in systems capacity to accommodate them. For CICS this may mean creating additional CICS regions, or larger regions, preparing to handle more end-users, or demanding more processing power or disk storage.

As CICS interacts with so many other subsystems, part of the analysis may be to understand the need to support new releases or functions of those subsystems. Similarly, even though application packages may be acquired more cheaply by buying them ready-made, instead of developing them in-house, they will need system resources and will need to be installed and maintained by system-support personnel. Any new software or hardware may require a CICS upgrade to perform effectively.

Forecasting

If your business is static and you are happy with your organization and its efficiency, you will probably also remain content with your computer systems. Your staff will simply keep the existing systems until they wear out. If your business is in any way dynamic or competitive, however, you will need systems that can make you more competitive and flexible, and that will allow you to take advantage of any opportunities as they arise.

CICS is a family of transaction-processing systems that allows almost unlimited growth. However, for maximum cost-effectiveness, you need systems to grow only slightly faster than your business, keeping one step ahead. In effect, you want to use the same sort of just-in-time ordering that you use for any other kind of commodity, though if your business often presents unforeseen opportunities you may want to maintain surplus capacity so that you can respond instantly to events.

It is the responsibility of CICS system-support personnel to monitor the state of the transaction-processing systems and forecast future work volumes. This activity is usually referred to as *capacity planning*. At the routine level, it involves monitoring transaction volumes and response times, and in analysing statistics that detail the use of particular system resources. If the analysis shows that growth is outstripping expectations, system-support staff may be able to take corrective action to control the growth, to absorb it in some way, or to bring forward equipment upgrades.

System-monitoring activity can also help to warn that the system is growing less rapidly than expected, and so could warn that planned updates can be delayed instead of brought forward. System monitoring like this is a form of process control, similar to that practised in most organizations that employ continuous processes. However, process tracking assumes that there is a plan against which progress can be tracked. Development of such a plan usually falls to the technical support team.

In many organizations, systems planning forms part of the total financial planning cycle of the whole organization. The department regularly, once or twice a year, will forecast the need for new hardware and software. Your system-support staff will prepare predictions for the CICS systems, showing current workloads and capacity, and predicting medium-term growth and hence systems requirements. They will study current technical trends and available systems, and will recommend actions to achieve the required growth. For CICS, they will probably review new versions or releases, new features or facilities, and show how using these will enable them to support additional terminals, or entire new applications, or to become more cost-effective.

The need for detailed study for real-time systems such as CICS can be very great, as there are so many variables. Not only can workloads increase rapidly and unexpectedly, but also new applications can interact with existing ones, causing special effects. There can be contention over access to data, processor time or network resources. System-support staff will consider whether new applications create a need for new CICS systems, or whether they can be absorbed by existing systems. They will sometimes have to decide whether to split single systems into multiple systems connected by MRO. In that case, they will need to model or prototype the multiple systems set-up, to ensure that the performance is suitable.

In some cases, research may show that system-capacity problems would be better solved by changes to applications. In such cases you will, of course, want to compare the cost of changing applications with that of upgrading hardware. Your systems-support team will typically provide cost data to support the case being stated.

Technological assessment

From their position at the 'leading edge' of technology, many system-support groups are accused of using technology for the sake of it. However, it cannot be denied that most technical leaders have managed to give their enterprises very great competitive advantage. Automatic tellers in banking, point-of-sale in retail, and now intelligent telephone switching, are examples of ways that technology has changed business over the years.

A key part of system support is ensuring that the enterprise's systems remain competitive, up to date and cost-effective. To this end, most system-support teams spend time reviewing new technology, to see what benefits are to be gained. We will look at the more strategic part of this work in Chapter 10. Here, we will consider the short-term focus on technology that keeps the current generation of systems viable and competitive.

Just as IBM's CICS systems develop gradually, through releases and by addition of 'features', so your systems should develop in small evolutionary steps. This requires a lot of planning work by your system-support staff. You have already seen that they will often decide to begin using a previously unused CICS facility. In addition, they will monitor new CICS releases or versions, to determine whether new facilities justify the cost of upgrading your systems to use them.

At a higher level, they will consider major technological changes outside CICS, such as architectural changes to the operating system: extended architecture or enterprise systems architecture, for example.

At a lower level, system-support staff will consider the advantages of new utilities that can improve productivity or reliability of staff. For example, they frequently run trials on new monitoring, systems management or debugging software. As with all other proposals, they have become accustomed to providing meaningful cost/benefit analyses to support their recommendations.

Inventory assessment

The system-support staff charged with taking a whole-system view will look at the viability of the installed CICS (and associated) software as well as the hardware and networks. In effect, this is the equivalent of inspecting plant and machinery in any other business, to see if it has become obsolete or inefficient. Strangely, it appears to be more difficult to convince managers of the need to upgrade software than it is to justify replacement of industrial hardware. Presumably this is because depreciation and deterioration has physical connotations, and cannot easily be related to intangible software. System software can become so out of date that it brings a competitive disadvantage. Besides lacking straightforward performance, it may not be able to make use of new hardware technology, and new architectures and application packages. As a result, a pitch for systems upgrades may have to be more polished than those for hardware or plant.

Cost/benefit analysis

In preparing a plan for investment in CICS transaction processing, system support will have to make detailed cost and benefit analyses. Where new application systems are to be developed at the request of client departments, funding may be agreed in advance. In addition, most organizations will automatically fund basic expenditure on system maintenance and running costs. For CICS this will probably cover installation of service tapes and system refreshes, support of existing end-users, and general running costs. In addition, most CICS teams will want to justify more costly projects, including installation of new releases. Some CICS users install new releases as a matter of course, confident that the benefits easily outweigh costs. However, others take time in assessing the benefits and costs, wanting to prove first that migration will be an advantage.

In recent years, MVS-based CICS support staff have had to assess several releases of CICS/MVS and several releases of CICS/ESA. Their VSE counterparts have had to assess two releases of CICS/VSE. Each will have considered the possible benefits and savings from moving to the new releases, comparing them with the undoubted costs of going through the migration process. For several releases, the costs clearly made the majority think twice, holding back. In particular, there were heavy costs associated with converting CICS macro-level programs to command-level. Yet it is clear that, for example, the third release of CICS/ESA is seen to bring such advantages that most users feel that they have to migrate. Most of these will have had to convince their management that there is a business case for migrating, as well as a technical case.

Managing projects

Having performed appropriate studies, prepared detailed proposals and persuaded you that they should proceed, system-support staff will draw up implementation plans to carry out the proposals. At this point they are probably starting the processes described earlier, in Chapter 7, beginning by installing a new release of CICS.

They will install the various hardware and software elements, in partnership with their counterparts in hardware, MVS, VTAM, database and other system-programming groups, then will integrate CICS systems and test the resulting configuration. They will design and carry out tests, to ensure that the system performs as expected.

Very often, the activities will include creating new systems to run alongside existing ones, perhaps connecting them one to another. Such interconnection adds a dimension to all CICS activities, from programming and operation through to performance planning and recovery design. In fact, it affects any CICS system-programming activity you can think of, and offers some of the most stimulating challenges. As it is such a broad, challenging and important subject in its own right, it gets the next chapter to itself.

9
Networks of CICS systems

This chapter is about communication between one CICS system and another—usually referred to as *intercommunication*—which has become vital to the continued evolution of transaction-processing systems (Fig. 9.1). After more than fifteen years of development, intercommunication has made CICS a catalyst for growth in enterprises of all sizes. Starting modestly with single CICS systems, users have been able to cope with enormous growth in demand for transaction processing, without losing the original look and feel of their systems.

Strictly speaking, we should have looked at CICS intercommunication in each of the earlier chapters, as it can affect the work of application designers, operations staff and system programmers. However, doing that would have added another dimension to each subject. As they were already complex, we have given intercommunication a chapter of its own. In the chapter we will consider the reasons for, and implications of, running multiple systems. We will then consider the environments in which intercommunication can take place, and the kinds of communication that are possible. Finally, we will look at the intercommunication networks that you can build.

9.1   Multiple CICS systems

Most CICS users keep more than one CICS system running at a time. The largest have well over a hundred in productive use at any time—all on the same computer! In some cases these systems will run entirely independently. More often than not, though, they are connected to operate in concert, as networks of cooperating systems.

Paradoxically, some users cite simplicity as a reason for running so many CICS systems. This is not as strange as it seems, because such users regularly create new systems on demand, to provide new transactions or to handle extra workload. When a new transaction is ready for testing, or for real use, a new CICS system can very easily be cloned to accommodate it, using predefined, model systems. If they occupy a separate CICS system, a new transaction's programs cannot interact with other programs and can therefore be easier to monitor and debug. If a program

150

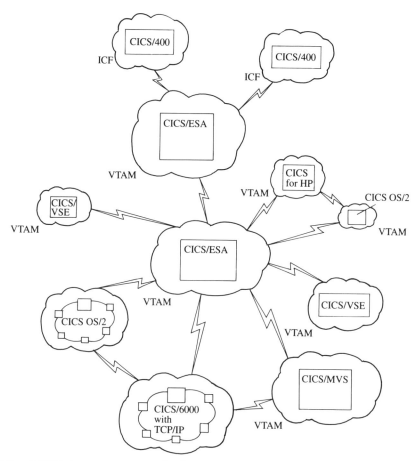

Figure 9.1. CICS intersystem communication.

manages to stop the system, it can be restarted without affecting other vital business transactions.

When an organization runs many CICS systems in parallel in this way, it does not have to link them, but can run them independently. However, most users connect many of their systems, giving each end-user access to distributed transactions without having to sign on to different systems—indeed, without having to know of the existence of different systems. CICS intercommunication, in the form of intersystem communication (ISC) or multiregion operation (MRO), links CICS systems so that they can look like one. We will look at ISC and MRO later. First, let us consider why you might need multiple systems.

Splitting systems

Many of today's major CICS users began by running single systems, then allowed them to multiply by splitting repeatedly. The splitting made it possible to address a number of challenges: of organization and security; of reliability; of constraint brought about by addressing limitations of computer hardware; and of performance. We shall consider each of these.

In many installations, a network of CICS systems has evolved with the underlying organization or workload. As additional departments have found uses for transaction processing, they have been provided with their own, separate systems. Sometimes, separation is intended to ensure security, segregating groups of users to restrict access to different kinds of data. At other times, it is seen as a way of simplifying accounting: recording use of a particular departmental system rather than recording the activity of individual members of staff. In addition, many users find operational reasons for separating systems: to allow some to be given higher priority than others; to allow entire applications to be started and stopped at different times; or to make it easier to introduce major new applications without disrupting existing ones.

Splitting systems helps to solve problems caused by unreliable programs. Programs that are designed and tested well usually run without error in production. Yet most installations have a few programs with a history of problems, and at any time there will also be a number of untested new programs. As you saw in the section on application programming, real-time systems are particularly vulnerable to rogue programs. To protect the system and other programs from their unpredictable effects, such programs can be kept apart in their own CICS systems (Fig. 9.2). At the same time, a program that is of vital importance to an organization may need to be isolated completely from other programs, placed in its own system to avoid the slightest risk of interruption.

Placing a CICS system in a region of its own brings another benefit—it has access to a whole virtual address space as large as the computer's architecture can support. Throughout the 1980s, until MVS/ESA removed existing limits on the architecture, this made it possible for CICS systems to continue growing faster than hardware technology would allow. This became vital, because users of mainframe CICS systems were experiencing the effects of what was known as 'virtual-storage constraint'. In short, massive growth in transaction processing led to contention for system storage between system software, control blocks and tables, and user programs, application packages and data. System efficiency suffered, as CICS spent more time managing storage and less on processing transactions. (In recent times, the same sort of constraint has been experienced on a smaller scale by users of personal computers, who encountered addressing limits under personal-computer operating systems.) To make more room, CICS users split their systems, running them in parallel, as separate system tasks, and spreading programs and data between them.

Sheer workload is often a concern for the largest users of transaction-processing systems. We saw in Part I how use of popular transactions often exceeds the forecast, and how effective programs stimulate demand for additional function. As a result, rapid growth can cause the most heavily used transaction-processing

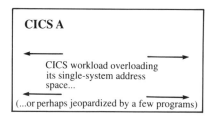

CICS A can be divided into a connected pair: CICS B + CICS C

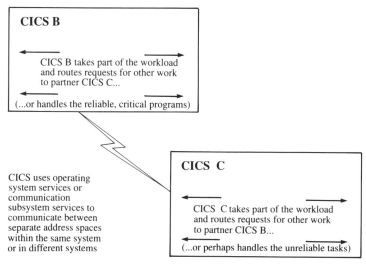

Figure 9.2.   Splitting CICS systems.

systems to outgrow the processing capacity of their computer systems. When this happens, the only options are to upgrade the computers, or to use more of them. When a system is running on the fastest machines available, there is no option but to add machines or to increase the amount of multiprocessing (say by upgrading from a 4-processor machine to a 6-processor). CICS intercommunication helps in this situation, allowing you to place different programs on different machines or processors, but allowing all users to have access to any of them.

CICS intercommunication provides a way of organizing transaction-processing systems to reflect the structure of your organization. It also helps to solve a variety of problems. It was conceived as a way of giving more freedom to system designers. It brings flexibility and room for growth, as it allows system designers to relocate transaction programs and data according to the changing needs of an organization. So, for example, you can selectively move programs, or data, or entire systems when user departments move or new equipment becomes available. Yet you can keep the separate systems linked to share common programs and data, or to give a single-system image.

Combining systems

It is becoming increasingly common for different departments or subsidiaries within an enterprise to specify and procure their own systems, getting the best solution for specific local needs. However, systems developed separately within an enterprise often grow together, eventually needing to be linked—to share data or programs, or to allow end-users to view them as a single system. CICS intercommunication facilities allow you to connect existing independent systems that are based on CICS.

Joining existing CICS systems within an enterprise is normal practice nowadays. The system-programming tasks are the same as those performed when splitting systems: establishing links and defining resources in each system. However, there will be different emphases during system design, as autonomous departments will want to control access to their systems, and to ensure data integrity.

The need for control and integrity is more obvious in the increasingly common use of real-time data communication between large enterprises. Point-of-sale systems, providing credit authorization and other services, are already taken for granted. Cross-enterprise transaction processing will become increasingly important as we advance into the twenty-first century, and will underline the importance of design considerations of present-day systems: reliability, security and integrity. As you will appreciate, this adds a dimension to the work of the system-support team.

As it becomes more common for CICS systems to be connected within and between enterprises, it becomes more likely that those systems will be running in different system environments. We shall look next at the environments supported and the kinds of communication they support.

9.2   Intercommunication environments

There are CICS systems designed to run under each of the following operating systems: MVS/ESA, MVS/XA, MVS/370, VSE/SP, VSE/ESA, OS/2, DOS, VM/SP, OS/400 and AIX. Others are promised, such as those designed for Hewlett-Packard systems. When connected to the same VTAM communications network, any CICS systems running under one of the listed operating systems can communicate directly with the others. For example, a CICS/ESA system can communicate with a CICS/400 system, or with another CICS/ESA system (Fig. 9.3(a)). This process is called intersystem communication, abbreviated to ISC.

Very large MVS and VSE systems, running on System/370 or System/390 processors, contain multiple regions.[1] It is common nowadays for users to run CICS systems in many regions at the same time, for reasons we discussed earlier. Being connected to the same VTAM network, such systems can use ISC to

(a)

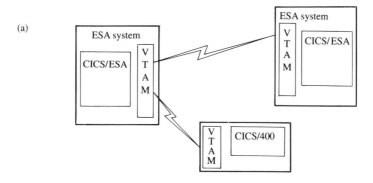

(b)

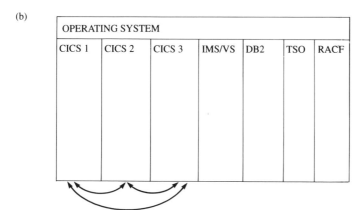

CICS A, B and C can coexist in the same machine. Each
can be independent of the others, but all can communicate using
interregion protocols, sharing workload.

In this figure, the systems coexist in an MVS system. Equivalent
configurations can be created for CICS/VSE and CICS/400. CICS OS/2
and CICS/6000 achieve the same result in different ways.

Figure 9.3.   (a) Intersystem communication (ISC). (b) Multiregion operation (MRO).

communicate with each other within the computer. Alternatively, they can use
special cross-region communication facilities built into CICS. Communication
using these facilities is known as multiregion operation, abbreviated to MRO
(Fig. 9.3(b)). In the same way, multiple connected CICS/AIX systems can use
'cross-region' communication through TCP/IP, and CICS OS/2 systems can
communicate with each other through a local area network, using either SNA or
NetBios protocols.

ISC and MRO are the underlying communication mechanisms between CICS
systems, and the differences between them affect the system specialists who have
to set up the systems. In most cases the application programmer is unaffected by
intercommunication, though there are a few exceptions which will become
apparent later. An end-user should not be aware of the CICS system itself, so
intercommunication should be completely invisible.

9.3   Modes of communication

Intersystem communication and multiregion operation provide two mechanisms for connecting CICS systems. On top of each, CICS provides five different modes of communication, each offering something different. The five modes are: Transaction Routing, Function Shipping, Asynchronous Processing, Distributed Transaction Processing and Distributed Program Link. We shall look at each in turn.

Transaction routing

Whatever your reason for having more than one CICS system, there will be times when terminal users on one system need to use a transaction owned by another system. Rather than duplicating the transaction and its supporting programs, or making the users logon to each of several systems, you can provide apparently seamless access from the end-user's terminal by using transaction routing.

As you already know, every transaction has to be defined to CICS before it can be used. With transaction routing, systems-support staff create the definition in the usual way, but specify that the transaction exists on a remote CICS system, naming the system on which it can be executed (Fig. 9.4(a)). The users of the transaction know nothing of transaction definitions, so will not notice anything unusual. CICS, on the other hand, will know not to start the transaction itself, and will send the entire request to the remote system.

Any subsequent interaction, for example messages or screen maps from the program requesting further input, or input from the end-user, will be passed between systems before reaching the user's terminal, but this passage will not be apparent to the user. Everything will appear as it would for a normal transaction.

The impact on the systems-support organization is slight. The definitions need to be created properly, and each system needs to be available and connected whenever the transaction is likely to be used. In addition, support staff need to know how to interpret debugging information when it relates to routed transactions. Otherwise, though, transaction routing creates few demands.

As a matter of interest, it is possible for a remote transaction not to be on the stated remote system, but somewhere beyond. If this is so, the stated remote system will also have the transaction defined as 'remote'. Any routed request will be passed on to yet another CICS system. This process will continue until the request reaches the system that *does* have the transaction. Once it starts to run, any communications will again automatically be passed back and forth along the communication path to the end-user. This will all happen transparently, as long as the transaction resides somewhere, the systems remain connected and the routing path does not cross itself. This repeated transaction routing is known as 'daisy-chaining', for reasons that are fairly obvious when you look at Fig. 9.4(b).

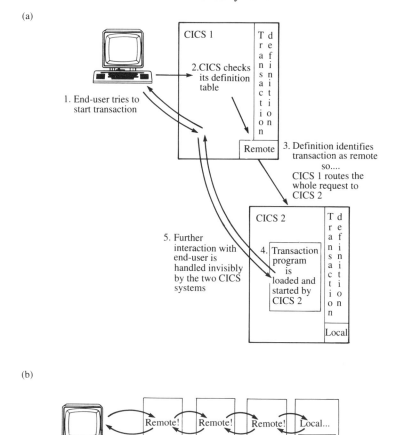

Figure 9.4. Transaction routing. (a) Simple case. (b) Daisychaining.

Function shipping

Whereas transaction routing is CICS's way of allowing several systems to share a single transaction and its programs, function shipping is a way of allowing programs on several different systems to share resources of other kinds, for example files.

With function shipping, a request for CICS to do something with one of its resources (for example, to read data from a file) is not satisfied by the local system, which does not have a copy of the file, but is sent to a remote system. The file's definition in the local system specifies that the file is remote, and names the system that owns it (Fig. 9.5).

The file request is sent to the remote system, which handles it as though it had been received in the normal way from an application program. Any results of the request are sent back, through the local system, to the program that made the

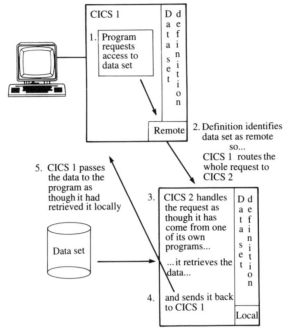

Figure 9.5.   Function shipping.

request. The application programmer and the end-user need not know that the program and file are remote from each other. Indeed, from time to time the data file may be moved between systems, sometimes being local, at other times remote. At all times, only the systems-support team will need to know where the data is kept.

Function shipping takes place in response to a command within a program. In this it differs from transaction routing, where the whole program is 'shipped' to another system.

As with transaction routing, end-users and application programmers should be unaffected by function shipping. The effects on the system-support organization are the same as for transaction routing, and again are fairly minor.

As a final thought on function shipping: it is possible for a transaction to be routed from one system to another, only to have a request for function to be shipped onwards to a third system, or even backwards to the first. As with daisychaining, this process should affect only systems-support staff, who need to define resources correctly in every system. End-users should not notice anything.

Asynchronous processing

Asynchronous processing is like a special kind of function shipping, in which the function to be performed is the execution of a program. During asynchronous processing, one program indirectly triggers execution of another program in a

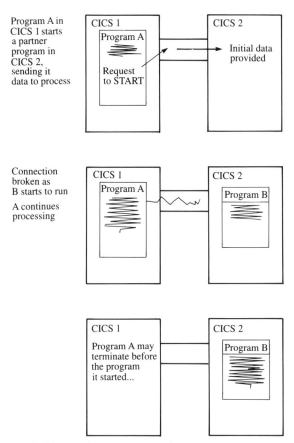

Figure 9.6. CICS asynchronous processing.

remote system (usually giving it some data to process), then breaks contact. After that, the two programs continue processing completely independently or 'asynchronously' (Fig. 9.6).

A typical example of the use of asynchronous processing is the concentration of printing programs in a single low-priority CICS region. Other regions, which contain programs but have no direct access to printers, route data to the printer region, naming the printer programs that should handle it.

Asynchronous processing is unlike transaction routing and function shipping in that a programmer knows that communication is taking place with another program during asynchronous processing because the process is triggered explicitly by a command in the program. The command names a transaction to be started, and may also specify the remote system on which it is to be started. If the started program is to be sent data for processing, the programmer will need to understand how to send it. He or she may also need to design a program to handle any responses.

In designing programs that use asynchronous processing, programmers have to pay special attention to overall transaction design. In particular, they need to ensure that there is no need for synchronization between the programs. In terminating after starting another transaction, a program trusts that transaction to complete satisfactorily.

Distributed transaction processing

This is the most sophisticated of the forms of intercommunication, and affects application design as well as system design. During distributed transaction processing, two or more programs engage in a conversation, cooperating to complete a transaction. In effect, the partner programs in the transaction comprise a single logical program, broken up and distributed among systems. The communicating programs do not both have to be CICS programs: one partner can be running on another system that uses the APPC protocols of the systems network architecture. For example, a partner can be a program running under the IMS/ESA transaction manager.

The distinguishing feature of distributed transaction processing is its need for synchronization. Once in contact, programs continue to communicate with each other until all cooperative activity is complete. In most cases, the programs making up the halves of the two-way conversation negotiate changes in data, each changing files or databases under their control. At the end of the exchange, both sides will confirm all changes, committing themselves. In a major business system, it is vital that such commitments are precisely synchronized, even if communication is broken or one of the systems fails. For this reason, application programs engaged in distributed transaction processing must be designed and tested with great care. Programmers have to learn new programming commands and concepts, designing programs that can negotiate for resources, or for control of a conversation, and can recognize and agree statuses.

Despite the extra complexity arising from the existence of a pair of application programs, system-support staff have no special work to do for distributed transaction processing. They have to ensure that systems are defined to each other, and that programs, transaction and terminals are properly defined on their owning systems. Yet they do not have to define remote resources in the way that they do for transaction routing and function shipping. They may expect to be asked by application designers to inspect proposed transaction designs, and will have to ensure the participating systems are connected before transactions are used. In addition, they may have to trace events that have taken place in the event of a problem.

Distributed program link

This is the newest form of CICS intercommunication. It was originally introduced with CICS OS/2 but later provided for CICS/ESA, CICS/VSE, CICS/6000

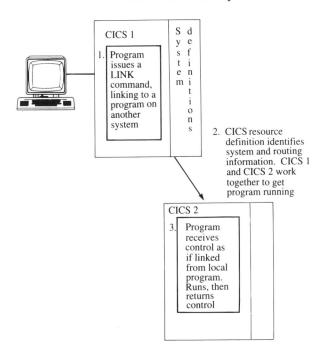

Figure 9.7. Distributed program link.

and CICS/400. It allows an application programmer to use an EXEC CICS LINK command to link to another program that resides on a remote system, awaiting return when processing is complete (Fig. 9.7).

Distributed program link allows programmers to design transaction programs that follow the client/server model for distributed programming. Originally, the command was designed for the workstation-based CICS OS/2, giving its users access to mainframe-based programs and databases. This is an ideal application of the facility, allowing transaction systems to make best use of the power of both the workstation and central mainframe. The LINK function has proved so useful that it has been provided on the CICS systems, for host-to-host linking as well as workstation-to-host linking.

Again, the system programmer needs to ensure that systems across which the link will be made are able to communicate when a request is made. Otherwise, the only significant impact will be in debugging, should a problem occur.

9.4 Networks of CICS systems

You should now have an idea of the range of communication techniques available to CICS systems, and the degree to which CICS systems can communicate across different operating-system platforms. Let us now look at the ways this ability to link systems can help system designers to create a network of systems, cope with enormous growth, and handle changes in the composition of an enterprise.

Connected machines

CICS systems come in all sizes, from the largest, supporting tens of thousands of end-users, to the smallest, with a handful of users. As we have already seen in Part I, use of new online systems usually results in rapid growth of need, often ahead of forecast. You can cope with very rapid growth by upgrading your processor to handle additional work. Eventually, if you started small, you can upgrade the entire system, say from CICS OS/2 to CICS/VSE or from CICS/VSE to CICS/ESA. However, many enterprises find that this kind of growth does not fully meet their needs: because of the way they are organized, because of the nature of their businesses or because of the way they are evolving. As well as allowing individual systems to grow, they need to allow the *number* of systems to grow, by adding new systems or by allowing existing systems to split and grow side by side. As the number of systems grows, so does the need for a degree of residual interconnection, and this is where the CICS family's interconnectivity comes into its own.

For example, consider a large corporation consisting of a number of fairly autonomous business units. Each unit may be given freedom to develop its own systems strategy, some choosing LAN-based systems, others mainframe or mid-range approaches, often basing decisions on the availability of applications. This will almost certainly result in diversity within the enterprise over time. This diversity can allow different parts of the business to make best use of the staff and resources that they have, while ensuring that their systems meet the specific needs of their sector. Using a centralized, host-based system could stifle such business units. However, to get the best value from the overall investment, a corporation will probably want key systems to communicate with headquarters' computers on a regular basis, providing business reports, sharing marketing data and allowing corporate-wide common information to be held centrally. In such a situation, CICS can be the binding agent (Fig. 9.8(a)). Its communication facilities allow users to connect their dissimilar systems, and its EXEC programming interface allows those systems to run common application programs or utility programs.

Another kind of enterprise, say an insurance company or a cooperative, may wish to maintain central control of the core business, but be able to do so while continuing to deal with widely distributed small groups of relatively independent users—agents or remote branch offices (Fig. 9.8(b)). In this situation, there is clearly a need for centralized transaction-processing facilities. There is also a need for independent local transaction-processing capacity in the remote branches. Such processing could be achieved using dial-up terminals connected to a central host, but as the data belongs largely to the agent or branch this may be inappropriate. Nowadays many branch offices or small businesses use powerful

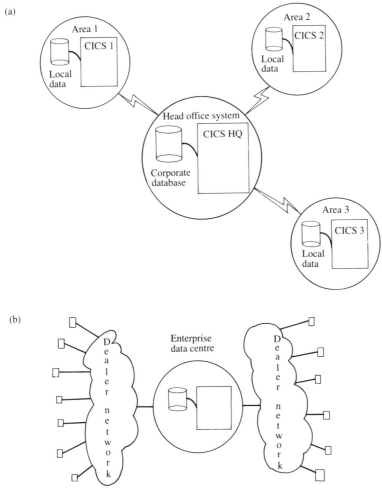

Figure 9.8. Examples of CICS networks. (a) Autonomous business units linked to corporate headquarters. (b) Enterprise serving a large network of independent business partners.

microcomputers or minicomputers to do day-to-day processing of customer data. Yet it makes sense to use the communication capabilities of these remote computers to give their users access, perhaps transparently, to services provided by the parent—or partner—company's central systems. Once again, the access can be achieved through CICS, which in its different forms can be the platform for running both local and central systems.

There are other scenarios that show the value of CICS's connectivity and programming capabilities. For example, a corporation that merges with, or takes over, other companies will need to merge or attach inherited information systems. For the reasons already considered, when CICS is used on some or all of the various systems it can be an important catalyst for convergence.

Within the same system

Even when an organization's information-systems policy is for centralization and non-programmable terminals, there is often a need to segment the workload, or separate systems owned by different business units. In some cases, this need may best be met by giving each department its own processor, and operating in the way described above: each department having local processing capacity, but all systems being connected so that they can share key business information. However, the most cost-effective, efficient and secure approach is often to use intersystem communication (ISC) or multiregion operation (MRO) to run a number of CICS systems in parallel on one or more shared mainframes, sometimes completely independently, sometimes loosely connected, to share key data.

A major advantage of centralizing processing on a mainframe system in a corporate data-processing department (the so-called 'glasshouse') is that system design and management can be made the responsibility of one specialist organization, allowing business units to focus on their own work without each one having to employ its own team of data-processing experts. System-support and application-programming teams focus their attention on the host-based systems and application packages that provide a tailor-made business solution. Other advantages are performance, data integrity and control, and security.

Transparent systems

One consequence of allowing business units to focus on their own work is that it is more important to spend time and effort on the design and provision of transparent systems. By this I mean systems that the users quickly learn to use, and can relate directly and intuitively to their day-to-day responsibilities.

Of course, intersystem communication, multiregion operation and related subjects cannot be allowed to intrude into the lives of end-users. So a key responsibility of CICS systems-support specialists is to design and support intercommunication in a way that it is transparent to users. They have to provide what is commonly referred to as a 'single-system image' for anyone who uses more than one system.

Most users need, at various times, to gain access to the order entry and inventory management applications: accounting personnel need access to the customer account applications and the payroll applications; strategy groups need access to market analysis data and accounting applications; management needs access to all applications. If each kind of application is managed by a different system, the challenge is to connect systems in a way that can give each user an impression that there is only one system. CICS provides many facilities for achieving this. You have already read about the key facilities, available as CICS intercommunication. In addition, there are user exits, including the dynamic routing exit.

9.5   Beyond the CICS network

CICS intercommunication through ISC and MRO clearly allows enormous flexibility within an enterprise. For new applications, CICS support for APPC and TCP/IP also allows communication with non-CICS systems. CICS therefore fits naturally into new kinds of transaction-processing networks.

As new CICS systems are created, they usually coexist with existing systems, which have to continue to run to support existing business. To help protect existing investment, CICS has evolved to coexist more effectively with other subsystems. In 1992 it was extended to include a front-end programming interface (FEPI), which helps to bring dissimilar systems together. Before that, CICS users had been able to consolidate various systems by using the PR/SM feature of MVS/ESA. We will look briefly at each of these features.

The front-end programming interface (FEPI)

The CICS Front-end Programming Interface (FEPI), pronounced 'feppy', is part of CICS/ESA, introduced in CICS/ESA 3.3. It provides a way of drawing together an enterprise's CICS/ESA and IMS/ESA systems. As its full name suggests, it is a facility that provides a programming solution to the problem of giving a single-system image to multiple systems.

FEPI is part of CICS/ESA, and provides extensions to the EXEC programming interface that allow programs running under CICS/ESA to act as intermediaries between end-users and a mixture of existing CICS/ESA and IMS/ESA programs. It can prove particularly useful when an enterprise is combining systems, or extending the use of existing systems to many users. When end-users are given access to a wider range of transactions, some on CICS/ESA, others on IMS/ESA, they need simpler interfaces to the systems. FEPI makes it possible to write single front-end transactions that conceal the various back-end transactions. The attractive feature of this approach is that existing programs do not have to be rewritten to achieve system convergence; the front end invokes the old back-end transactions in their existing form.

A front-end transaction can be a simple program that displays menus and routes transactions according to input. On the other hand, it can provide additional function of its own. It can provide a single, unified image for all transactions or it can provide different images for different audiences. So, for example, different groups of end-users used to different styles of initial displays could have their own front-ends, to give a feeling of continuity.

PR/SM

Before systems could be linked at the level of application programs, through FEPI, many CICS users had been consolidating CICS and non-CICS subsystems on single multiprocessor systems. The PR/SM feature introduced with Enterprise Systems Architecture/370 (ESA/370) made it possible to consolidate not only subsystems but also entire System/370 systems on a single machine. This allows users of powerful systems to get greater benefit from multiprocessors.

PR/SM (often pronounced 'prism'), the processor resource/system manager, makes it possible for a multiprocessor machine to be partitioned so that it acts as two or more entirely separate processors. As each one can run its own copy of a System/370 or System/390 operating system, you can run dissimilar operating systems on the same processor complex. For example, the same machine can run MVS/ESA, MVS/XA and VSE/ESA at the same time.

For CICS users, PR/SM makes it possible to run successive releases of system software in parallel prior to migration. It also adds a dimension to CICS intercommunication: CICS systems can use ISC to work together across PR/SM partitions.

9.6   Multisystem strategies

As you can see from this chapter, CICS system design and programming is multidimensional. As well as coping with all of the activities described earlier in this book, the staff in a dynamic, growing enterprise will have to plan for and deal with the added dimension of intercommunication. For every task described in Part III, they will need to add consideration of intercommunication. So, for example, they have to consider performance, security, recovery and operation. Intercommunication also produces new interfaces to be set up, monitored, maintained, tuned and debugged. So CICS staff become involved even more in considerations of VTAM, security managers, other CICS products, database managers and so on.

The extent to which your system-programming staff will use these CICS intercommunication facilities depends upon your overall transaction-processing strategy. Their readiness to take up new transaction-processing technologies will depend very much on how you invest in your systems strategists. They are the subject of the next chapter.

Note

[1] Or 'partitions' or 'address spaces'. Throughout this chapter 'region' has been used.

10
Systems strategy

By carrying out the activities described in Chapters 7, 8 and 9, your systems-support team will keep your systems vital, and so ensure that your business can run smoothly in both the immediate future and the mid-term. However, a successful business plans for long-term health and growth, investing in forecasting, research and development. Effective investment in data processing, particularly transaction processing, has been shown to give very large returns on investment; ineffective use brings corresponding penalties. CICS's key role in many businesses means that experienced CICS staff often play an important part in planning the future of their enterprises.

CICS strategists can prove invaluable where the world of business meets the world of advanced information technology. They need to understand the needs of both worlds at a number of levels. In the business world, CICS strategists need to appreciate the trends and competitive pressures in their enterprises' industries or business sectors. On a human level, they need to understand the people that will be using the systems they provide: staff, management and even customers. They need to appreciate the financial pressures and something of the current corporate strategy, the related strategic goals and the tactical steps on the way to fulfilling the goals.

At the same time, in the world of technology, CICS strategists need to understand the trends that could benefit CICS, its users or its applications. Almost all data-processing and communications technology somehow relates to CICS, so strategists need to remain in touch on all fronts.

Leading CICS strategists are generally viewed with respect by the information-technology industry. They are often consulted by IBM for views on requirements relating to CICS and associated products, for example databases, security or operating systems. Their views are also much sought in specialist forums, such as user groups.

In this chapter, we will consider the different areas in which advanced strategic planning is essential. In each case, we will look at subjects only in general terms, to show the kinds of work performed by the specialists. In some cases, our predictions will be reasonably accurate. However, experience shows that CICS systems people are creative enough to confound almost all predictions.

10.1   Business needs

A constant theme of this book is that CICS is evolving continuously in response to business and technical pressures. Those same pressures influence your technical planners, driving them to find new ways of using the transaction systems.

In the course of normal business, enterprises are responding more than ever before to market pressures. They know that they have to compete with each other for customers. This means that they have to provide better or more cost-effective goods and services, on time. Not only do they have to provide them—they also have to be seen to provide them, showing promptness and efficiency without excessive charges.

Opportunity

A common way of improving the cost-effectiveness of a data-processing installation is to do more work, spreading fixed costs more widely. Ideally, the core business of an enterprise should keep its systems fully occupied; in reality, many organizations have spare capacity, especially outside peak working hours. At such times, the organization can handle additional transactions, maybe for outside organizations. CICS strategists are best placed to detect and quantify spare capacity. They can also judge the impact of new workloads, ensuring that they do not begin to affect existing work.

Once established, this kind of additional business can grow to become a significant revenue-earner. In fact, some data-processing organizations have become full businesses in their own right. CICS frequently plays the part of catalyst in this kind of business success story. The spark of enterprise will be provided by another element—say a technological advance such as mobile telephony—but CICS is frequently the component that allows a team to make something of the possibilities.

There are many examples of this 'secondary industry' effect. Most common are the highly successful data-processing service subsidiaries that have grown from data-processing departments of large companies. Other examples include mail-order businesses, credit agencies and consultancy organizations that started small but have grown explosively.

Opportunist organizations have tended to benefit from having talented staff with sufficient technical knowledge to recognize a fit between technological advances and business opportunities. We will look at the kind of technical considerations that currently offer the greatest opportunities.

Efficiency and service

To achieve efficiency and give effective service to users, strategic planners continue to look for new ways of harnessing technology and new ways of applying proven technology to different parts of the business process. So, for example, they need to consider ways of improving efficiency of members of staff, perhaps by providing them, or their customers, with specialized workstations. A long-standing example of this is the banking teller machine that has relieved counter staff in banks of some time-consuming routine tasks, by giving customers direct access to a special kind of terminal. The growing power of personal systems makes it easier to build such specialized devices.

Organizations with a large range of business interests are beginning to find that their customers expect another kind of efficiency—that of communication between component businesses. So, for example, the customer of a major insurance company may expect to conduct a number of personal insurance-related transactions at one time. The customer sees the transactions as closely related—by self. This may be in conflict with the traditional company view of the transactions—that of a series of separate transactions, to be handled one by one by different departments: life policy, house policy, motor policy, holiday insurance, motor claims and so on. Similarly, in the banking business, a customer expects to be recognized as a single portfolio of accounts, whereas the bank may be used to seeing him or her in pieces, as a current account, a mortgage account, a savings account and so on. In future, the company that cannot deal quickly and efficiently with a complex enquiry could lose business to more effective competitors. This brings a need for systems convergence and a way to make it easy for unsophisticated users to work with many separate systems, some old, some new: a task for which CICS is perfectly suited. As we will see later in this chapter, the CICS strategist will be able to see technical solutions to all of those business questions.

The drive to provide more 'one-stop shopping', as this is sometimes called, encourages cooperation between enterprises. So, for example, point-of-sale has brought banks and retailers together, initially to allow cashless purchase. The connection also allows 'purchaseless cash', with shops being able to supply cash, automatically debiting customer accounts. Similar cooperation allows banks to work more effectively with insurance companies. It is no coincidence that banks figure strongly in these examples. They have themselves had a long history of cooperation through information systems. Networking facilities have for a long time enabled them to complete complex interbank transactions. The newer services simply embrace the banks' other partners—their customers, both large and small.

The same kind of cross-enterprise aggregation happens for other reasons. In recent times, corporate takeovers, mergers and alliances have become more commonplace. However, regardless of the reasons, aggregation has major implications for system planners, who need to decide how to connect different kinds of hardware and software. Where CICS exists in both enterprises, merging systems should be relatively straightforward. As the variety of systems grows, such exercises will inevitably become more challenging, despite the growing use of open systems. We will see later what technical implications this has for the CICS strategist.

Efficiency and organization

At the same time as organizations have been coming together, some of the more monolithic establishments have shown signs of the reverse, moving towards separation of business units to form looser coalitions, devolving management control. The end result is approximately the same as convergence: a collection of discrete business units, connected whenever there seems to be a common purpose.

This loose clustering of business units can make growth easier to manage, and could become crucial as we enter the twenty-first century. The trend towards a global marketplace, with fewer trade barriers, encourages companies to set up subsidiaries outside their home countries. Separate units will need to be independent inasmuch as they have to adapt to national differences. However, they need to be connected to parent companies for corporate reporting and control, and to realize the benefits of economies of scale.

Similarly, corporate mergers mean that corporations have to be able to connect dissimilar systems, so that they can communicate freely. Increased levels of takeovers in recent years have presented many organizations with the challenges of systems integration. In some cases, the approach has been to impose one set of standards. Entire data-processing organizations have been disbanded, or converted to use systems from another vendor. In other cases, the different systems have been retained, and the challenge has been to find ways of connecting them to give optimum communication and control. This second challenge is similar to the cross-enterprise connection described in the previous section.

The 'open' approach to use of systems is becoming more popular as organizations find ever-larger numbers of possible solutions to business problems, and install a variety of dissimilar systems. The provision of CICS on a wide variety of platforms, including UNIX systems, provides an excellent opportunity for full flexibility when designing corporate systems. As CICS becomes the common element in a wider range of system platforms, so the CICS system specialist will become key to the efficient use of the systems.

One systems-support need in the immediate future is for CICS to extend its ability to serve, so that almost any subsystems can attach themselves to the central, corporate systems. The leading systems staff are already defining how they would like this to be done, basing their definitions on their knowledge of how businesses and subsidiaries are organized, and how existing systems will evolve in the coming years. They will use their deep knowledge of all of the topics that we have reviewed so far. Factors that will influence them include their attitude to open systems, the need to accommodate a variety of communications architectures, choice of data technology and systems-management challenges. We will look at these and other related issues in the rest of this chapter.

Value

Enterprises are at last beginning to see systems in the same way as they see plant and machinery. CICS specialists have to be able to provide cost and benefit analyses for the solutions that are based on CICS. Such analyses nowadays have to compare:

- CICS-based solutions with non-CICS equivalents
- Solutions on a variety of different CICS platforms
- Solutions based on different features within the same CICS platform.

In many cases, a new business system will fit neatly into an existing CICS mainframe. Often, though, there will be cases for distributing the work. CICS strategists have to make recommendations based on considerations of cost, flexibility and organization. Their task is in one way made more difficult by CICS: there are usually several choices of solution with CICS. Yet the growing openness of CICS provides significant freedom to change platforms over time. So, for example, a new system can be developed and tested—even used in production for a time—on a mainframe CICS system, then later transferred to a departmental or distributed system, when the specification has been decided.

Systems are also being viewed like plant and machinery in another way. Like those assets, the value of a software system diminishes over time, and the system needs to be refurbished. This can, like plant replacement, be expensive and can be difficult to justify. Systems specialists for CICS have to spend time convincing first themselves and then management that new technology is good value for money, and that migration to new releases will be cost-justified.

10.2   Technology responses

CICS has evolved with, and sometimes even ahead of, industry. Its broad range of facilities and interfaces keeps it adaptable, so that it can be used to meet most needs that arise. Whenever new needs arise, it is rapidly extended to meet them, too. The system is therefore equal to most challenges, but only when applied by strategists who know its capabilities and understand the technical challenges. In the following sections we will look briefly at some of the major technical matters of importance to strategists.

Standards and architectures

As the number of available systems and applications has become bewildering, organizations have introduced international standards to provide a degree of compatibility. Your system strategists need to help to define your policy on standards, and to know how these fit in with your long-term plans for transaction processing.

Many CICS users have been used to IBM's established standards, introduced as proprietary architectures or at least as IBM-controlled standards. For example, the long-standing proprietary System/370 architecture, now the System/390 architecture, to which IBM's largest mainframe computers conform, is designed and written by IBM itself, though it is documented fully and is used by other computer manufacturers. In a similar way, IBM controls the development and publication of other standards: the systems network architecture (SNA), which defines how conforming products such as terminals and computers communicate, and the systems application architecture (SAA), which is a set of interfaces, conventions and protocols that make it easier to achieve consistency at the application level, across a variety of different systems. CICS has long been among the first subsystems to use new features of these architectures, consistent with its roles of application enabler, communications subsystem and operating system within the operating system.

Nowadays, some organizations, particularly government agencies throughout the world, insist on using IBM-independent standards, so that they are free to choose software and equipment from a wider range of suppliers. This means that they favour open systems, communications architecture embodied in inter-national standard, such as the OSI model, plus a variety of long-established standards, such as X.12 and X400 for communication and ANS COBOL and SQL for programming languages. In addition, some bodies favour a number of de facto standards, such as the use of TCP/IP for communication in UNIX environments, or conformance to the distributed computing environment model developed by the Open Software Foundation. Your strategists will need to define a strategy for standards that can accommodate your future needs, taking into account the decisions that your business partners and clients will have made. For example, if your partners decide to adopt a communications strategy based on OSI, your strategists will need to ensure that your systems can at least communicate with OSI subsystems. Similarly, if your organization wishes to bid for government contracts that have to be based on open standards, your organization must be ready to accommodate that need while fitting in with your existing inventory of systems.

Choice of communications technology

Sitting at the centre of data-communications networks, CICS systems are ideally placed to use new communications technology. Of course, CICS communicates through telecommunications subsystems, such as VTAM, so it is shielded from the raw technology.

As we saw in the last section, communication using the SNA protocols implemented by VTAM no longer satisfies all users. Some prefer TCP/IP, mostly for UNIX systems, and others prefer OSI. CICS/6000 communicates through TCP/IP or SNA. CICS OS/2 communicates through SNA or NetBios token ring protocols. CICS/400 and CICS/VSE use SNA. As the most likely candidate for central server, CICS/ESA supports SNA communication but has also been tested with the prototypes of an OSI adaptor and a TCP/IP adaptor.

Your systems strategists need to identify the mix of CICS products that could form your future product base for transaction processing, to understand the range of communication options offered by the CICS family as a whole, and so to see the relationship between your enterprise's communications strategy and its transaction-processing strategy. In addition, they need to relate your enterprise's communications plans to those of business partners and clients.

Communications promises to be among the fastest-changing technologies into the twenty-first century, offering vastly greater communication capacity at much lower cost. With the increased capacity, telecommunications companies can offer additional services to their customers. Such services could form key elements in future applications. As a result of these possibilities, communications technology is likely to be a key driver for change in transaction processing. To remain competitive, an organization must anticipate the new working methods, applications and customer services that could be the natural by-products of the new technology. Its success in doing so could have a significant influence on its future. With CICS systems as the application platforms controlling this communication, the CICS specialist becomes key to the success of the project.

Data technology

The rate of change in the communications world in the late 1990s will probably make changes in data storage and management seem relatively pedestrian. However, the management of data will become increasingly important if your organization begins to distribute transaction processing across a variety of systems, or opens up communication channels with systems in other organizations.

Easier and cheaper communication is already making distribution of data more acceptable. Your CICS specialists will have to study the way your CICS network is likely to evolve, and to predict the way this should influence placement of data. They have to advise client departments on the most appropriate location of data, and methods of data management, for their applications. They also need to educate user departments in the need to back up data and introduce procedures for recovery in case of disaster. They need to ensure that the freedom that comes with distributed processing does not result in loss of organization and data integrity.

You saw in Chapters 8 and 9 that CICS specialists are already expected to be experts in distributed systems, data integrity through logging and recovery, and related topics. They are therefore natural consultants when considering distributed system management.

Choice of CICS systems

As CICS becomes available on new systems, strategists need to be able to choose the best systems for any new application. Having been brought up with CICS/OS/VS and CICS/MVS, or CICS/VSE, they will often first consider using those systems for new applications. However, system solutions based on CICS OS/2, CICS/6000 or CICS/400 will sometimes provide the best value for money, either because the systems themselves are less expensive or because such systems are already being used and can accommodate transaction processing as well. Even so, in most cases the choice will not be one between having one CICS or another. New systems will typically coexist with existing ones. With CICS services common to them all, it is possible to connect the systems at a later date, extending the scope of services to all users through intercommunication.

Long-term decisions about purchasing and using systems will be made only after exhaustive study of the alternatives by strategists. The final choice will often depend on many things beside cost. For example, your strategists need to determine what skill levels are needed to support particular systems; how remote systems are to be maintained and operated; what equipment is already installed in each location. Yet the CICS dimension means that any decision made at the outset need not be final: intercommunication and the extensive portability of CICS programs allow changes of direction.

CICS intercommunication

Chapter 9 showed the full range of options for communication between CICS systems. The power of CICS intercommunication cannot be overstated. It has been the means by which CICS systems have been able to grow in power for the last decade, outstripping the growth in processor power. At the same time, it has provided the growth in ways that are flexible enough to accommodate organizations of all size and description. It has now become one of the key means of bridging the communication gaps between CICS systems on different architectures: System/370, AS/400, RISC System/6000, OS/2 and, most recently, on Hewlett-Packard systems.

Of all the technologies that the CICS strategist needs to embrace, CICS intercommunication is probably the most important. Successful intercommunication design depends upon a sound communications base, and demands a sound system-management strategy, but the strategy itself is a vital part of the transaction-processing strategy of any large organization. Referring back to the discussion of devolution and aggregation in Chapter 9, either approach will depend upon CICS intercommunication.

The system strategist has to analyse the organization's transaction processing needs, deciding whether the needs are to be met within a small number of large processors, or distributed throughout the whole enterprise on smaller systems, or a combination of both. He or she then needs to understand the need for connectivity and the relationships between the connected systems: whether they are peers or have an hierarchical relationship.

System topologies

Having established the requirements, the strategist will consider the merits of various system topologies. For example, consider Fig. 10.1, which shows only four out of many possible situations but which helps to show the kind of choices that are being made regularly. The figures within Fig. 10.1 show collections of connected CICS systems.

Figure 10.1(a) shows a group of independent CICS systems, running on any mix of operating systems, each largely independent. In this set-up, the systems communicate with each other only occasionally, when they need to give their own users access to transactions or data on connected systems. This represents fairly standard use of CICS intercommunication. The communication could be between CICS systems running in different regions of the same processor, or within different regions of a logical partition under the PR/SM feature of MVS/ESA, or within separate processors. It could even be on different operating systems, for example CICS/ESA and CICS/6000.

Figure 10.1(b) shows a CICS OS/2 token ring configuration, with a server machine providing local transaction-processing resources, but connected to a CICS/ESA system for access to major corporate databases. The CICS OS/2 system could as easily have been a multi-user CICS OS/2 system with non-programmable workstations.

Figure 10.1(c) shows a common, and fairly simple, configuration. In this, every application occupies its own region. As new applications are created, new regions are started to accommodate them. A simple 'menu' transaction routes transaction requests to the appropriate handling region. This structure is commonly used on CICS/ESA mainframe systems, but clearly would work equally well with multiple connected CICS systems of other kinds. Although this may sometimes make inefficient use of system resources, it certainly provides a simple and relatively easily maintained structure. It may therefore be the cheapest configuration to design, operate and maintain.

Figure 10.1(d) shows a series of CICS systems running in cooperation in different regions or systems. In an MRO configuration, the CICS systems would

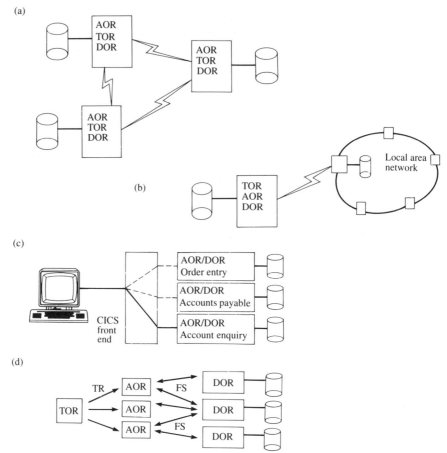

Figure 10.1. CICS configurations. (a) Systems largely self-sufficient. Connected for limited interchange. (b) Independent (departmental) LAN with host connectivity for access to database. (c) Entirely independent application/data-owning regions. Front-end CICS performs intelligent routing. (d) Full TOR/AOR/DOR configuration, with transaction routing and function shipping.

simply be in different address spaces of the same processor; in an ISC configuration, they could be in different address spaces on the same machine or different machines. In any case, we will refer to the location as a CICS region. A terminal-owning region (TOR) handles all terminal input and output, but routes transaction requests to one of three application-owning regions (AORs) for processing. These in turn route program requests for data access to data-owning regions (DORs). The seven-region complex of CICS systems (otherwise known as a CICSplex) replaces a single CICS system.

These are just four of many possible topologies, any of which may have relevance for your organization. They could have included CICS/6000, CICS/VSE or CICS/400 systems instead of the ones shown. The key point is that the CICS strategist will need to understand all of the possibilities and review the options whenever a new system or application is proposed. This decision will be added to those on whether to choose MRO or ISC; whether to use CICS/ESA only or to distribute the workload to departmental systems; which CICS systems to use; and how interenterprise communication is to be implemented.

Single-system image

An additional intercommunication consideration for the CICS strategist is one that we considered in Chapter 2. The application end-user needs to see the CICS system as a single-user system. It may offer a menu of applications, but it should behave as though each terminal user has the system to himself or herself. As the world of open systems encourages enterprises to choose systems according to their suitability for particular applications, so it becomes vital to provide acceptable front-end 'menus' to hide the details of routing and connection. As you have seen, the use of CICS terminal-owning regions can provide this effect. Furthermore, in mainframe systems where CICS/ESA and the IMS transaction manager are running applications side by side, the CICS front-end programming interface (FEPI) allows you to create the same effect for CICS and IMS together.

This front-end 'camouflage' conceals successive layers of complexity, giving end-users a very usable interface. However, it can do nothing to hide the complexity from the system-support team. That brings us to the next challenge for the strategist: system management.

10.3   System management

In Chapters 7 and 8 we looked at the work of the system-support staff, relating it to a simple, single CICS system. In that context, the work of defining resources, handling messages, processing system data sets and journals, and so on, seemed fairly straightforward. In Chapter 9, we considered ways in which many CICS systems can be created and combined to form a CICSplex, sharing resources. We did not review the many ways that this would change the day-to-day system support tasks.

As your CICS systems divide, or combine, you quickly discover the need for a system-management strategy. Or, at least, your staff quickly discover the need! In a single CICS system, individual resources need to be defined before they can be used. In a CICSplex, they need to be defined within any system that will use them, either directly or through transaction routing or function shipping. This almost-clerical task can become huge in a large network, so requires careful planning and a well-defined process.

Similarly, a simple matter such as the handling of CICS messages or dump data can become a major issue when there are hundreds of systems producing data to be handled. In fact, many routine matters pose special challenges in the multi-CICS environment. And the challenges can become greater as some of the systems themselves become simpler. Departmental transaction-processing systems are usually designed to work with minimum intervention. As a result, all messages and administrative operations must be handled remotely, from a central site. Problem resolution must be done from there, too.

The establishment of a system-management strategy is a major project in its own right. It is clearly intimately related to almost everything we have discussed so far in this chapter—perhaps in this book. There are CICS facilities and related products to help systems-support staff to establish a framework for system management. Your strategists need to understand these facilities, their strengths and limitations, and to develop the best management strategies for your configuration. As systems proliferate and communications networks expand, they need to develop an architecture within which to develop. An early need, becoming increasingly important for more sophisticated users, is for a naming convention for systems and the resources they share.

Application development policy

Although application development is often held to be the responsibility of a separate application-development department within an organization, the systems-support group will often need to provide guidance and occasional education.

System-support personnel are usually among the first to see details of a new release of CICS. Certainly, they are the first to study the release in depth. As a result, they are first to discover major impacts on application developers, and to draw up action plans. So, for example, they will have been first to recognize the withdrawal of the macro-level programming interface in CICS/ESA, and will have had to prepare appropriate strategies for handling it. The guidance from IBM was clear: macro-level programs should not be migrated to CICS/ESA. They should either be converted to command-level programs or be maintained for the foreseeable future on CICS/MVS systems that can be connected to follow-on release of CICS/ESA. System strategists will have assessed the extent of use of macro-level programs within their systems, probably using the macro-detection utility provided by IBM, will have assessed the costs and benefits of conversion, then will have made appropriate recommendations to the application-development teams.

On a more general level, strategists will help with application reviews, and will consider alternative approaches to application development. For example, they will survey and assess application-development productivity aids, such as application generators and screen painters, or debugging aids. More radically, they may challenge the need for in-house development capability, arguing in some cases that application packages are more cost-effective.

Vendor products

System strategists will study alternative system packages as well as application packages. By system packages I mean those ancillary products, produced by both IBM and other vendors, that help to make CICS systems easier to operate, manage, secure or debug.

Some of the packages used with CICS are seen by their users as indispensable system components. Consequently, it is essential that versions of the packages are ready in time for use with any new release of CICS. System strategists need to keep such packages under constant review, to ensure that they are being developed and maintained properly, and that they are the best in their field.

As more of CICS code becomes available only as object code, it becomes more important to ensure that packages are fully able to migrate to successive release of CICS.

10.4   Summary

You can probably tell from this description that the system strategists typically have extensive experience of CICS, of its applications, and of systems generally. They are often able to contribute to the technical debate, through participation in user-groups. In addition, they keep in touch with IBM and other CICS specialists, sharing experience and knowledge. These people are the subject of the next chapter.

11
CICS worldwide community

As you discover more about CICS, you appreciate the skill, knowledge and enthusiasm of the professionals that work with it. All three attributes are developed mainly through experience, but there are plenty of opportunities for developing through others. Apart from formal education, almost all involve contact with other professionals, especially with some of the thousands of recognized experts, both IBM and non-IBM (Fig. 11.1), who provide education, advice and sometimes example.

In this chapter, we look at the kinds of experts that can prove most effective, and the forums that provide most contact with them.

11.1   IBM support staff

Your system designers and application-programming designers, and your system-support team, can call on a wide range of experts within IBM. The experts cover

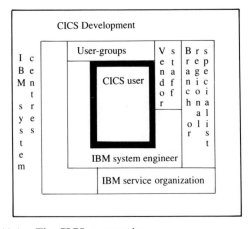

Figure 11.1.   The CICS community.

180

hardware and software. For software, the first contact is usually the IBM system engineer, the SE.

The system engineer

You will be familiar with the idea of the system engineer, your assigned IBM representative from the local branch office. The system engineer is analogous to a medical general practitioner. He or she has a good general understanding of your system and your business needs, and knows, or can find out about, different products and services that can help you. Like a general practitioner, he or she is competent to help and advise in most areas, has knowledge in depth on a few, and calls on a wide range of specialists to provide more specific support and advice when necessary.

As CICS is often a key element in an installation, an IBM system engineer will usually know most of your key CICS system-support staff personally, meeting them regularly. He or she will keep abreast of advances in CICS-related technology (for example new releases and features) and will be able to track down technical information from a variety of databases. From time to time, the system engineer will also prepare and present recommendations on strategy, based on his or her understanding of your business, systems and staff.

If you need more detailed technical support than your system engineer can provide, he or she will call in a more knowledgeable colleague. Each marketing region has access to CICS specialists who can offer services to customers through their branch offices.

Depending on the nature and complexity of your needs, you will get the services of one or two experts or an entire team. For example, you may need advice on how to upgrade a series of applications, a need that could be met by a single CICS specialist. On the other hand, you may need help deciding what products to use to meet particular needs. Or you may want a complete strategy review. In these cases, you probably need help from a variety of hardware and software experts, including a CICS technical specialist.

The CICS technical specialist

CICS technical specialists exist throughout the IBM organization. Sometimes they are system engineers with extensive experience gained as support staff working with CICS users, often having been programmers in their own right. In other cases, they are members of IBM's system centres, and spend most of their waking hours working with CICS and CICS users: answering users' questions, giving education or briefings, and conducting reviews of application or system designs.

System engineers who become expert often reinforce their expertise by becoming involved in design reviews for many different customer situations. At times they become involved in early support programs, after which they can advise other system engineers who begin supporting users who follow later. When such early experience is seen as particularly valuable to the wider user community, IBM system engineers spend time documenting it in one or more technical bulletins, assigned for the task to one of IBM's international technical support centres, in Washington, New York and Santa Teresa in California. CICS bulletins are also sponsored by other centres, including for example those in Greenford in England and Böblingen in Germany. Technical bulletins are generally highly regarded, being based on direct experience of the author.

Some American system centres, notably the one in Dallas, Texas, have permanent staffs of long-standing CICS experts. These provide full-time support for IBM's marketing and support personnel. They perform almost all kinds of support function, from briefing customers to providing online help-desk support for system engineers. These systems centres remain very close to CICS Development, meeting to understand future plans, and feeding back to Development the latest impressions and requirements they have heard from the customers they meet.

The systems centres necessarily work in different ways, according to geography. In Europe, for example, each country organization has its own challenges, so the organization differs from that in America. Nevertheless, projects initiated in one country eventually benefit users in other countries. For example, system-centre bulletins sponsored by IBM's World Trade organization, perhaps sponsored from Europe, are available from IBM worldwide. At the same time, staff from, for example, the Dallas System Center can be found in Europe, giving advice to user-group meetings, technical conferences and so on.

The electronic question-and-answer service provided through system engineers (known as QAT, ASKQ, EQUAL and RETAIN at different times and in different parts of the world) is possibly the best example of two-way sharing of technical expertise. This allows system engineers anywhere in the world to share the answers to technical CICS questions. As they are raised, questions are routed automatically to technical specialists in the system centres, and those specialists research and respond, if necessary engaging in longer dialogue to get more detail. Where there is no immediate solution, a system engineer can act as a channel for passing the requirement to CICS Development.

11.2   Consultants

The support and advice provided by system engineers and their IBM colleagues will help you to handle short-term operational and planning needs. For more comprehensive projects, or for strategic planning, you may want to commission the services of consultants.

IBM branch offices can arrange consultancy services. Sometimes these will be provided by system centres, as described in the last section. At other times, entire project teams can be assembled, from system-centre staff, developers and even non-IBM specialists.

Of course, IBM is not the only organization capable of providing consultancy services for CICS users. The use of CICS is so widespread, and the range of related packages so comprehensive, that there are many experts available throughout the world. Some specialize in CICS system consultancy. Others, primarily vendors of ancillary products or of education, have built up significant secondary businesses from consultancy. So, for example, a leading developer of a software package used with CICS will advise users migrating to a new CICS release. His or her expertise will have been acquired by direct experience of updating the software package to work with the new release. In the same way, an IBM consultant's expertise may have been acquired while helping a customer during an early support program for CICS.

11.3   Bureau services

Bureau services may be viewed as the ultimate form of consultancy, providing the hardware, software, system support and operations support that you need to install your systems and keep them running. IBM is one of a number of organizations that can provide such a service. It will install and maintain specified systems within IBM facilities, saving you from having to invest in equipment, space and staff of your own. If necessary, you can even have your applications installed and maintained.

Many CICS users want to keep control of their systems, applications and data, so do not want to use the services of a third party in this way. However, it is sometimes necessary. For example, an organization may need to implement a new CICS system too quickly to be able to build a suitable project team or to assemble the necessary equipment. It may simply not have room for the expansion. Or it may not wish to make a long-term investment in hardware, software and staff until it is certain that a project will be successful. In these circumstances, it may decide to use bureau services.

There is a halfway house between running your own systems and having them created and managed by a bureau. Called 'facilities management', it generally involves hiring an outside organization to provide all the staff and expertise to take over management of established premises, equipment, programs and data. A number of organizations, notably IBM itself, provide facilities-management services. CICS often features among the systems requested as part of such services.

Subcontracting these kinds of services has been common for a long time. Some of the biggest and most sophisticated users of CICS systems, using all of the facilities described throughout this book, are facilities-management organizations and bureaux.

11.4   Service organizations

IBM's software maintenance organization, nowadays an arm of IBM's Development organization, provides a ready source of CICS consultants. The organization's primary aim is to provide rapid relief to users who are having problems with their use of CICS systems, but the specialists who provide this relief are world-renowned experts in CICS and its use. They frequently work alongside system-centre experts to provide comprehensive advice and guidance. Sometimes they form part of IBM project teams providing design reviews or other consultancy services.

However, the CICS service organizations in IBM spend most of the time helping customers to solve problems. As we saw in Chapter 7, problem analysis is extraordinarily challenging in an online real-time environment. The almost infinite capacity for tailoring CICS ensures that every CICS system is unique, and that different problems will occur in each, or the same problems will have different symptoms in each.

Your system-support staff will handle most problems. When they have explored every possible solution, they will contact IBM to describe the problem and see if there is a known remedy. IBM staff search for solutions within a database of known problems. If the problem is known, they will supply a solution to your staff. If the problem has not previously been encountered, it will be reviewed by IBM staff expert in the diagnosis of CICS problems. These people, in the IBM support centres, carry out research in depth to understand a problem. If necessary, they ask for detailed data, perhaps dumps of system-storage contents. They may ask your system-support team to try to recreate a particular problem, to gather more data. In most cases, these experts will find the solution to your problem. If they cannot, though, they pass the problem directly to CICS Development, who will review the problem in even greater depth and identify a solution, which may involve minor modifications to CICS. So a customer can rapidly be put in touch with CICS developers if there are serious problems.

The existence of a major support organization ensures that there is a pool of expertise in diagnosing real-time CICS problems. It also means that a particular problem need be discovered only once; the symptoms and solution are stored on a database for future reference.

11.5   Education consultants

Throughout this book I have referred to CICS education in various forms. Education on CICS is, not surprisingly, closely related to consultancy services and provision of CICS utilities.

Over the years, IBM itself has provided extensive education services. It has now established a separate company in America, called Skill Dynamics, to specialize in high-quality education. The demand for CICS-related education is so great that many non-IBM organizations also provide CICS education. The expertise gained by companies that develop CICS utilities (for example, performance monitors, debugging tools or application packages), or those providing help with system installation or migration, can often benefit less-experienced CICS users. For this reason, consultants and package developers often document their experiences in the form of books or education classes.

11.6   User-groups

CICS specialists of all kinds benefit from membership of the very active CICS projects within IBM user-groups around the world. User-groups are nowadays a fairly commonplace phenomenon, reflecting the variety of proprietary and open systems in common use. However, IBM user-groups have a long history, very widespread membership, and much experience. They provide a way for users of advanced IBM hardware and software to share knowledge and experience, and to convey their thoughts and needs to IBM. CICS projects within the user-groups have had an enormous effect on the evolution of CICS over the years. In this section, we will look at each of the groups that are currently active, and show the range of activities and interests.

Although user-groups exist throughout the world, they follow the direction set by the SHARE and GUIDE organizations that started in America. These groups each provide a critical mass of expertise, knowledge and interest, making it possible to convene large conferences several times each year. The conferences are forums for presenting and hearing technical papers, seeing new products and meeting fellow experts. Although each of the user-group organizations is independent of the others, most are connected by being affiliated to the International User-Group Council (IUGC). For CICS, the connections are particularly strong. Since 1986, IBM's Hursley Laboratory in England has been the venue for an annual CICS Joint User-Group Project meeting. This is an opportunity for the CICS project-management teams from a number of user-groups to meet and exchange information. It has allowed the groups to agree and convey joint messages to IBM's development team. At the same time, it has made it possible to agree a joint programme for preparing and exchanging study papers and surveys, thereby avoiding duplication of effort, maximizing exchange of information and extending the scope of surveys. We shall say more about the project later.

IBM Hursley is a willing contributor to the CICS projects. As part of IBM, it is merely a guest at any meeting, but it takes its responsibilities seriously, having staff permanently assigned to work with each user-group. The staff attend all meetings, arrange for guest IBM speakers, and ensure that user-group requirements are understood and addressed properly by Development.

Each user-group offers an excellent opportunity for your technical staff to keep in touch with latest technology and ideas, to exchange experiences with counterparts in other corporations, and to meet some of the developers of CICS itself.

Systems-support and application-support staff are likely to get most out of attending CICS project sessions, though high-calibre programming staff can learn a lot.

The Appendix contains addresses of the user-group organizations. We shall look briefly at each here.

GUIDE International

GUIDE International is a North American user-group that meets three times every year, each time in a major city. It has more than 2000 member institutions, and its main meetings attract up to 4000 delegates. It was among the first groups to be formed, starting in December 1956.

A GUIDE group meeting takes place in one of the hotel districts of a large American city, taking over several large hotels for a whole week. The agenda for any meeting includes 1500 or more sessions, including user-experience sessions, product descriptions, working sessions to formulate requirements, and question and answer sessions. Informal sessions, over dinner or drinks, allow individual delegates to learn from each other.

Any GUIDE conference includes sessions on CICS. The majority of them are run by the CICS group, which usually holds most of its formal sessions in a CICS headquarters' hotel. Most other sessions that concern CICS are sponsored by the VSE project, as CICS is a major component of the VSE/SP system package. From time to time, other project meetings arrange sessions on CICS, or on CICS-related topics. For this reason, and because CICS personnel tend to need a wide knowledge of a variety of products, there are good reasons for CICS personnel to attend non-CICS sessions. For example, they could benefit from presentations on database products, security products, and programming languages and compilers.

The divisions within GUIDE are:

- Application Enabling Environment Division
- Automated Business Solutions Division
- Business Applications Division
- Communications System Division
- Database/Data Communications Division
- Information Systems Management Division
- System Software Division.

The CICS group is part of the Database/Data Communication (DB/DC) division. It sponsors a large number of sessions during the week of a conference, covering the entire family of CICS products, reflecting its concern for the consistency and integrity of interfaces across the CICS family. The group focuses on system-support issues, so application-programming staff would be better occupied attending programming-related sessions run by the Application Enabling Environment Division. Hundreds of delegates attend CICS sessions throughout the week. In the largest general-interest sessions, major CICS users may describe their experiences in installing new products or implementing major transaction systems, or well-known IBM speakers may provide education or announce new products.

At smaller sessions, experts speak to special-interest groups. In addition, there are 'working sessions', at which participants continue work on ongoing projects or papers. All meetings are sponsored by one of the CICS Project groups. There are six of these:

- CICS Futures
- CICS Requirements
- CICS DOS/VSE
- CICS Performance
- CICS Communications
- CICS Systems management.

At some time during the week, the CICS project holds a large open-session meeting at which delegates can ask questions on any subject. The same meeting hears, and votes on, requirements raised by individual GUIDE members. As a result of the voting, requirements are passed through the parent GUIDE organization to IBM's User Group Relations department, and hence on to CICS Development.

SHARE Inc.

SHARE Incorporated is the oldest user-group organization in the computer industry. Formed in 1955 by a group of scientists and engineers, its first meeting was held in Santa Monica, California, and was attended by 47 delegates from 22 organizations. The founders' companies were users of the then new IBM 704 computer, and realized that by pooling knowledge and effort they could get more from their new systems.

Nowadays, SHARE holds four meetings every year, two 'majors' that have essentially the same form as described earlier for GUIDE meetings, and two 'interims' at which project leaders and major participants decide on direction, and review the statuses of ongoing study papers. SHARE's focus has traditionally been on large systems, based on MVS and VM, notably omitting the smaller VSE-based CICS users. For this reason, CICS/VSE users usually belong to GUIDE. Nevertheless, SHARE groups do focus more heavily nowadays on small and mid-sized systems, such as those based on OS/2, OS/400 and AIX.

SHARE has grown enormously since the first meeting in 1955. It now boasts a membership of about 2400 institutions, and its major meetings attract anything up to 6000 delegates. Like GUIDE meetings, major SHARE conferences take place in large American cities' hotel districts, with the major meetings taking over several hotels for a whole week, and providing delegates with the problem of choosing between 1600 or more different sessions. The smaller interim meetings are often held in smaller cities, as the number of delegates is much smaller.

The formats of meetings, and their management, is very similar to those of GUIDE. Although the style and atmosphere at the two sets of meetings is slightly different, the format of the week and the nature of the sessions is very similar.

The divisions within SHARE are:

- Application Architecture and Data Systems Division
- Communications Division
- Integrated Technologies Division
- Management Division
- Operating Systems Support Division.

The CICS project, primarily for system-support staff, is part of the Data Systems Group within the Application Architecture and Data Systems Division. Application-programming staff will generally fit better into the Application Enabling Group within the same division.

Like GUIDE, SHARE's CICS project runs sessions all week, mostly in its headquarters' hotel. The project's stated goals are to provide an exchange forum for CICS users, dealing with such subjects as technical education, product update information, performance measurement and tuning, maintenance, and migration pitfalls and recommendations. Hundreds of delegates attend CICS sessions during the course of a week's meetings, and submit and vote on a range of requirements. Between meetings, active project members work together to produce study papers, which they present at later sessions.

SHARE Europe

SHARE Europe has its headquarters in Switzerland. It has a membership of approximately 500 organizations in 28 countries throughout Europe. Members include all kinds of organizations: from government departments to universities; from industry and commerce to service bureaux.

SHARE Europe holds two week-long conferences every year. The conferences are held in major European cities, and attract as many as 600 delegates. SHARE Europe meetings are very similar in style and form to their North American equivalents, and are conducted in English.

CICS itself does not have a separate project, instead being covered within the Database Project. There are several CICS sessions at every meeting, and the CICS Development organization from the Hursley development laboratory is always represented. Otherwise, the conferences give the same opportunity as G.U.I.D.E. for delegates to attend a variety of different sessions, from database to languages.

G.U.I.D.E.

The European G.U.I.D.E. organization was formed in 1959, as an offshoot of the American GUIDE International organization. It is now fully independent, and has its own headquarters in Switzerland, but remains affiliated to GUIDE International.

G.U.I.D.E. has a slightly different approach to meetings, with added emphasis on 'local' meetings, each country having its own group. This is important mainly because of the different languages spoken from state to state. Although the country meetings are smaller, and hence less ambitious, than the typical American meetings, many of the participants naturally get more from sessions given in their own languages.

G.U.I.D.E. holds two major meetings every year, the Spring Conference and the Autumn Conference, bringing together attendees from all European countries. At these meetings the organization offers presentations in a variety of languages, but provides simultaneous translation into four languages (French, German, Italian and English). The main theme of the conference is addressed by a series of meetings comprising The Symposium. In addition, a variety of special-interest divisions run alternative sessions in parallel with the symposium. These sessions include many about CICS or which are closely related to CICS.

The main divisions within a symposium are:

- Application and Information
- Database/Data Communication
- Data Centre/Systems Programming
- Management.

CICS subjects are covered mostly within the Database/Data Communications Division. They include presentations by both CICS users and IBM personnel from Development or IBM Support. Unlike the case in US GUIDE or SHARE meetings, CICS sessions do not run all week. As a result, delegates are better able to attend useful sessions on CICS-related products and subjects, such as IMS, VTAM or design of distributed systems. They may also like to share some sessions with their application-programming colleagues in the Application Enabling Environment Division.

Individual countries have their own regional G.U.I.D.E. organizations, each with its own constituent working groups. The regional organizations have their own written objectives and agendas.

There are currently regions for the following countries:

Austria
Belgium
France
Germany
Israel

Italy
Netherlands
Nordic countries

- Denmark
- Finland
- Iceland
- Norway
- Sweden

Portugal
Spain
Switzerland
United Kingdom.

The divisions of the overall organization are mirrored within many of the individual countries' user-group organizations. That is, the groups are subdivided into divisions roughly related to Applications, DB/DC, Data Centre and Management. Some of the countries' groups are subdivided by working group, mirroring the overall G.U.I.D.E. working groups. In some countries, each working group schedules one or more meetings each year. The country group also meets every year, and provides input to surveys and resolutions representing the whole of Europe.

COMMON EUROPE

COMMON EUROPE is the largest IBM user-group, with about 9000 members spanning 15 countries throughout Europe. It has traditionally held no direct interest for staff working mainly on CICS, because its focus is mainly on smaller systems: System/36, System/38, AS/400, OS/2 and VSE/SP. Nevertheless. it is likely that CICS activity will grow as CICS OS/2 and CICS/400 become used more widely.

COMMON US

COMMON US was formed in 1960, and is the second-largest of the user-groups, having a membership of more than 3600 institutions. As with COMMON Europe, it is probably best described as a 'mid-range' group, catering mainly for users of medium-size systems such as System/36, System/38 and AS/400. In recent times, it has begun to deal with RISC System/6000. It has also had an interest in VSE systems. Until now it has had little or no dealings with CICS. As the new CICS systems become more popular, this may change.

COMMON Australasia

COMMON Australasia has its roots in the first Australian user-group, which was formed in Sydney in the 1960s. It began life as the IBM Computer Users'

Association. It was renamed COMMON NSW (New South Wales) in 1990, led by a committee of representatives from the Melbourne and Sydney groups. The committee was later expanded to include a representative of each of seven state user-groups.

Affiliated groups are organized and funded independently of COMMON, but maintain a close relationship. The individual groups share articles of association and have adopted the same code of ethics. Each of the groups holds frequent local meetings, both collectively and through special-interest groups, such as AS/400 groups. The national COMMON group organizes an annual national conference, and coordinates the requirements-gathering and submission process.

GUIDE Latin America

GUIDE Latin America first met in 1985, in São Paulo, Brazil. Nowadays, it meets twice a year: in Rio every May, and in São Paulo every October. Its membership includes approximately 260 enterprises. Between them, these send about 800 delegates to each of the five-day GUIDE meetings, and they have about 150 different sessions to choose from during the week.

GUIDE Latin America does not have a separate CICS project, but its CICS-related content has grown over the years. At the beginning of the 1990s, CICS topics occupy 1.5-days worth of meeting sessions. Presentations include some by staff from IBM Hursley in England.

Australasian SHARE/GUIDE

The Australasian SHARE/GUIDE user group serves IBM's user community in Australia and New Zealand. It is affiliated to many of the other groups around the world, but has especially good working relationships with groups in the Asia and Pacific region. By synchronizing meetings, the groups make best use of visiting speakers from America and Europe. Members of the CICS Project of Australasian SHARE/GUIDE also play a very active part in the CICS Joint User Group Project, and have done so since it was formed in 1985.

Australasian SHARE/GUIDE holds two major conferences each year: one in August or September, the other in February or March. Like their American equivalents, the conferences take place in large cities, taking over large hotels and conference facilities for four days at a time. Most meetings take place in Australian cities, but some are held in New Zealand. Special-interest groups also hold smaller regional meetings during the year.

The major meetings of Australasia SHARE/GUIDE attract up to 700 delegates from approximately 200 member organizations. As with other user-group conferences, their activities are organized along project lines, with the projects forming divisions. There are four divisions:

- Application Enabling
- Communications
- Information Technology Management
- Systems Management.

The CICS project forms part of the Application Enabling Division. The project covers all aspects of CICS and its environment, and is usually of interest to users of both MVS and VSE CICS systems. It has CICS sessions scheduled throughout the conference, and a good CICS session will be attended by 100 or more people, despite constant competition from other projects. Like others, the CICS project gathers and submits requirements to IBM that reach Development in Hursley.

Other projects within the Application Enabling Division provide valuable CICS-related sessions. In particular, the IMS and DB2 projects are of interest. For the application programmer, the Application Engineering Project covers CICS issues, too.

Japan GUIDE/SHARE

This organization was formed in 1968, and at the start of 1992 it had a membership of over four hundred enterprises. It has six divisions:

- Operating Systems
- DB/DC
- Network
- Software Engineering
- Office System
- Management.

The CICS group exists as part of the DB/DC division.

Japan GUIDE/SHARE general conferences are held twice each year. In addition, the user-group holds three technical seminars each year.

Speakers at the conferences include both Japanese experts and visiting speakers from both IBM Hursley's development team and IBM US's marketing and support consultants. Presentations given in English are relayed in Japanese.

As with other user-groups, Japan GUIDE/SHARE helps its members and influences IBM strategy by submitting requirement resolutions, forming study groups and producing white papers. Study groups that were active most recently covered the subjects:

- Effective use of CICS/ESA Version 3
- Cooperative processing between CICS and CICS OS/2.

Other Asia/Pacific groups

There are active, though smaller, user-groups throughout the Asia/Pacific area. As with Europe, the variety of national languages has encouraged the development of national user-groups. These are:

- Singapore SHARE/GUIDE
- Korea SHARE/GUIDE
- Hong Kong SHARE/GUIDE
- Philippines SHARE/GUIDE
- The SHARE/GUIDE Association (Malaysia)
- China IBM Computer Users' Association.

Both Thailand and Indonesia may soon have user-groups of their own. The Appendix gives the names and addresses of contacts for more information on these groups.

The CICS Joint User Group Project

Since 1985 the CICS groups from GUIDE International, SHARE Inc., G.U.I.D.E. Europe and Australasian SHARE/GUIDE have worked together in an alliance called the CICS Joint User Group Project, or CJUGP (pronounced 'see-jug-pee') for short. This project has enabled the groups to identify common strategic issues concerning the CICS products, to synchronize their activities, and to share the workload of conducting surveys of members and of preparing requirements papers for submission to IBM. The project is composed of CICS project leaders from the four organizations. It meets for a week every year in IBM's Hursley laboratory, where its members discuss their groups' issues and activities with CICS product planners, managers and development programmers.

Over the seven years of its existence, the CJUGP has had a major influence on CICS product directions, particularly in respect of CICS/ESA Version 3. The influence has been exerted largely through the strategy papers that the group has delivered to IBM. These include:

- Object Code Only CICS Implementation
- CICS and Cooperative Processing
- Auditing CICS Systems
- CICS Repository Requirements
- CICS as a Network Switch
- High Transaction Rate Constraints
- Remote Site Backup and Recovery
- CICS Reliability, Availability and Serviceability
- CICS Security
- Continuous System Operation
- Automated CICS Operations
- CICS Single System Image
- Resource Manager Interface
- System Programmer Workbench
- CICS Systems Management
- CICS Performance Management.

As the CICS product family grows to include platforms such as AS/400, RISC System/6000 and non-IBM systems, the CJUGP is certain to see the need for continued cooperation.

11.7   Building on the community

As you can tell, CICS staff are part of a worldwide community of experts. The accumulated knowledge of the enormous number of data-processing experts, combined with the wide range of channels and regular meetings for sharing that knowledge, provides a professional support structure unprecedented in technological history.

Many of the experts provide services that will save you from having to keep a large body of your own experts. You can hire consultants, from IBM or from other organizations, whenever you need them. However, if you do any more than simply run software packages, you will need to retain at least a small staff of competent CICS technical specialists. Their worth to your organization will be multiplied many times by contact with peers in the community of experts.

If you can afford to let your technical support staff attend technical conferences, user-group meetings, or IBM briefings regularly, or even from time to time, you will almost certainly benefit from their experience. The formal presentations by IBM staff, with opportunity for questions, can help them to get your strategy in perspective. Presentations by other CICS users allow them to benefit from others' experiences. Just as importantly, though, participation in working groups can ensure that your business needs and technical strategy influence the groups' recommendations on CICS to IBM. As you will see in the next chapter, the possibilities for the future are immense, and you need to ensure that your organization has an opportunity to influence IBM's direction where it affects you.

Part IV
Past, present and future

12
CICS—past and present

In this chapter we will look at the history of CICS (Fig. 12.1), seeing the evidence of, and some of the reasons for, its enduring success. We will then look at the history of the CICS-based Olympic systems, whose four-year cycles provide interesting snapshots of CICS's evolution up until the present day.

12.1   The beginning

CICS has always developed in response to its customers' needs. It emerged in the 1960s, in response to demand from various customer-oriented industries that were beginning to see the power of mainframe computers and were impatient to harness that power. These companies saw that they could improve business efficiency using the new computing technologies, but only if programmers could be allowed to devote most of their time to the business logic of programs. They needed help from subsystems to free programmers from the very complex, and therefore more time-consuming, real-time programming activities such as interpreting input communications data streams, building output data streams, acquiring storage to hold programs or data, coordinating shared use of the computer, and many other things. CICS, with its wide range of services, proved to be exactly the system they needed.

The first CICS system, produced in 1968, was designed to run on System/360 computers. It used OS/360 as its operating system, BTAM as its terminal access method program, and ISAM and BDAM as its data access methods. It provided support for both local and remote IBM terminals of the day, such as IBM 2260s, 1050s, and 2740s. A system could support about 50 terminals. In 1969 CICS/OS became one of IBM's first program products. Its effectiveness was immediately apparent to a wide range of commercial users, who started to use it in large numbers.

Users of the smaller but more numerous System/360 DOS systems demanded a similar CICS system. IBM adapted the CICS/OS design to produce two products, CICS/DOS–ENTRY (CICS/DOSE) and CICS/DOS–STANDARD (CICS/DOSS). These were announced in September 1970, and were shipped to

Date	MVS	VSE	OS/2	OS/400	AIX	Other
1968	CICS/OS Ann.					
1969	CICS/OS Av.					
1970		CICS/DOS Ann.				
1971		CICS/DOS Av.				
1974	CICS/OS/VS Ann. and Av.	CICS/DOS/VS Ann. and Av.				
1975	CICS/OS/VS 1.1.1 Ann./Av.	CICS/DOS/VS 1.1 Av.				
1976	CICS/OS/VS 1.2 Av. 1.3 Ann.	CICS/DOS/VS 1.2 Av./1.3 Ann.				
1977	C/O/V 1.3 Av.	C/D/V 1.3 Av.				
1978	C/O/V 1.4 Ann.	C/D/V 1.4 Ann.				
1979	C/O/V 1.4.1 & C/O/V 1.5 Ann.	C/D/V 1.5 Ann.				
1980	C/O/V 1.5 Av.	C/D/V 1.5 Av.				
1982	C/O/V 1.6 Ann.	C/D/V 1.6 Ann.				
1983	C/O/V 1.6.1 Ann. and Av.	C/D/V 1.6 Av.				
1984	ISC TR-1.6.1					
1985	C/O/V 1.7 Ann.	C/D/V 1.7 Ann.				C/C R1 Av.
1987	CICS/MVS 2.1 Ann.	C/D/V 1.7 Av.				C/VM Ann.
1988	C/M 2.1 Av.		CICS OS/2 Ann.			C/VM R1 Av.
1989	C/MVS 2.1.1 & Data Tables & CICS/ESA 3.1 Ann.	CICS/DDM Ann. for C/D/V	C OS/2 Av. C OS/2 1.20 Av.			C/VM R2 Av.
1990	C/E 3.1 Av.	CICS/VSE 2.1 Ann.				
1991	C/E 3.2.1 Av. C/M 2.1.2 Av.					
1992	C/E 3.3 Av. Shared DTs Av. FEPI Av.	CICS/VSE 2.2 Ann.	Statement of direction on CICS OS/2 for OS/2 V2	CICS/400 Ann.	CICS/6000 Ann.	CICS for HP Ann.
1993		CICS/VSE 2.2 Av.	CICS OS/2 V2 Av.	CICS/400Av.	CICS/6000 Av.	CICS for NT statement

Key: C/O/V = CICS/OS/VS   C/D/V = CICS/DOS/VS   C/VM = CICS/VM   C OS/2 = CICS OS/2
C/E = CICS/ESA   C/C = CICS/CMS   C/M = CICS/MVS   HP = Hewlett-Packard
NT = Microsoft Windows NT   Ann. = announced   Av. = available

Figure 12.1.   CICS—the first twenty-five years.

their first customers in August 1971. At about the same time, CICS was extended to allow users to write CICS application programs in COBOL and PL/I as well as assembler language.

12.2   Mapping the way forward

In the early 1970s, IBM 3270 display devices became available, providing much more sophisticated handling of display data. CICS was extended to handle the new kind of data stream used by the devices, providing application programmers with new basic mapping support (BMS) to handle the data streams. BMS allowed programmers to handle display data as a series of fields, rather than as complete screenfuls. Not only did this relate more closely to the way data was viewed and handled within programs, it also allowed selective update and transmission of parts of screens, making communication more efficient.

12.3   The first age of growth

The early signs of commitment to new technology must have endeared CICS to its users, because their numbers continued to increase. The CICS commitment was underlined by the provision, at the beginning of the 1970s, of access for CICS users to IMS hierarchical databases. Soon after that, CICS embraced the radical advances that came with the System/370 architecture that replaced System/360. Both CICS/OS and CICS/DOS were redesigned to use the virtual-storage capabilities of the new architecture, breaking free from the shackles of real storage limits. The virtual-storage versions of CICS, CICS/OS/VS and CICS/DOS/VS, both became available in 1974. Each product promised source-level compatibility for programs developed to run on its pre-virtual-storage equivalent, a policy adopted by successive releases.

The new OS/VS and DOS/VS operating systems were accompanied by data and communications access methods for the virtual-storage environment: VSAM and VTAM. CICS was modified to work with these, too, resulting in Release 1.2 of both CICS/DOS/VS and CICS/OS/VS. In addition, by early 1973 both CICS/OS/VS and CICS/DOS/VS provided database access through the DL/I data language.

12.4   CICS goes European

During this time, the product was transferred to Hursley, England, where plans were drawn up to keep the product at the forefront of transaction processing. The advances over the next few years confirmed CICS's leadership, and positioned it for its role as an engine of business. First, in 1976, Release 1.3 introduced a new command-level programming interface. This is the EXEC CICS interface that remains in use today. It replaced the old assembler macro-language facilities of early CICS systems with a set of commands that proved much more acceptable to programmers who were used to high level programming languages such as COBOL and PL/I.

In 1978, CICS/VS Release 1.4 introduced the EDF debugging aid. More importantly, it provided the first of the changes that were to make CICS so important in distributed processing and communications: intersystem communication and shared database support were introduced. A year later, multiregion operation was announced. At the same time, CICS provided distributed trans-action processing support through VTAM for SNA parallel sessions, support for IBM 3279 colour displays, support for the RACF security product, the CECI command interpreter, and the new master terminal transaction, CEMT.

So, by the start of the 1980s, CICS had many of the elements that make it so versatile today. Its naturally usable programming language, its support for almost all new device types, and its ability to link to other systems through ISC and MRO, made it irresistible to customers and to companies developing application and system packages for industry. By this time, though, the very large user population began to find that whole businesses depended on CICS. As a result, they needed CICS to permit near-non-stop operation. They also wanted assurances from IBM that it would continue to support and enhance CICS.

12.5   Availability releases

In 1982, IBM began to satisfy both needs when it announced Release 6 of both CICS/OS/VS and CICS/DOS/VS. The new release introduced the first layer of RDO—which allows system support staff to define resources to CICS and install them ready for use without having to stop CICS and restart it. This was the first in a series of moves to allow CICS to remain running continuously. Furthermore, CICS began to use the new extended architecture (31-bit addressing) of the MVS/XA operating system. This underlined IBM's commitment to continued investment in CICS, which seemed to have been the subject of debate among some users since CICS had moved to England.

In 1983, CICS/OS/VS 1.6.1 extended the use of MVS/XA and began to make use of IMS/VS data sharing and DBRC; two years later, CICS/OS/VS 1.7 and CICS/DOS/VS 1.7 both advanced the cause of continuous operation by providing RDO for terminals and dynamic allocation for files. In addition, CICS/DOS/VS provided a print spooler, called the 'report controller', to enable users to control printed output more efficiently.

In the same year as CICS 1.7, IBM announced a new member of the CICS family. CICS/CMS was a small-scale CICS system designed to run under the conversational monitor system of IBM's VM operating system. It was intended as a development and test environment for CICS application programmers. In the event it was short-lived, as its successor, CICS/VM, was announced the following year. CICS/VM was a full-scale transaction-processing system, designed to be used to process production transactions as well as for program development and testing. Sharing many of the application-programming and intersystem-communication capabilities of the mainframe CICS systems, CICS/VM made it possible to combine transaction processing in a personal-computing environment with full access to major commercial systems on connected systems.

The emergence of CICS OS/2 in 1988 probably ensured that CICS/VM did not gain popularity in the way that might have been expected. CICS OS/2 is a production-grade CICS system for OS/2-capable computers, and like CICS/VM it is capable of communicating with host-based CICS systems. As a result, it has many of the advantages of the VM environment: single-user or multi-user systems; a base for personal computing; ideal as a development and test environment, but capable of production use and of connection to other systems.

The year 1988 saw the announcement of CICS/MVS Version 2 as well as CICS OS/2. CICS/MVS was the successor to CICS/OS/VS, a direct descendant of the original CICS system. Initially, its main claim to fame was its provision of a degree of software fault-tolerance, known as the extended recovery facility. This allowed a partially-started CICS system to act as 'reserve' for a production system. In the event of a total CICS failure, it could complete its startup process and take over from the failing system. CICS/MVS underwent a significant number of improvements in the first three years of its life. Many were concerned with improved connectivity, supporting additional CICS family members. Others were designed to increase the reliability and performance of the system. Ultimately, they were intended to provide a very stable base from which to plan more revolutionary change.

12.6   Age of enterprise

CICS/MVS has been viewed by many as a simple evolution of CICS/OS/VS. In fact, it holds an important and pivotal position in the development of CICS from the old, macro-level system of the 1970s to the family of compatible, connectible application enablers of the 1990s. Its importance did not really become clear until 1989, when CICS/ESA (the third version of CICS) was announced. CICS/ESA was to be a restructured product, designed for continued evolution. In its first release, it continued to support many old functions, such as the obsolescent macro-level programming interface. However, IBM warned that these old functions' days were numbered and that programs using them should not be used on the new CICS/ESA system. Instead, such programs should remain 'in quarantine' on CICS/MVS systems. In this way, they could remain available to CICS/ESA users, through CICS intercommunication, but would not inhibit technological advances to CICS/ESA.

CICS/ESA was announced only months after IBM's new Enterprise Systems Architecture (known in short as ESA). Like the virtual-storage operating-system architecture changes of the 1970s and the extended-architecture extensions of the 1980s, the new architecture increased capacity for systems growth, in effect adding a new dimension to System/370 computing. It allowed users to define enormous numbers of address spaces, each up to 2 Gigabytes in size, as well as data spaces capable of acting as virtual 'warehouses' of data. It also offered PR/SM, a hypervisor function allowing a user to segment a multiprocessor machine so that it could run several operating systems at once, or even a mixture of similar and dissimilar systems, for example VM, MVS and VSE.

For very large enterprises these changes removed barriers to total system growth. CICS/MVS was able to run on the new operating system immediately, and CICS/ESA was designed from the outset to use MVS/ESA functions. Once again, CICS was at the leading edge of computer technology.

12.7   Explosion

Since 1989, there has been what amounts to an explosion of activity in CICS. CICS/ESA's emergence was followed almost immediately by that of CICS/VSE Version 2, designed to run on the VSE/ESA operating system. The new version replaced CICS/DOS/VS, which IBM has since stopped marketing. It was desperately needed by VSE-based users of CICS, who were bursting all system limits and needed extra scope for growth. CICS/VSE gave extra room for growth, and also provided the same extended recovery facilities as CICS/MVS. In 1992, CICS/VSE's second release was announced. This brought CICS/VSE back to the close relationship with CICS/MVS that it had enjoyed until 1987. It provided even more scope for growth, by supporting 31-bit addressing in programs and by giving improved connectivity. It also met many long-standing usability needs.

CICS/VSE's revitalization meant that it reestablished itself as the production CICS system found on VM systems. This, as well as the growing sophistication of the CICS OS/2 system, and the appearance of CICS on the RISC System/6000 and the OS/400 systems, meant that CICS/VM was no longer necessary, and IBM stopped marketing it in 1992. At about the same time, IBM and Hewlett-Packard surprised the industry by announcing that they were jointly developing a CICS-based system for Hewlett-Packard systems. Shortly after that, IBM announced its intention to develop a CICS offering for Windows NT.

12.8   Packages

In the 1990s, therefore, there has already been a proliferation of CICS systems. At the same time, the vast number of ancillary CICS products has continued to grow. In the 1970s, very large numbers of application packages and utility programs emerged to form the 'CICS industry'. The producers of the packages revitalized their products for CICS/ESA, redesigning them to work with the restructured CICS. At a time when many of them are now proving themselves in the world of ESA, they are being joined by ancillary products from IBM itself: a migration aid called CICS/AMA, and new releases of the established products like the SDFII screen generator, the CICSVR recovery utility and so on.

In addition, there are countless program packages for use with CICS systems. Some are applicable worldwide; others, such as taxation or accounting packages, are developed on a country basis. They have evolved with the systems, and many have been brought up to date to use command-level programming and modern databases. The newest packages are being designed to run on a wide range of CICS family members, taking advantage of the potential for massive growth in the number of corporate CICS systems needing prepackaged application software.

As we saw at the start of the book, the application program is the reason for having a CICS system. And the proven reliability and upward compatibility of the CICS programming interface is largely responsible for the system's enduring success. While providing this compatibility, CICS always manages to evolve, embracing successive technologies. This is perhaps best illustrated by an example, so for the rest of this chapter we will consider a slice of CICS history.

12.9   CICS and the Olympic Games

We have looked at CICS in abstract terms throughout this book. Despite considering a number of applications and configurations, it may still be difficult to visualize CICS in action. It is therefore appropriate to consider a very public case study: the use of CICS in Olympic Games. You cannot call this a 'typical' case, as there is no such thing as a typical CICS system or program. However, most of the requirements met by the system, and most of the programs, are typical of business requirements and programs. The end-users of the Olympic systems are in many ways typical of the wide range of users of modern systems: a mixture of permanent professionals and complete novices.

CICS and the Olympic Games have a 16-year history, characterized by steady evolution close on the heels of technology. The data systems for the 1992 games provided state-of-the-art transaction-processing services through CICS, and were based on experience gained with CICS systems developed over the years since 1976. In July of that year, IBM Canada used CICS to provide Olympics support systems for the XXI Olympiad in Montreal.

That first large-scale system was based on CICS/OS/VS 1.1.1, and had to support a meeting of 12 000 competitors, competing in 5000 events, covering 21 sports. Two IBM System/370 Model 145 computers were used to drive more than 100 IBM 3270 display terminals and printers, providing a round-the-clock results and information service. In today's terms, the achievements seem modest, especially as the system did not gather data automatically, or drive scoreboards, or provide information direct to television viewers. Data had to be entered manually at event sites, and then had to be read and transcribed by journalists before being used for copy or commentary. Nevertheless, the system made it possible to share results almost as they emerged, and to get biographical data at any time.

In 1984, CICS was used at both the XIV Winter Games, in Sarajevo, and the XXIII Summer Olympic Games, in Los Angeles. For the Winter Olympics in Sarajevo, Yugoslavia, new Olympic CICS systems were designed, based on CICS/DOS/VS and DOS-DL/I. In a display of CICS portability, when they had completed their task, the Sarajevo systems were supplied to IBM Canada, where they were modified to run on CICS/OS/VS, using IMS/VS as a database manager. This system, extended to provide additional services, became the system for 1988's XV Winter Olympics, held in Calgary. At its peak, Calgary's CICS/OS/VS 1.7 system was to handle more than a million transactions each day, supporting about a thousand terminals. Olympic officials used IBM PCs at each of the sports venues to feed results to CICS, which in turn fed the IMS/VS database. After the results had been reported, checked and approved, they were sent to all Olympic sites to be printed. Results were also extracted regularly from the IMS/VS database and copied to a DB2 database, from where media personnel and officials could extract any data they wished, as they wished. Later in the year, in Seoul, South Korea, CICS again formed the basis of the Summer Olympic Games' systems.

The most recent games, in 1992, show best how CICS systems have advanced in only 16 years. They provide an excellent example of the power, applications and adaptability of CICS systems. Furthermore, they show two different approaches to the same technical problems. We shall look at them in more detail.

Albertville

The XVI Winter Olympic Games systems in Albertville comprised a network of CICS systems. At the centre of the system were two IBM 3090 mainframe processors, between them running four CICS/MVS 2.1.1 systems (Fig. 12.2). Attached to the four CICSs, mostly through the 200 local area networks, were 1750 IBM PS/2 workstations, 1150 of them running CICS OS/2 1.20.

Together, these workstations allowed the Olympic organization to serve and manage the staff, competitors and journalists, and to record, report and analyse results in real time, across 16 Olympic sites. There were four main elements in the system: a games management system, a results service system, an information service and an electronic mail system. It is estimated that during the two weeks of the Games more than 40 000 people, or end-users, became CICS OS/2 users for the first time. The users included staff of the Olympic organization, competitors, reporters and broadcasters, and ordinary spectators. They gained access to a variety of systems and data through 1750 LAN-attached PS/2s.

The results service system

The system that became most publicly visible throughout the Winter Games was the results service system (Fig. 12.3), which was responsible in part for displaying results on millions of television screens worldwide. It acted as a workstation server and database machine, collecting input in the form of timer data and judging scores, and supplying real-time results data to score boards, journalists and television screens.

At each site, pairs of PS/2 computers collected data from electronic timers, and used application programs running under CICS OS/2 to compile the data and deliver it, by function shipping, to the CICS/MVS results system on the central systems. Also at each site, input from judges was entered at PS/2 computers that were connected as terminals to the central system. The central system gathered all input data and updated the results-system central database, which was managed by IMS/VS. On the outbound side, application programs running under

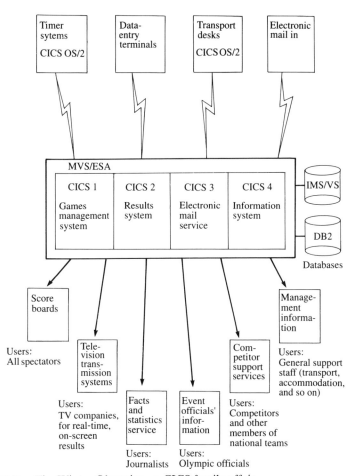

Figure 12.2. The Winter Olympics—a CICS family affair.

CICS OS/2 systems at each site extracted certified results from the database, processing them and presenting them in a variety of forms: on illuminated scoreboards at the event sites; as displayable overlays for television company transmission; on results monitors to be used by television commentators; as printed results sheets; and on results monitors for Olympic staff.

The games management system

With 40 000 people to manage, the Winter Olympic Games organization had a considerable administrative challenge, even without the events themselves. The logistic challenge of receiving, accommodating, feeding and transporting all of these people was enormous. This was handled by CICS OS/2 systems connected to the central games management system, running under CICS/MVS and using DB2 as its data repository (Fig. 12.4).

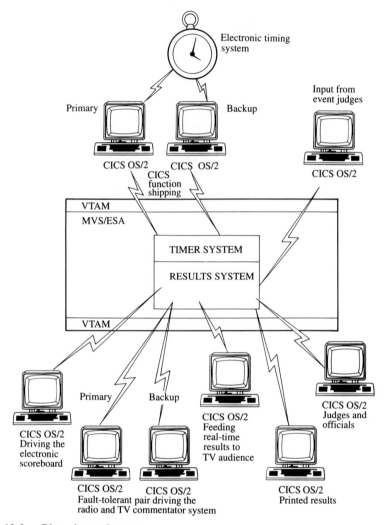

Figure 12.3.   Olympic results system.

A major task of this system was 'accreditation', or keeping track of bona fide staff and competitors, a particularly important task considering security concerns. The CICS OS/2 systems allowed staff to handle registration, checking credentials and then printing bar-coded badges, using data from the central database. Subsequently, other programs checked bar codes, and hence controlled and tracked movement of badge-holders. Yet other programs controlled the use of transport, ordering transport when requested, and printing transport orders as they were needed. At all times, data could be uploaded to the central database or downloaded to the PS/2 systems, ensuring that everyone was working with the same data.

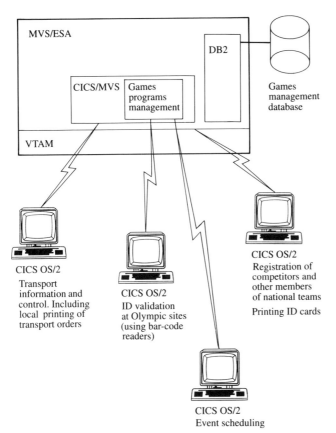

Figure 12.4.   The games management system.

Information and mail systems

There were two other major systems at Albertville, both serving more general information needs of the competitors and journalists. They were accessible from the same workstations, which were arranged in local area networks, and used Touchscreen displays for simplicity and ease of use for potentially-naive users. The first of the two systems provided a sophisticated information service, covering sporting events, biographical information, transport schedules, weather reports and general news. Again, access to the system was through CICS OS/2 systems running on PS/2 computers. These systems used the external call interface to communicate with the presentation manager, and used distributed program link commands to get messaging and administrative programs running on the central systems.

The second system provided an electronic mail service. This allowed officials and members of the media organizations to communicate with each other, regardless of which site they were visiting. They could leave electronic mail messages and they could search OfficeVision address books to identify and locate other users through their system user identifiers or local pager identifiers. In all, there were more than 100 000 messages sent during the Albertville games, and more than 200 000 calls were made to address books. In addition, the electronic mail system provided an electronic paging service. Selected users carried pagers, which were activated as part of the registration process, and so could be summoned to a workstation when an important message was waiting.

The electronic mail system was provided by the host-based OfficeVision/MVS product, which supported AS/400 systems as well as the hundreds of LAN-based PS/2 systems.

Maintenance and management

One interesting operational feature of the overall system used at Albertville was the overnight administration and maintenance. Any changes in locally-held programs or data could be downloaded to all distributed systems when they were restarted each morning. The first activity at restart was to check for upgraded components on the LAN server machine. These in turn were distributed to each LAN server overnight, from a master server machine. This system-management process did a lot to help prove the viability of the heterogeneous, distributed CICS network.

Follow that!

The snow dust had barely settled on Albertville when the team began to plan for the next Winter Olympic games, in Lillehammer, Norway, in 1994. Those games will almost certainly be recorded and reported by a combination of CICS/ESA Version 3.3 and CICS OS/2 Version 2. The existing transaction systems have been migrated to CICS/ESA 3.2.1, and are being moved again, on to CICS/ESA 3.3.

Barcelona

Like the Winter Olympics, the Summer Olympic Games have traditionally had CICS at the centre of their systems. The most recent games, the twenty-fifth, in Barcelona during the summer of 1992, used CICS/ESA Version 3.2.1 in combination with OfficeVision/MVS and DB2. The configuration differed from that used in Albertville, in that its network of PS/2 systems did not use CICS OS/2.

As with Albertville, the immediate end-users of the systems were the Olympics' staff members and officials, the athletes and their national team support staff, and journalists and commentators. The data and transactions were similar to those of Albertville, too. In the background, systems coped with registration of team members, management of accommodation, and tracking and transportation. More visibly, other systems helped to manage and schedule events, to measure, record and report results, and to provide large amounts of data for journalists and commentators: results, biographical details and statistics.

Besides gathering data from the various event sites, the central CICS systems had to drive real-time reporting systems. The CICS Results system collected results, then redistributed them to printers at each site, to the databases at the centre of the enquiry systems, and to the world press agencies (through telephone lines). Even though a lot of processing had been moved from the host to the network of powerful workstations, the central system continued to be driven hard. The transaction rate reached a peak of 885 949 in a single day.

Like the Winter Games, the Summer Olympics grow steadily, Olympiad by Olympiad. In Barcelona the systems had to serve a vast crowd of about 120 000 short-term end-users. Their network of PS/2s had to cover more than 80 sites. There were about 4600 PS/2 systems in the network, arranged in a series of token ring local area networks.

The networks of PS/2s converged on two IBM System/390 processors, housing eight CICS/ESA systems, running together using MRO (Fig. 12.5). The two processors were kept at a secret location close to the centre of the games complex. A third, backup, processor was housed at another secret location, several miles away. The CICS systems ran on only one of the machines throughout the games. The second machine was a communications network manager, but had enough spare capacity to take over the most vital functions if there was a serious failure in the main CICS machine. The third, remote, machine was available in case of major failure or damage affecting the whole of the main site. Its database was backed-up daily using data carried between sites on tape cartridges. In the event, there was no significant failure, so neither level of backup was needed. In fact, there was only one minor problem in any system based upon CICS during the fourteen days of the games. On that single occasion, the failure was countered quickly by automatic restart using the CICS/AO program.

There were 28 CICS systems in the main CICS processor. Eight of them formed the CICS part of the Olympics production system. The others were development, integration and acceptance systems. In the production system, a terminal-owning region handled all communication with the network, on behalf of the application-owning regions. The CICS systems in the application-owning regions shared the transaction workload (Fig. 12.6). Pure administration tasks were handled by two CICS systems: one processed only accreditation transactions, as these were seen as critical; the other handled remaining administrative tasks, such as accommodation, transport and medical needs.

At the other end of the application spectrum, a separate CICS region handled collection and redistribution of results data, taking input from sites, storing it, and relaying it to other sites and to the information systems used by the press and commentators. The commentators viewed information at Touchscreen display PS/2 computers connected to the award-winning SICO system developed by IBM. These information systems were provided by two other CICS regions. Between

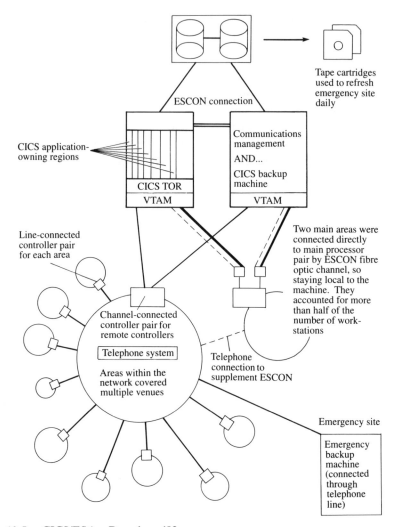

Figure 12.5. CICS/ESA—Barcelona '92.

them the information systems allowed random access to results data, statistics, biographical data, and information on weather, transport and so on. The system designers chose to run parallel information systems for two reasons: to ensure a degree of fault-tolerance, and to share the transaction workload at times of peak activity. Transactions were routed according to terminal identifier and, for a few (commentator) transactions, transaction identifier.

In addition, following the example of earlier games, there was an extensive and heavily used electronic mail system. This ran in a separate CICS region. Finally, there was a paralympics games system running alongside the main system. This was a small-scale replica of the main Olympic system, designed to manage the World Paralympic Games. Although the paralympics (Olympic Games for the

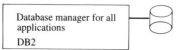

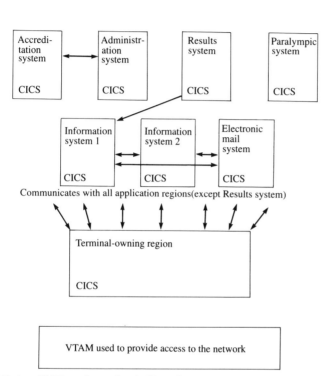

Figure 12.6.   CICS configuration in Barcelona.

physically handicapped) were not due to start until September 1992, the administrative systems were already operating, and ran independently during the two
weeks of the main games.

As you can tell, the scale of the undertaking was vast. Yet the equipment and
software used to create the basic systems was standard. As CICS users regularly
discover, by using CICS as a framework, designers were able to construct a real-
time system to meet all their needs, and to support the latest technologies in sport
and communication. Most importantly, they were able to provide instantly-usable
systems for unsophisticated end-users of all nationalities. For the first time,
graphical interfaces and Touchscreen displays, supporting multiple languages,
were used to make information systems accessible to a huge range of cultures and
abilities. All of this effort for two weeks of furious activity! The system is now
being upgraded so that it will be ready to qualify for a place in the next Olympics,
in Atlanta in 1996. By then, who can say what technology it will have to
accommodate?

13
Ever onward—the future of CICS

There are some who would question the utterance of 'CICS' and 'future' in the same breath. They see emerging technologies, such as personal workstations, local area networks, advanced communications, open systems, and so on, as alternatives to CICS transaction processing. CICS has always been associated with mainframe systems, and the demise of the mainframe computer has been predicted with glee for years by industry-watchers. Yet CICS has quietly side-stepped such debates and adopted the causes of rightsizing and openness as its own. Seeing them as opportunities rather than threats, CICS has grown into a family of systems, spanning a variety of platforms and offering business solutions for all sizes of enterprise. While introducing truly entry-level systems at the low end of the marketplace, it has kept pace with technological developments in its traditional mainframe world. Meanwhile, being part of IBM's Networking Systems line of business, its development remains in step with communications technology and international standards. It therefore remains ideally placed to take advantage of any developments, host-based, distributed, or any combination of the two, according to the needs of users of information technology.

As you have seen throughout this book, CICS uses underlying hardware and software subsystems to provide the services it needs. The symbiotic relationship between CICS and its supporting systems stimulates continued evolution and viability of all of them. At the same time, it allows CICS to concentrate on developing to meet specific transaction-processing needs, embracing appropriate new technologies rather than competing with them. In addition, it provides its users with a set of general-purpose transaction-processing services, rather than a finished system. By selecting ready-made application packages, or designing some of their own, users can mould it precisely to almost any business situation, present or future.

In predicting the future of CICS in the world of information technology, therefore, it is appropriate to look first at the evolution of businesses and of the base technologies that they will use. So for the rest of this chapter we will look at:

- How we can expect the marketplace to evolve
- How end-user and data-processing populations will change

- What other technological changes we can expect
- What effect these things will have on the CICS family.

13.1   The transaction-processing marketplace

The use of computerized transaction processing has been growing steadily for twenty years, across the world and throughout all segments of industry. It has traditionally been the province of large and medium-sized companies, because only they have been able to afford large-scale commercial computer systems with the processing and communications power needed to handle typical transaction workloads. In the 1980s, advances in hardware technology made powerful systems accessible to small business. Now that suitable environments exist, CICS is evolving to run on small OS/2 systems and RISC System/6000 systems. This represents a potentially enormous change in the characteristics of the CICS user population. Tens or hundreds of thousands of very small CICS systems will soon outnumber the established host-based systems, and often will be used by a new class of user.

In the early years, availability of transaction processing for smaller systems is outstripping improvements in systems integrity and ease of use. Systems still need skilled staff to design, install and operate them; further advances will be needed to make transaction-processing systems *easy* for the average small business to set up and use.

We will look here at the developing needs of different CICS users, divided for convenience into three classes: small, medium and large. The development of the CICS family will reflect the needs of all three classes, and we can expect improvements introduced for each to filter across to the others, setting common standards and providing benefit for the whole transaction-processing community.

From little acorns . . .

Smaller companies have started to recognize the value of transaction-processing systems. Having invested in stand-alone microcomputers in the 1980s, they can now see the advantages of joining them together. Once they have created networks, small users will naturally begin using them to process transactions, probably using ready-made application packages.

Small users cannot afford to employ teams of system programmers, or application programmers, or operators. In fact, they expect their newer, more powerful systems to reduce or limit the number of staff they need, not increase it. They will want to train one or two members of staff to carry out routine operations in addition to other duties, but they will expect systems to look after themselves most of the time. They will expect application packages to be instantly usable, and to need minimal education for users. In fact, they will expect a transaction-processing system to be as usable and unobtrusive as a PC software package—for example a word processor or a LAN-based file manager. They will want any transaction-processing package to run on the mixture of machines that they are already using, adding value to an existing investment in equipment, without disturbing normal business.

Such minimalist data-processing organizations may not expect massive power and sophistication from their new systems, but in some respects they will assume, by default, more of their systems than is expected by traditional CICS users: greater ease of use; full reliability, so that the systems are not prone to failure; almost no need for system administration during normal use; automatic recovery from, and notification of, problems and faults. These attributes will become essential, as small startup organizations will have no on-site technical support staff to solve day-to-day problems.

There could be hundreds of thousands of such small-business users worldwide by the early years of the twenty-first century. Many will grow rapidly as a result of their use of transaction processing, to become medium and large users. They will expect to be able to grow without restraint, handling extra workload by expanding their established transaction-processing systems, or by moving them smoothly to larger, more powerful machines or operating systems.

Despite their size, startup companies will be interested in intersystem communication from an early stage. To be more precise, they will be encouraged by business partners to be interested from an early stage. Banks, suppliers and customers will encourage them to use common business communications: transferring data, funds and orders through shared networks, to improve efficiency, reduce costs and provide better service.

To saplings . . .

As a small transaction-processing system grows, supporting more users, handling more data and running more transactions, it undergoes several changes. First, it becomes indispensable to the organization that it serves, with parts of the business depending upon it totally for continued efficiency. Secondly, its data becomes more valuable, and needs better protection. Thirdly, and partly because of the other two, the system's administrative workload becomes more significant. As a result of the changes, a system begins to need dedicated staff to ensure efficiency, security and continuity, and to carry out system-management tasks, including maintenance, operation and planning.

For medium-sized businesses, although transaction processing may become vital, the need for a dedicated support team will be difficult to accept. Users will want to retain the simplicity and low costs of their early days, running transactions without a thought for underlying issues. Perhaps more significantly, there will not be enough system programmers to go round. Consequently, today's growing businesses will demand CICS systems that eliminate many system-programming tasks and simplify those that cannot be eliminated. To minimize the need for extra staff, administration tasks will have to blend with those of the underlying system. So, for example, CICS/400 will need to become even more integrated with other AS/400 system software, maintenance and procedures; CICS/6000 will need to become more integrated with those of AIX.

The need for smaller CICS systems to grow closer to other parts of the platform is two-fold. First, and most obviously, CICS needs to become easier to install and integrate with the system. More importantly, it needs to be readily usable by anyone who is familiar with the platform and decides to add CICS as an option.

For any given platform, closeness of CICS to the underlying systems will not be enough in itself. Already, users are wary of anything that ties them to a given manufacturer's hardware. Consequently, CICS users will not want their use of CICS on one platform to preclude their subsequent adoption of, or conversion to, other hardware; that is, they will want openness. In running on a wider variety of operating systems, CICS is furthering this cause of openness. As an application-enabling layer that spans systems based on UNIX, *and* System/370, System/390 and plug-compatible systems, *and* OS/400 and OS/2, it provides the most open transaction-processing system available. Nevertheless, its users will want it to become even more open, making sets of transaction-processing function and services available on every appropriate platform.

When users of the CICS family begin to exercise their freedom of choice, they will discover the need for communication between dissimilar systems, and the need to manage dissimilar systems as a single entity. Members of the CICS family already provide intersystem communication, as you saw in Chapter 9. However, they do not yet provide enough help in managing multiple, similar systems, let alone dissimilar ones. As they begin to expand their systems, users will want painless incremental growth, with easy system management and operation. They will want to be able to install systems, operate them, manage their environments, and ensure their security and integrity, all without having to expand their organizations significantly, without having to have a team of administrators for each system, and without having to consider technical details traditionally the concern of the system programmer. They will want to be able to organize systems in ways that reflect the structure of their enterprises.

Despite aiming for ease of use, medium-sized systems are likely to need some specialist system-planning and design support. As the size of a system, its workload and the complexity of its connections increases, so do the penalties for poor capacity planning or poor choice of hardware or software. Larger systems usually manage more valuable data, so data loss is more likely to prove catastrophic, and data logging and recovery planning become vital. Yet we have seen that growing organizations will be reluctant to have large, permanent teams of specialists, and will want 'load-and-go' systems that need minimal attention. To cope with this conflict, small and medium-sized companies will typically employ as few system-support staff as possible, and will hire consultants to plan significant changes or carry out trouble-shooting. They will expect CICS systems to be more self-sustaining, more forgiving, and better at communicating their needs or problems. So, for example, users will want more helpful advice about the state of their systems: measurements that show clearly how a system is performing, whether that is acceptable, and what action to take if it is not. A system that is nearing its capacity limits will be expected to issue warnings, summarizing performance trends, correlating these with statistics, and suggesting causes and remedies in time to stop the trend affecting end-users. The warnings and instructions will have to be clear and precise enough for the user to take action, or in a form that can be interpreted easily by visiting consultants.

To tall oaks

Today's preoccupations of medium-sized, growing CICS users are surprisingly similar to those of many established, and sometimes very large, CICS users, differing mainly in scale. From a transaction-processing point of view, many large enterprises are becoming coalitions of small and medium internal business units, each with its own procurement policy and application needs. Rather than attaching hired experts to each unit, large CICS users will use their own centralized teams of system-support staff as home-grown consultants. This is in fact not very different from the existing role of a typical large team of CICS system programmers. However, the difference lies in the scale of the challenge faced by the teams. As systems are dispersed across networks, the support task changes significantly. Many systems have be monitored, controlled and maintained, some from afar; consultants and operators may be miles—even time zones—from end-users. System support staff and operations staff handling anything but the smallest networks will be too stretched by new responsibilities to continue doing all of the routine tasks in the way they do today. They will need the same improvements in system and network management services, statistics, problem reports and so on as smaller users. Traditional CICS support staff may initially resent the dilution of their familiar responsibilities, but they will quickly see that it frees them to do more productive and satisfying work.

The need to manage tens, hundreds or even thousands of CICS systems at the same time has been with traditional CICS system programmers for a decade. As you have seen, a sophisticated CICS system-support organization may manage hundreds or thousands of CICS systems (connected or independent). The systems can be running on different platforms, sharing the same processing system, or be in different processors within a PR/SM complex, or in different machines in the same building, or in machines scattered around the world. Although CICS users operate very large numbers of systems successfully today, their task is not easy, and pressure for increased ease of use will increase in the 1990s.

Corporate users of personal workstations have begun to realize that they use only a tiny fraction of their processing power; most of the time workstations are idle, waiting for work. By contrast, more obviously expensive mainframe computers are usually force-fed with work to make them cost-effective. Organizations will try to find ways of redistributing processing workload, increasing the amount of distributed processing, and thereby deferring upgrades of mainframe processors. This process of redistribution will generate new requirements for improved cooperative processing facilities, and better operational characteristics, including maintainability.

Despite growth in the use of CICS on distributed systems, the future of the traditional host-like CICS system is in little doubt. The centrally-developed and centrally-maintained system is ideal for organizations with large numbers of mainstream employees, who need the services of a system but need to avoid any technical understanding. It needs central support, but the cost of a system-support organization can sometimes be dwarfed by the cost of inexperienced staff trying to manage their own workstations. Even when individual departments have their own processing systems, they will continue to need transaction-processing support from shared server machines from time to time, and the server for a large network will need enormous processing power. Whether this continues to be provided by System/390 systems remains to be seen, though the likelihood is that users will want it to be; enterprises have so much invested in such systems that entire businesses, probably the world's economic system, would be jeopardized by an attempt to change.

We can expect the emergence of small-scale CICS systems to influence the development of the mainframe systems, providing new and innovative approaches to old problems. However, the drive for improvement will not be one-way. Pressures for change continue to come from the largest, and usually most experienced, mainframe users. Although they are seen mostly to focus on technical challenges—capacity, performance, growth and so on—the larger users have begun to show greater impatience with usability of CICS systems. They are already demanding usability changes to complement the functional and performance enhancements that they have received over the years. They are under pressure from cost-conscious internal auditors and managers, and are beginning to question the cost of implementing systems, of migrating and upgrading them and of administering them.

13.2   The community

We have looked at the direction of individual enterprises. We will now look at the different user populations that comprise such enterprises, and see how they are likely to change. The nature and characteristics of the users will affect the development of the CICS family almost as much as the changes in businesses themselves. We will see changes in the nature of end-users, of application programmers, and of system programmers.

End-users

Chapter 2 started by looking at the end-users of CICS applications. These are likely to be the drivers of the next phase of transaction-processing evolution, so we will look at them first here.

We have seen in Chapter 1 that the end-user has gone through an evolution in the quarter-century life of CICS. The back-office user has been joined first by the front-office user, then by remote, distributed office users and the general public. However, even now, the general public's use is fairly limited and unambitious, and so has plenty of scope for expansion. For the office worker, new working methods suggest possible changes in patterns of transaction processing.

Clearly, telecommunications are providing significant pressure for change at the turn of the twentieth century. Satellite and cable communications seem to shrink the world a little more every year. Optical technologies make global communication cheap and attractive for everyone. The technologies waiting to capitalize on these advances will create new business and new ways of life. Video telephones that enable you to hear and see a caller are just coming onto the market. This itself is impressive, but one step onward, IBM's Person to Person/2 system allows voice, video image, graphical data and text data to be shared in real time by PS/2 workstations connected by telephone. This means that the user of a workstation can hold full teleconference sessions from his or her desk. A session can include playback of prerecorded video sequences, real-time input from video cameras, shared use of sketchpad windows and shared access to data. This is a perfect setting for use of CICS systems, which can process participants' *ad hoc* enquiries, providing results that can be shared and discussed in real time. CICS therefore remains relevant, despite the completely new environment. What is more, its involvement need not require any new CICS technology, as its own programming services allow users to adapt CICS to the new environment.

Whereas some desktops are getting busier, others are being left vacant for long periods. The use of portable telephones means that mobile workers have less need to return to their bases. The PCRadio, a combination of rugged personal computer and portable telephone, can be a roving CICS terminal, connecting through wireless local area networks into major networks, and thereby gaining access to the rest of the network, and any associated CICS system. Many PCRadio users are certain to need transaction-processing support: querying databases and carrying out simple data-entry tasks. Potential users are countless: police patrols, gas or electricity metering staff, car rental agents. This change in working pattern can occur without necessarily affecting CICS. By subcontracting communications management to other subsystems, CICS has avoided the need to change with every technological advance. Of course, the new methods and work-patterns may nevertheless prompt development of new applications with special character-istics, or extensions to CICS's programming interfaces.

Other desktops are being relocated, as the practice of working at home becomes more commonplace. A distributed workforce has many of the characteristics of a distributed system, and its transaction-processing needs will best be met by exactly the services provided by the CICS family. A home-worker (or a travelling worker, for that matter) will be someone who can work efficiently in relative isolation, but who needs residual contact, probably to retrieve or provide data for a central database, or to communicate directly with other members of an organization. For example, a home-worker might be involved in telephone marketing, market intelligence, or help-desk activity. Such a worker will probably work with a home-based workstation, data local to the workstation (uploaded to or downloaded from a host computer at intervals), and workstation-based application programs. When these are not enough, the programs will need to communicate with programs or databases on remote host systems, probably without the worker realizing. From time to time, programs will need maintenance, updates and so on, through downloading from host systems.

Personal computers are commonplace in the home—even before home-working is common—and most homes in the western world already have tele-phones. Consequently, much of the technology of home-working is available to the general public as customers as well as employees. This provides an oppor-tunity for businesses to develop new services, or adapt old ones, based on the new technology. Home banking is already relatively well-known, and home shopping is a likely future growth area. Future advances that will almost certainly grab the imagination of the public will link telephone users to databases and ordering systems. They will, for example, allow a consumer to: search inventories and price lists before deciding where to order goods; order goods, theatre tickets, aeroplane tickets or hotel rooms; order, and receive electronically, digitally-recorded films, books or music. All of these will be done without leaving home, and will be paid for by automatic transfer of funds between banks.

Where the world of the public meets the world of business, there continue to be advances in transaction processing. The most rapid advances are coming with cheaper and more sophisticated telephony. The combination of computer-controlled switching, voice synthesizers and touch-tone telephones allow a telephone handset to become a CICS terminal, supporting keyed input and audio output. Suddenly, every telephone user has become a potential end-user, every touch-tone telephone a terminal.

All of these technologies have the same effect: they bring an ever wider audience of end-users into the world of transaction processing. Without excep-tion, the technologies can be exploited today, using the existing services of CICS. However, their emergence changes the nature of the CICS workload, and will impose new demands on CICS: to support new data streams or formats, to conform to new architectures, to absorb new workloads, or to make possible advances in interface design or performance.

Application programmers

Changes in the characteristics and needs of CICS end-users will be seen most often by members of the application-programming team. They will have to design new classes of programs to meet the demanding needs of relatively naïve members of the public. At the same time, they will have to design dialogues for use with new kinds of device, for example telephone keypads and voice synthesizers. Their programs will need to be less intrusive, less impersonal, more responsive and more forgiving of errors.

The constant demand for new transaction-processing business systems already keeps programming staff fully busy. In fact, the need for new programs, combined with the need for running repairs and extensions to existing ones, has historically outstripped the availability of qualified staff. Application-program backlogs *can* be addressed by employing more programmers, but only if such programmers are actually available for hire. The constant need for staff, combined with a continued shortage, will generate requirements, each in turn creating additional requirements for CICS.

Some users will decide to reduce their reliance on skilled application programmers. They will want increasingly sophisticated programming interfaces that enable ordinary employees to create simple programs. Their reasoning will be that existing professional staff members are often highly educated, skilled in their own fields, and therefore better able than anyone else to specify applications, even though they may not be computer-literate. Many CICS users already use 'fourth generation language' application generators that run with CICS. These can be used by relatively inexperienced programmers to achieve higher productivity at lower cost. The next logical advance will be the use of 'fifth generation' languages—expert systems—to cut out the need for programmers as interpreters. Expert systems will behave like the application analysts of today, interviewing staff from client departments to determine their program needs, building prototypes from standard building-blocks of program code, then testing the resulting programs to see if they meet expectations. In time, programs built in this way could become efficient and usable. For the immediate future, though, they are likely to be less efficient and effective than purpose-built traditional programs. They will therefore not be used for some years in business-critical transactions, or in systems where performance is of overriding importance. Yet they could soon provide the best hope for organizations with impossible deadlines or severe staff shortages.

Many CICS users will continue to produce programs in-house, using ordinary (third generation) languages to achieve efficient, optimized code. However, they will want to be able to use the best available programmers, regardless of programming language, so they will want CICS to support a wide range of programming languages. They will want to be able to mix the use of different languages.

In future, a transaction-processing application will be designed for client/server operations *because of* the balance of skills in a department. As personal computers and powerful workstations have become commonplace, the population of programmers trained to write workstation code has grown explosively, while the population trained in mainframe programming skills has grown modestly in comparison, though there is a large existing population. In future, organizations will have access to a nucleus of specialist System/390 programmers, plus a very large population of programmers with workstation programming skills. This will encourage analysts to separate programs into parts that require knowledge of real-time transaction-processing design (servers) and parts that do not (clients). The servers will often run on System/390 systems, and will be similar to traditional CICS programs, but will have less interaction with the end-user, focusing instead on data-related activities, such as locking files to prevent multiple access, recording updates in case of failure, assuring security and so on. Clients will handle anything that is essentially single-user activity, such as dialogue with the end-user, input validation and manipulation of data after input or before output.

The world of personal systems will encourage another trend in CICS programming: the growing use of prepackaged software. Such packages are already commonly available for CICS. They range from full business solutions, for example hospital-management systems, through to single applications, such as account receivable programs. Many organizations have resisted using prepackaged software, for a number of reasons, including three notable ones: it cannot precisely meet their needs, so requires at least a little tailoring; its continued development and maintenance depends on another organization, whose business priorities may not always coincide with those of its customers; they know that there is always a security risk in letting outside agencies know more than they already do about parts of their systems. Nevertheless, most executives are now used to personal systems, and can see the value-for-money advantages of the packages that they buy for themselves. Many will not be persuaded that the benefits of in-house development justify its cost.

Of course, any of these alternative approaches to CICS programming presupposes the continued existence of the CICS programming interfaces. Even fifth generation languages will, underneath it all, be CICS programs designed to use the CICS programming interface. Application programmers, whoever employs them, will expect CICS to be more helpful and more forgiving. The CICS command language has developed over many years until it now allows programmers to write more robust code. However, it is still possible to create rogue programs, as we saw in Chapter 5. Programmers will expect mainframe CICS systems to evolve to prevent common programming errors, including potentially catastrophic ones, such as storage violations.

Increased portability of CICS program source between CICS platforms will give rise to increased pressure for the same set of languages to be supported on every platform. It will also increase demand for greater consistency in the EXEC CICS programming language across the different platforms. In addition to improvements in portability, programmers will expect consistent intercommunication interfaces, designed to be simple in concept. An example of what will be needed is the relatively new distributed program link CICS facility that makes it possible to design cooperative processing applications that span systems, but that appear simply to link to each other in the normal way. As it becomes possible, and commonplace, to link many hundreds or thousands of CICS systems into a homogeneous or heterogeneous network, so programmers will want CICS to find ways of keeping its single-system image, so that they can continue to program in the familiar way, and run existing programs without change.

Systems support

The pressures for change in the world of system support appear at first quite different at the high and low ends of the marketplace. Traditional large CICS users often seem preoccupied with the minutiae of system function, while low-end users want systems to be easy to install and manage. However, this appearance is deceptive. Large users do value CICS's rich and flexible set of services and interfaces, but to use them fully they need CICS to relieve them of the less interesting tasks that can take up so much time.

Small users need CICS to be easy to install and maintain because they cannot afford the traditional CICS support team, or cannot find suitably-skilled staff. Very large users need the same because although they have CICS support staff, they need them to develop and maintain very sophisticated, probably highly distributed, systems. Consequently, they need them to spend more time on leading-edge projects and less on routine tasks.

Large CICS users are more inclined than ever to install CICS as part of a CBIPO installability package. This removes some of the variables in the installation process, but still leaves an enormous number of options before a user can have a working system. Users will expect packaging to improve, and will expect CICS to do more to make the subsequent processes simpler. So, CICS will be expected to make customization and tailoring simpler. This could be achieved in a number of ways, but all will have to be aimed at eliminating processes, guiding users in making choices, or providing working examples that need only minimal tailoring.

CICS/ESA users will expect their CICS system to emulate CICS/VSE, which blends in with the VSE/System Package, using its more usable interfaces and procedures. CICS/VSE will itself learn from the work done to make CICS/400 and CICS/6000 blend even more effectively into their operating-system environments.

CICS systems on all of the platforms will need to simplify decision-making, by being more helpful: providing more and better defaults, more samples, inter-active dialogues-even expert systems. So, for example, users will expect CICS, wherever possible, to learn about its system resources by interrogating other subsystems, rather than through explicit user definition—making more use of autoinstall and similar initiatives. Likewise, instead of receiving error messages about CICS limits being exceeded, users will expect the system to analyse the reasons and take corrective tuning action. Similarly, instead of receiving messages specifying system or program errors, users will expect CICS to rectify the errors without intervention.

The aim of system-support staff will be to free themselves from chores. This will leave smaller users' staff to pursue their own business, and will free large-system staff to handle more complex challenges. In particular, it will make it feasible to create, manage and maintain very large CICS complexes, without needing enormous teams of system programmers. Of course, creating such complexes will generate additional demands. Support staff and operations staff will find that they need new ways of administering systems. In very large networks, they will want to view the totality of all systems and networks—getting a 'view from a mile high'. Such a view will have to cover all of the usual CICS concerns: performance monitoring and tuning, debugging, operational tasks.

The very large networks of CICS systems may be homogeneous networks of either CICS/VSEs or CICS/ESAs, connected by ISC or MRO. On the other hand, they may have the added dimension of a mixture of different CICS systems, based on MVS/ESA, VSE/ESA, OS/2, AIX, OS/400 and non-IBM operating systems. In such cases, staff will have to learn how to handle the side-effects of interaction between dissimilar systems, say between CICS/ESA and CICS/6000. For CICS system programmers, this will be nothing new. Traditionally, they have been used to handling cross-product interactions—with IMS/VS, DB2, VTAM and so on.

Nevertheless, with system images proliferating, a system specialist checking parameters will not wish to use CICS system-management facilities in their present forms. Trying to route CEMT requests to one CICS system out of a hundred connected systems is already very difficult. Handling millions of console messages every day would be out of the question. Almost all other management functions would be equally impossible without new facilities: resource definition, debugging, performance analysis, application of maintenance and so on. So, CICS will have to provide system-monitoring and control functions that allow growing numbers of CICS images to appear as a single system for control purposes, but allow each system to be singled out for treatment whenever necessary. Where possible, management of CICS systems will have to be seen as part of management of the system as a whole: operating system, communications access methods, databases and so on.

13.3   CICS and other products

CICS's development will be influenced, as was its past, by advances in technology, both hardware and software. Its most obvious influences have traditionally been mainframe hardware, operating systems and access methods. However, through these CICS has indirectly supported countless minor advances. In this section, we will speculate on the technologies that CICS will embrace, either directly or indirectly, in the foreseeable future.

General technology

CICS has always been opportunistic. It has embraced almost every advance of information technology during its 25 years, and will continue to do so. We have already looked at some of the advances that we might expect to become very successful in the next few years:

- Video telephones
- Person to Person/2 conferencing
- PCRadio
- The use of telephones as terminals.

By continuing its policy of supporting any necessary extensions to architectures and data streams, CICS ensures that programmers can use new technologies as they emerge. In addition, CICS's flexible and extendable programming interfaces will continue to allow other technologies to adapt to CICS. Emerging products and technologies show the potential.

The most exciting predictions usually surround the most futuristic technologies. For example, there is often speculation about imaging and holography, anticipating applications such as being able to view a new house through 'virtual reality', or being able to examine goods from an electronic catalogue in three dimensions. Both of these would require database and data communications interactions, so could need the coordinating skills of CICS.

Such visual output technologies are likely to be less universally useful in the CICS environment than audio (both input and output) and visual input. For example, voice input is likely to be very popular with the general public in high-street applications. Voice recognition is just reaching the level of sophistication at which it can be commercially useful. Of course, audio output is already quite usable, and is in regular use in telephony and some consumer products. Visual input to systems is not yet very sophisticated, though bar-code readers are in common use in the retail trade and in warehousing. Future advances could include complex pattern recognition, bringing the ability to recognize end-users through physical characteristics such as fingerprints or facial appearance, thereby providing the ultimate security check.

These new technologies will need new kinds of terminal, which will in turn handle a different kind of data. Yet the CICS role will remain the same: supporting new applications and terminals, providing the application 'glue' that will hold database and data communications together.

Communications technology

The CICS glue continues to 'stick' because it evolves with both database technology and communications technology. It continues to evolve today, even as the pace of communications technology quickens.

Just as the EXEC CICS language has for years shielded programs from details of networking (through VTAM, BTAM or TCAM), it has made it possible for the same programming commands to be used without change in the OS/2, OS/400 and AIX environments, even though the underlying communications access methods are TCP/IP or NetBIOS rather than VTAM. The same approach will allow the EXEC CICS language to function in the Hewlett-Packard systems and any other CICS systems that follow. It will allow new networking protocols to be introduced and used by any CICS without affecting existing programs. As a sign of what may become possible: IBM's CICS Development organization has already tested CICS/ESA systems successfully in an environment using a large OSI communications network. In other trials, it has carried out tests on a TCP/IP sockets interface for CICS/ESA, showing in the process that CICS can participate in TCP/IP networks effectively.

Despite these developments, CICS will continue to evolve to match and exploit advances in its traditional networking partner, VTAM. For example, it will evolve to make best use of the emerging protocols of Advanced Peer-to-Peer Networking (known as APPN). This will make it easier for CICS users to connect and operate a variety of different peer systems. Such connectivity will become increasingly important as interenterprise communication becomes more widespread. These advances ensure that CICS/ESA and CICS/VSE are relevant to a new generation of communicating systems. At the same time, the continued use of traditional SNA allows enterprises to maintain and build traditional, hierarchical networks wherever their structure makes central control and administration much simpler.

The growing power of CICS as an engine of communication is already recognized by developers of communications applications. IBM itself is showing the direction in some of the application packages it provides. For example, IBM's expEDIte/CICS product is one of a family of products that provide electronic data interchange on a wide range of system platforms. Similarly, OfficeVision/MVS provides electronic mail capability from within the general suite of office support applications.

Data management

At the other end of the database/data communication partnership, CICS remains close to leading-edge data-management technology. It will continue its policy of using advances in data-management technology as they emerge. As CICS networks become larger and more heterogeneous, they will need more efficient ways of sharing data. In some cases, the efficiency will come through establishment of clear client/server relationships. However, in other cases, centralization of data within a mainframe CICSplex will be unacceptable. CICS will have to deal with both distributed data and highly-centralized data. Its intercommunication facilities suit it equally well to both models.

When data is needed simultaneously by different distributed (CICS and non-CICS) subsystems, the systems will need enhanced data-sharing facilities. The data-sharing capabilities of database products will doubtless be extended, and CICS products will have to evolve at the same pace. In time, VSAM and other file-management products will need to fit into such a data-sharing environment. Again, CICS will have to work with VSAM to make best use of any changes.

As the CICS network expands, it is inevitable that databases and files will be shared more widely. They will also be distributed to a greater extent. The totality of data in the network will be viewed as a single logical database, despite being distributed widely. This will, of course, introduce challenges for CICS system strategists, security administrators and database administrators: ensuring that in creating more dynamic and heterogeneous networks they do not create opportunities for a breakdown in data integrity or security.

13.4   CICS outlook

The needs of its users and the pressures of related technology will shape much of CICS's future. However, CICS has never been a passive participant in data processing. Major advances in CICS technology, such as command-level programming, MRO, and ISC, have been the result of creativity and foresight. Other such changes in future will ensure that CICS continues to be the answer to (as yet) unknown questions. Because of their nature, these changes cannot be discussed in this book. However, we can look at other technical changes to CICS that will keep it vital to all segments of the industry.

Family feeling

The CICS systems of today have much in common with each other, and can share portable application source code. Even so, there is room for improvement, as each CICS product supports a slightly different subset of the full CICS facilities. Over time, we shall see IBM bring the systems closer together, so that for all practical purposes they can provide full application portability. IBM has begun to document the different CICS interfaces in great detail, showing common base functions applicable to all products, and identifying differences. This documentation of the CICS family's language will accelerate the move towards common interfaces.

Individually, the different CICS systems will develop to make better use of underlying operating-system and hardware technologies. Just as CICS/OS/VS evolved to accommodate virtual storage, extended architecture, enterprise systems architecture and so on, to become CICS/ESA, so it will evolve further. Its MRO and ISC capabilities allow it to make use of multiprocessing machines, and will continue to do so as the number of processors grows. In the mid-range, CICS/VSE will also continue to evolve, taking advantage of improvements in the VSE system while matching many of the CICS extensions being introduced in CICS/ESA. CICS/VSE's relationship with CICS/MVS is similar to that of CICS/DOS/VS with CICS/OS/VS: two almost-identical systems, differing mainly when environment-specific differences offer advantages. This close relationship will strengthen throughout the 1990s, enabling CICS users on the System/390 platforms to benefit from the provision of common services and interfaces, the portability of programs, and the consequent effectiveness of vendor-developed application packages.

Like CICS/ESA and CICS/VSE, other CICS systems will evolve with their operating systems. CICS OS/2 is already demonstrating this through its enhancement to use OS/2 Version 2. CICS/400 and CICS/6000 will do so, too. At the same time, a common operating system layer (or 'kernel') for workstations will make it possible for workstation-based CICS systems to be developed once-only for several platforms.

Are we talking?

Programming and portability is fine, but, as we have seen, the future is being driven by communication. End-users will want to hop between systems. A multinational corporation will want to use its entire worldwide transaction-processing and data inventory as a single, always-available, system. This is already possible.

All of the current CICS systems can be interconnected. However, they need some improvements. Over time, they will come to use open interfaces, able to communicate with non-IBM CICS systems, and non-CICS IBM systems, as well as each other. The distributed program link capability will be provided on more CICS platforms, allowing CICS systems to run programs in direct response to input from such non-CICS systems. Each CICS will implement remote procedure call in the same way as is already done on other systems. CICS will thus comply with recognized client/server standards. CICS intercommunication will become universal.

Networks of CICS systems within, and between, enterprises will accommodate all existing CICS products, as well as any others that comply with the published architecture. Within single enterprises, large CICSplexes, probably centred on CICS/ESA hubs, will cooperate to process the total workload more effectively. The established TOR, AOR, DOR approach to forming CICSplexes will evolve to allow optimization of routing and workload-balancing. Where necessary, intelligence in the CICS network will recognize faulty components, bypass them and later recycle them when repaired. At times of highest workload, the CICS network will be able to initialize extra systems to process transactions, quiescing them when the workload diminishes again.

13.5   What will not change?

Throughout this evolutionary change, CICS will continue to provide elements of stability and certainty. It will continue to provide one of the richest sets of programming facilities and interfaces of any transaction-processing product in the world. These are the elements that have kept it at the forefront of transaction processing for a quarter of a century. They are the essence of CICS, and will ensure that the system goes on serving existing and future users. In addition, three attributes will make it indispensable.

The first is its fundamental nature: it is, to use those original words, a database/data communications system. In other words, it provides controlled access to a database through a data communication network. CICS access will always be achieved under control of application programs, and CICS will provide simplified programming interfaces to make things simpler for programmers. That is CICS's purpose, and it will continue to fulfil it. It will continue to support an enormous variety of terminal devices, and will continue to allow any data-resource managers to attach themselves.

The second is its dependability: supporting existing programs and terminals release after release.

The third is that it is a 'one-size-fits-all' product. There will be a CICS for everyone. However many new functions are added, you will still be able to design, code, test and run simple transactions on the largest or smallest systems. . . .

13.6   Back to the future

More than ten years ago there was a rumour circulating among CICS users that IBM was planning to withdraw CICS in favour of an alternative product. Since then, the number of CICS licenses has more than doubled, and the number of CICS images running at any time has risen a hundredfold. To paraphrase Mark Twain: the report of CICS's death was an exaggeration!

Rumours about the future of CICS surface at intervals of three or four years, usually accompanying the emergence of a new technology. The reports arise from a basic misunderstanding of the nature of CICS. Even now, workstations and open systems are cited as pretenders to the transaction-processing throne. Yet, as you have seen, CICS has embraced them as it embraces all new technology, from 'glass teletypes' to programmable workstations, from mainframes to laptops. It has become an open-system enabler, spanning platforms of many sizes and architectures. CICS thrives on new technology, and so is destined to evolve at the pace of the information-processing and telecommunications industry. The first twenty-five years of CICS have helped to spread strands of enterprise throughout the world. The second twenty-five years will start by bringing the strands together, towards an all-embracing CICS network.

Appendix
User-group information

This appendix gives the contact addresses and numbers of the main user-group organizations, and was correct in July 1993. Presidents and officers of user groups usually serve for a period of one year, so some names may change. For the latest information, contact the user-group administration office in Chicago, USA, or G.U.I.D.E. headquarters in Switzerland. The fax number of the office in Chicago is listed under the entries for SHARE Inc. and GUIDE International. The organizations will be glad to provide further information about membership, meetings and projects, on request.

The telephone and facsimile numbers are given as they would be dialled from the United Kingdom (using prefix 010).

GUIDE International

Headquarters: Ms Bonnie Engle Kampa
401 North Michigan Avenue, Chicago, Illinois 60611-4267, USA
Tel: 010 1 312 644 6610
Fax: 010 1 312 321 6869

SHARE Inc.

Headquarters: SHARE Inc.
Ms Lynne M. Schwartz
401 North Michigan Avenue, Chicago, Illinois 60611-4267, USA
Tel: 010 1 312 822 0932
Fax: 010 1 312 321 6869

G.U.I.D.E.

Headquarters: G.U.I.D.E. Headquarters
Kurt R. Thomas
Schindler Informatik AG, CH-6030 Ebikon, Switzerland
Tel: 010 41 41 33 28 27
Fax: 010 41 41 33 39 62

G.U.I.D.E. Region managers

Austria: Heimo Braun
Amt. der O.Oe. Landesregierung, Kaerntnerstr. 16, A-4020
    LINZ, Austria
Tel: 010 43 732 6584 3112
Fax: 010 43 732 6584 3198

France: Yves Deroual
C.N.R.O., Centre Technique National, B.P. 300, F-06808
    Cagnes sur Mer Cedex, France
Tel: 010 33 93 22 33 01
Fax: 010 33 93 22 36 87

Israel: Katriel Zimet
Bar Ilan University, Computer Center, P.O. Box 16654,
    Il-Tel Aviv, 61164, Israel
Tel: 010 972 3 34 94 02
Fax: 010 972 3 34 44 46

Italy: Dino Tuchtan
Cassa Di Risparmio Di Verona Vicenza Belluno e Ancona,
    Via Garibaldi 1, I-37121 Verona, Italy
Tel: 010 39 45 808 11 16
Fax: 010 39 45 800 09 05

Netherlands: Martin Visser
TIME-WARNER B.V., Otto Heldringstraat 5, NL-1066 AZ
    Amsterdam, Netherlands
Tel: 010 31 20 510 42 69
Fax: 010 31 20 617 50 77

Portugal: Drª Maria Manuela Veríssimo Mendes
Direcção-Geral Dos Serviços de Informática Do Ministério
    Da Justiça, Av. Casal Ribeiro, 16 P-1096 Lisboa Codex,
    Portugal
Tel: 010 351 1 35 61 061
Fax: 010 351 1 35 57 208

Switzerland and   Viktor Kornfein
Liechtenstein: CITIBANK, Postfach 244, CH-8021 Zurich, Switzerland
                    Tel: 010 41 1 205 71 54
                    Fax: 010 41 1 205 71 88

United Kingdom: David C. Saville
                    49 Mungo Park Way, Orpington, Kent BR5 4EE, England
                    Tel: 689 823639 (Country code 44)
                    Fax: 689 823639 (Country code 44)

Australasian SHARE/GUIDE Ltd

Headquarters: Mrs Ella Leithner
                    Australasian SHARE/GUIDE Ltd, P.O. Box 62,
                        Turramurra, New South Wales 2074, Australia
                    Tel: 010 61 2 449 6848
                    Tel: 010 61 2 449 7325

President: Mr Dave Botherway
                    President of Australasian SHARE/GUIDE Limited,
                        Coles Myer Information Services, L3M8, P.O. Box 2000,
                        Tooronga, Victoria 3146, Australia
                    Tel: 010 61 3 829 6410
                    Fax: 010 61 3 829 6211

SHARE Europe (SEAS)

Headquarters: Mr Marc Cattaneo
                    SHARE Europe (SEAS), 48, route des Acacias, CH-1227
                        Carouge/Geneva, Switzerland
                    Tel: 010 41 22 300 3775
                    Fax: 010 41 22 300 1119
                    IBMMAIL: GB5HE58F

COMMON Europe

Head office: Meggie Mohr
                    Bonländer Strasse 20, 70771 Leinfelden-Echterdingen,
                        Germany
                    Tel: 010 49 711 79 55 62
                    Fax: 010 49 711 79 77 340

COMMON US

Headquarters: Mr Rand Baldwin
                 401 North Michigan Avenue, Chicago, Illinois 60611-4267,
                   USA
                 Tel: 010 1 312 644 6610
                 Fax: 010 1 312 321 6869

COMMON Australasia

Administration: Ray Matterson
                 Administration Manager, COMMON Australasia,
                   P.O. Box 64, Chatswood, NSW 2057, Australia
                 Tel: 010 61 2 975 6133
                 Fax: 010 61 2 975 6356

GUIDE Latin America

Headquarters: GUIDE Latin America, Indira Alonso,
                   Rua Dr Mario Cardim, 482 Vila Mariana, CEP 04019,
                   São Paulo SP, Brasil
                 Tel: 010 55 11 575 9692
                 Fax: 010 55 11 573 7071

Japan SHARE/GUIDE

President: Mr Minoru Nakata
                 Japan GUIDE/SHARE, c/o IBM Japan Ltd,
                   19–21 Nihonbashi Hakozaki-cho, Chuo-ku, Tokyo 103,
                   Japan
                 Tel: 010 81 3 3808 3755
                 Fax: 010 81 3 3664 4766

Other Asia/Pacific user-groups

Hong Kong: Mr James Tang
                 Chairman, Hong Kong SHARE/GUIDE,
                   Astec International Limited, Kaiser Estate, Phase 2, 6/F,
                   51 Man Yue Street, Hunghom, Kowloon, Hong Kong
                 Tel: 010 852 765 3333
                 Fax: 010 852 363 0441

Korea: Mr Song Yol
                      President, Korea SHARE/GUIDE, Executive Managing
                          Director, Hanjin Data Communication Co., Yoido-dong,
                          Seoul, Korea
                      Fax: 010 822 786 9471

Malaysia: The SHARE/GUIDE Assoc. (Malaysia), 15th Floor,
                          Plaza IBM, 1,
                          Jalan Tun Mohd Fuad, Taman Tun Dr Ismail,
                          6000 Kuala Lumpur, Malaysia
                      Tel: 010 60 3 717 7788
                      Fax: 010 60 3 717 2188

Philippines: Ms Teresita B Tan
                      President, Philippines SHARE/GUIDE, c/o Bank of the
                          Philippines Islands (BPI), 5/F BPI Condominium Center,
                          8753 Paseo de Roxas, Makati, Metro Manila, Philippines
                      Tel: 010 63 2 816 9756
                      Fax: 010 63 2 818 9059

Singapore: Mr Eugene Sing
                      President, SHARE/GUIDE Association (Singapore),
                          c/o DBS Bank Limited, 6 Shenton Way, DBS Building,
                          Singapore 0106
                      Tel: 010 65 321 5489
                      Fax: 010 65 223 6062

Glossary

Access

The ability to read or update a system resource, such as a file.

Access method

A program or set of programs for moving data between main storage and input or output devices. For example, VSAM is an access method for retrieving or storing disk data; VTAM is an access method for transferring communication data to and from terminals.

ACF/VTAM

IBM's program that controls communication in a computer network. It uses IBM's SNA protocols to pass data between computers, terminals, terminal controllers, printers and other devices.

Address space

The storage within a computer that a program can identify, and therefore gain access to, by numeric address.

Advanced Communications Function/Virtual Telecommunications Access Method

See ACF/VTAM.

Advanced peer-to-peer networking

See APPN.

Advanced program-to-program communication

See APPC.

AIX

IBM's implementation of the UNIX operating system.

Analyst

A person who analyses problems, breaking them down into a form that can be solved by programming.

ANS COBOL

An implementation of COBOL that conforms to the standards for the language agreed by a committee of the American National Standards Institute.

AOR

Application-owning region. A CICS system in a multiregion operation or

235

intersystem communication environment. It specializes in loading and running programs, where a TOR or FOR specializes in terminal or data communications.

APPC

Advanced program-to-program communication. An implementation of the SNA LU6.2 communication protocols, which are used to communicate between programs or systems.

Application

A particular use to which an information-processing system is put: for example a stock control application, an airline reservation application or an order entry application. Often used as a synonym for application program.

Application development

The process of developing or producing application programs.

Application generator

A program that produces application programs semi-automatically. Following specifications, such a generator can be used by less-skilled or overworked programmers to improve their productivity.

Application program

A program written to serve a CICS system's end-users in their regular business activities.

Application programmer

A person who designs and codes an application program.

Application-owning region

See AOR.

Application-programming interface

A set of programming commands and services provided by CICS for application programs to request transaction-processing services. Usually called the command-level or EXEC CICS interface.

APPN

Advanced peer-to-peer networking: a networking protocol that allows computer systems to communicate as peers rather than as 'master' and 'servants'. The protocol is better suited to client/server applications than its hierarchical equivalent, SNA.

Architecture

The description of the logical structure, formats, protocols and operations that represent the essence of a hardware or software data-processing system. Having an architecture allows system developers to develop a common understanding through common standards. For example, the Systems Network Architecture, defined by IBM, provides a common framework for developers of telecommunications systems.

ASCII

American National Standard Code for Information Exchange. An international standard for communicating character and control data within and between information systems.

Assembler

A program that converts assembler-language programming statements into executable form. Other languages use compilers to achieve the same effect. CICS programs written in assembler language have to be translated before they can be assembled, and have to be link-edited after being assembled.

Assembler language

A programming language that is closely related to the machine language of the computer system on which it is used.

Asynchronous processing

A form of communication between CICS systems. One CICS system initiates the communication, starts a program in the second system to do some work on its behalf, then breaks off contact.

Autoinstall

The facility that enables CICS to accept unsolicited sign-on requests from previously undefined terminals. This dynamic 'registration' process can save very large amounts of CICS storage and eliminate the need for some regular administrative processes, but calls for extra programming.

Automated operation

Getting programs to handle many routine operations tasks. This can reduce the number of staff needed to run a system, reduce the chance of operator error, and provide almost instantaneous responses to situations.

Availability

The degree to which a system or resource is ready when needed to process data.

Back office

Administrative organizations, hidden within an enterprise, that do not regularly have face-to-face contact with customers or the general public.

Backing-up

Making a copy of a data file that can be used if the original file becomes damaged.

Backout

The process of restoring to a previous state all or part of a system, usually after a failure of part of the system or a program.

Basic mapping support

See BMS.

Basic Telecommunications Access Method

See BTAM.

Batch

A collection of data prepared for processing as a unit, with no intermediate interaction by an operator. In batch processing, similar data items that need identical processing are grouped in batches so that the same program can process them in rapid succession. Batch processing is ideal for work that can be planned in advance, and for data items that can be held until a suitable time for processing arises. A bank might process a day's cheques as a batch overnight.

BDAM

IBM's Basic Direct Access Method. A program for handling communication data, used by CICS.

Beta test

An early release of a program to its users. Similar to the early support programs used by IBM.

BMS

A CICS facility that makes it possible to separate the complexity of display-screen formatting from everyday programming. It leaves programmers free to concentrate on program data and logic rather than screen layout for different terminal types.

Bottleneck

A system queuing phenomenon that degrades performance.

BTAM

IBM's Basic Telecommunications Access Method: a program that can handle terminal communication on behalf of CICS/VSE and CICS/MVS systems. Often pronounced 'beetam' or 'bakertam', this access method has now been largely replaced by VTAM. It is not supported at all by CICS/ESA.

Byte

A sequence of eight adjacent binary digits (bits) that are operated on as a unit. One or more bytes represent characters or data values, or form computer instructions.

C

A programming language designed for a wide range of system and commercial applications.

C/370

A form of the C language implemented on System/370 systems.

Call

An instruction that enables one program to start another, anticipating an eventual return. For CICS users, an instruction that can also request DL/I services.

CallPath

IBM's product that links computerized telephone exchanges with application programs, allowing calls to be routed and rerouted under program control, and transactions to be initiated according to input. CallPath can run on CICS/VSE and CICS/MVS.

Capacity planning

Planning the performance and storage requirements of a system. This usually involves analysis of current processor loading and capacity, and use of storage, and projections based on understanding of planned programs and data.

CBIPO

Custom-Built Installation Product Offering. An IBM offering that provides a number of MVS-based software products as a prebuilt, ready-to-install package. CICS/MVS and CICS/ESA systems can be received as part of a CBIPO.

CD-ROM

See compact disc.

CECI

The CICS command-interpreter transaction. It enables programmers to build CICS commands interactively at a CICS terminal, and to execute them to see the results.

CEDA

A CICS transaction that can be used to define resources interactively, then to make the definitions available to the running CICS system. Once the system has access to the definitions, it can use the resources they define.

CEDF

A CICS transaction that starts CICS's debugging facility, the execution diagnostic facility (EDF). EDF allows a programmer to test a CICS program on a live CICS system, stopping at CICS commands to check that they operate effectively.

CEMT

A CICS transaction that makes it possible to monitor, check and control the live CICS system. It allows an operator to check and adjust the value of CICS settings, to enable and disable certain functions and resources, and to start and stop the system.

CICS

IBM's customer information control system—a transaction-processing system.

CICS OS/2

The version of IBM's CICS designed to run on the OS/2 operating system.

CICS PD/MVS

A program designed to help system programmers to analyse system dumps to solve CICS-related problems. Versions were produced for both CICS/MVS and CICS/ESA. In 1993, IBM announced that the program was to be withdrawn in favour of an almost identical product produced by the Compuware Corporation.

CICS Problem Determination/MVS

See CICS PD/MVS.

CICS system definition

See CSD.

CICS/400

The version of IBM's CICS system designed to run on the AS/400 family of computers.

CICS/6000

The version of IBM's CICS system designed to run on computers using IBM's AIX operating system.

CICS/AMA

IBM's CICS application migration aid, designed to help convert CICS macro-level programs to command-level programs.

CICS/CMS

The version (now obsolete) of IBM's CICS system for VM's CMS environment. Used for program development and testing.

CICS/DOS/VS

Version 1 of IBM's CICS system for the VSE operating system environment. Originally designed for the System/360 DOS operating system, it became CICS/DOS/VS on the introduction of virtual storage systems for System/370.

CICS/DPPX

The version of IBM's CICS system for IBM's DPPX operating system.

CICS/ESA

The version of IBM's CICS system for the ESA/370 and ESA/390 operating system.

CICS/MVS

The version of IBM's CICS system for the MVS environment. Originally designed for MVS/XA, it is now used mainly under MVS/ESA.

CICS/OS/VS

Version 1 of IBM's CICS system for the MVS operating system environment. Originally designed for the System/360 OS operating system, it became CICS/OS/VS on the introduction of virtual storage systems for System/370.

CICS/VS

IBM's CICS for virtual storage systems. A generic term for IBM's CICS/OS/VS, CICS/DOS/VS, CICS/MVS, CICS/VSE or CICS/ESA systems.

CICS/VSE

A version of IBM's CICS system for the VSE/ESA environment; successor to CICS/DOS/VS.

CICSPlex

A CICS complex; a group of interconnected CICS systems.

CICSVR

IBM's CICS VSAM Recovery program, which provides forward recovery and batch backout of the VSAM data sets used by CICS/ESA.

Client/server

A form of data processing that involves a partnership between two systems or programs. One system, the client, requests services or data; the other, the server, provides them.

CMS

Part of the VM virtual machine system that acts as an operating system. Usually known by its abbreviation CMS. CICS/CMS was developed to run under CMS.

COBOL

The most commonly used business programming language. Available on all CICS systems.

Code

Programming statements (noun). To write a program using such statements (verb).

Command

A CICS instruction similar in format to a normal programming-language statement. CICS commands usually begin 'EXEC CICS'. Database access commands start 'EXEC DLI' or 'EXEC SQL'.

Command interpreter
   See CECI.

Command language translator
   See Translator.

Command-level interface
   The programming interface that uses CICS commands beginning 'EXEC CICS'.

COMMAREA
   A storage area that is used to pass data between successive CICS tasks started from the same terminal, or by successive programs within a CICS task.

Committed action
   An action that cannot later be reversed. Uncommitted changes can be reversed (backed-out) if a failure occurs in a program, in data input or output, or in the system itself.

Communication area
   See COMMAREA.

Compact disc
   A plastic disc that can hold massive amounts of data, and from which data is read using laser light.

Compilation
   The act of using a compiler to process a program.

Compiler
   A program that converts programming statements, in a programming language such as COBOL, into executable form. The original program statements, written in a programming language such as COBOL, PL/I, C/370 or assembler, are known as 'source code', and the product of the compiler is known as 'object code'. The object code cannot actually be executed until it has been 'link-edited', or made ready for loading. CICS programs have to go through another process before being compiled: they have to be translated.

Complex
   A CICS complex is a collection of connected CICS systems. They may be connected by ISC, MRO or a combination of both.

Console
   A terminal from which a large computer system is controlled. Although a system may have many terminals, only a few, maybe only one, will have the status of console. In effect it is the system's 'helm'.

Conversation
   An exchange between two partners, usually an end-user and a program.

Conversational
   A mode of execution for CICS programs. A conversational program continues to exist throughout the time that the system waits for a response, from an end-user, to its (the program's) last output. Contrast this with pseudoconversational.

Conversational monitoring system
   See CMS.

Cooperative

> Cooperative processing is a mode of execution of CICS programs in which the programs cooperate with each other to achieve a desired result.

Corruption

> Damage, usually to data, that makes it unusable or incorrect.

Crash

> A disastrous failure. A system crash involves failure of a system, perhaps CICS or the operating system. A 'head-crash' is the failure of a magnetic storage disk drive that destroys the disk, losing some or all of its contents.

Credit authorization

> Checking a customer's account to ensure that he or she is creditworthy.

Cross-region

> In multiregion operation, the ability of two or more CICS systems to communicate despite residing in separate regions or partitions of the operating system.

CSD

> CICS system definition. The repository of all of the resource definitions. Held in a file, and managed and used by the CEDA transaction and the DFHCSDUP batch program to define resources to CICS.

Customization

> Making changes to a system (such as CICS) by providing substitute or supplementary programs. CICS provides immense scope for customization, allowing its users to tailor it in countless ways.

Cutover

> The point of change from a development or test CICS system or application to a production CICS system or application.

Daisychaining

> In CICS intercommunication, the chain of sessions that results when a system requests a resource in a remote system, but the remote system discovers that the resource is in a third system and has itself to make a remote request. Such a daisychain need not stop at three systems, but could theoretically go on indefinitely, provided its path does not cross itself.

DASD

> Direct-access storage device. Synonymous with magnetic disk.

Data access

> The act of getting a piece of data, updating it or simply reading it.

Data integrity

> The protection of data items in a database while they are available to any application program.

Data Language/I

> See DL/I.

Data set

> The major unit of data storage and retrieval, consisting of a collection of data in one of several prescribed arrangements.

Data stream

Information transmitted through a data channel in a read or write operation.

Data table

A file whose records are held in main storage.

Data-owning region

Often called a DOR, this is a CICS system in a multiregion operation or intersystem communication environment. It specializes in handling data access, where a TOR or AOR specializes in terminal communications or program loading and execution.

Database

A collection of interrelated or independent data items stored together. A database usually has a well-defined form and is managed by a sophisticated program known as a database manager.

Database 2

IBM's relational database management system, accessed by CICS application programs issuing SQL requests.

Database administrator

A person who manages the installation, operation and maintenance of a database.

Database Control

See DBCTL.

Database recovery

The function of restoring user data sets, starting with a backup copy and applying all changes made to each data set after the backup was taken.

DB2

Database 2. IBM's database management system for relational databases in the MVS/ESA environment. CICS programs can access DB2 data using EXEC SQL commands.

DBA

Database administrator. A member of staff in a large installation who is responsible for database systems.

DBCTL

An interface between CICS/ESA and IMS/ESA that gives CICS programs flexible access to IMS DL/I full-function databases and to data-entry databases.

DBM

Database manager. A program that maintains, and provides access to, a database. For example IBM's IMS or DB2, or non-IBM DBMs such as Adabas or IDMS.

DCE

Distributed computing environment. A layer of software that provides additional services, in addition to those of basic AIX, that facilitate distributed computing. Developed by the Open Software Foundation (OSF).

Deadlock
> A situation in which processing cannot continue because each of two elements of the process is waiting for an action by, or a response from, the other.

Deadly embrace
> A situation in which two or more tasks prevent each other from completing, each waiting for a resource (usually data) already in use by the other.

Debug
> To remove faults ('bugs') from programs.

Despatching
> See Dispatching.

Device independence
> The capability of transaction programs that use BMS to communicate with terminal devices without having to know details of their physical characteristics.

DFP
> Data Facility Product. A data-management product produced by IBM. It includes, among other components, IBM's VSAM access method.

Disk Operating System/Virtual Storage
> See DOS/VS.

Dispatching
> Setting a task running. Operating systems are said to dispatch tasks, one by one. CICS dispatches its own tasks.

Distributed computing environment
> See DCE.

Distributed program link (DPL)
> A CICS function that allows programs on different systems to link to each other.

Distributed transaction processing
> See DTP.

Distributed processing
> The act of sharing processing work between two or more systems.

Distribution tape
> The magnetic tape on which mainframe systems such as CICS are supplied.

DL/I
> A database access language used by CICS to get at hierarchical databases managed by DL/I DOS/VS or IMS. Usually known by its abbreviated form, DL/I.

DL/I DOS/VS
> IBM's DL/I database system used in the VSE environment.

DOR
> Data-owning region; a CICS system in a multiregion operation or intersystem communication environment. It specializes in handling data access, where a TOR or AOR specializes in terminal communications or program loading and execution. DOR is synonymous with FOR.

DOS

Disk operating system. A personal-computing operating system. This was the original name of the operating system that evolved to become VSE.

DOS/360

An early form of IBM's operating system DOS/VS that became integrated into VSE.

DOS/VS

IBM's mainframe operating system of which VSE is an extension. A low-end operating system for personal systems.

DPPX

An operating system designed for the IBM 8100 system.

DTP

A kind of CICS intercommunication, in which processing is distributed between transactions that communicate synchronously with one another over intersystem or interregion links.

Dump

See Transaction dump and System dump.

Dynamic addition

The process of adding resources to a system while it is running. See CEDA, which describes the transaction that CICS uses for this.

Dynamic transaction backout

The process of restoring uncommitted changes made by a transaction to recoverable resources following a failure of the transaction for whatever reason.

Dynamic transaction routing

Routing terminal data to an alternative transaction at the time the transaction is invoked.

Early support programme

IBM's term for the period, early in a product's life, when early users are given support in case of problems. Equivalent to the 'beta test' used by other vendors.

EDF

The execution diagnostic facility of CICS, which makes it possible to test CICS programs interactively.

EDI

Electronic data interchange.

Emergency restart

The CICS backout facility for an automatic restart following a system failure.

Emulate

To simulate or mimic another program or device.

Encina

A set of products from Transarc Corporation that provides transaction-processing services in the DCE (distributed computing environment) on top of AIX. CICS/6000 uses the services of Encina to provide CICS services.

End-user

Anyone using CICS to do a job, usually by interacting with an application program (transaction) by means of a terminal.

Enterprise Systems Architecture/370

A trademark of IBM. See ESA/370.

Enterprise Systems Architecture/390

A trademark of IBM. See ESA/390.

ESA/370

A trademark of IBM, synonymous with Enterprise Systems Architecture/370; the IBM hardware architecture for mainframe computers of the late 1980s and early 1990s. An evolutionary development of the MVS operating system, following MVS/370 and MVS/XA.

ESA/390

A trademark of IBM, synonymous with Enterprise Systems Architecture/370; the IBM hardware architecture for mainframe computers of the 1990s. An evolutionary development of the MVS operating system, following ESA/370, MVS/370 and MVS/XA.

ESP

See Early support programme.

EXEC

Key word used in CICS command language. Most CICS commands begin with the keywords EXEC CICS, EXEC DLI, EXEC SQL, ...

EXEC interface

See Command-level interface.

Execution diagnostic facility

See EDF.

Exit

An exit from and return to a CICS module at a stated functional point. The user can insert code at these points to enhance the program.

Extended addressing

The use of 31-bit addresses (above the 16 MB line)

Extended recovery facility

A facility that can reduce the time lost through system failures.

Feature

A part of an IBM product that can be ordered separately by a customer.

FEPI

Front-end programming interface. A feature of CICS/ESA, introduced in Version 3 Release 3, that enables you to combine existing CICS and IMS application systems to give a unified appearance to end-users.

File

For CICS, a data set.

File-owning region
See FOR.

FOR
File-owning region; a CICS system in a multiregion operation or intersystem communication environment. It specializes in handling data access, where a TOR or AOR specializes in terminal communications or program loading and execution.

Forward recovery
The process of restoring a backup copy of data and bringing it up to date by reapplying changes made to the file since the backup was taken. It makes it possible to recover from the effects of severe failure, such as physical damage to magnetic disks.

Front end
The part of a system, or set of systems, closest to the end-user. Very often, the front end of a CICS system is designed to be very user-friendly, hiding complexity or improving overall system reliability.

Front-end programming interface
See FEPI.

Front-end transaction
In an intercommunication environment, the transaction that acts as go-between for the end-user and other system transactions.

Front office
The part of a business or commercial enterprise that has daily contact with customers.

Function shipping
The process, transparent to the application program, by which CICS accesses resources when those resources are actually held on another CICS system.

Generator
A program for designing and coding transaction programs for CICS. Usually referred to as an 'application generator'.

Glass teletype
Slang for a display terminal.

Glasshouse
Slang for a large, centralized data-processing organization.

Global user exit
A point in a CICS module at which CICS can pass control to a user-written program (known as an exit program), and then resume control when the program has finished. When an exit program is enabled for a particular exit point, the program is called every time the exit point is reached.

Hardware
The physical parts of a computer or network.

Hierarchical
In referring to databases: a database that has a tree-like structure. Such a

structure is simpler and often more economical than a relational structure, but requires careful design, and is less flexible.

High-level language

A programming language, such as COBOL, C/370 or PL/I, in which each statement is converted by a compiler into one or more machine instructions. A high-level language is more application-oriented and less machine-oriented than assembler language. CICS application programs must be processed by the CICS translator before compilation. The output of the compiler is an object module which must be processed by the linkage editor to produce an executable load module.

High-level programming interface

For CICS, a synonym for EXEC level interface.

HLPI

High-level programming interface.

Host computer

The primary or controlling computer in a data-communication system.

IBM-compatible

A computer that simulates IBM's original well enough to be viewed as equivalent.

ICCF

The Interactive Computing and Control Facility of VSE.

IMS Database Control

See DBCTL.

IMS/ESA

The latest in IBM's evolutionary line of hierarchical databases produced by IBM. A successor to IMS/VS.

IMS/VS

An old version of IBM's IMS hierarchical database manager.

Industry-specific

Something that has relevance to only one industry or industrial sector; for example an application package applicable only to the airline industry.

In-flight task

A task that is in progress when a CICS system failure or immediate shutdown occurs.

Information Management System

A database manager used by CICS to allow access to data in DL/I databases. IMS provides for the arrangement of data in an hierarchical structure and a common access approach in application programs that manipulate IMS databases.

Infrastructure

For CICS, the associated hardware, software and service industry that has evolved around the product itself.

Initialization

Actions performed by the CICS system to construct the environment in the CICS region to enable CICS applications to be run.

Input

Something that is put into a computer system: messages from an end-user at a terminal, data from a disk drive and so on.

Inspect

To review program code thoroughly, using a formal process.

Installation

A particular computing system, in terms of the work it does and the people who manage it, operate it, apply it to problems, service it and use the work it produces. Installation can also refer to the task of making a program ready to do useful work. This task includes generating a program, initializing it, and applying any changes to it.

Integrated Services Digital Network

See ISDN.

Integration

The act of unifying two or more parts of the system.

Integrity

See Data integrity.

Interactive

Pertaining to an application in which each entry entails a response from a system or program, as in an enquiry system or an airline reservation system. An interactive system may also be conversational, implying a continuous dialogue between the user and the system.

Intercommunication facilities

In CICS, a term embracing intersystem communication (ISC) and multiregion operation (MRO).

Interpretive

Referring to a programming language: one for which program code is decoded and executed instruction by instruction, without discrete compilation and link-edit processes.

Intersystem communication

See ISC.

ISAM

An early form of data-access method.

ISC

Intersystem communication. Communication between separate systems by means of SNA networking facilities or by means of the application-to-application facilities of VTAM. ISC links CICS systems and other systems, and may be used for communication between user programs, or for sending CICS requests to remote CICS systems.

ISDN

Integrated Services Digital Network. A technology that uses digital networks to carry digitized forms of a variety of data. It allows video, data and sound information to be carried simultaneously.

JES
> IBM's Job Entry System. A subsystem of an MVS operating system that accepts, submits and controls work to be done by the system.

Job control language (JCL)
> Control language used to describe a job and its requirements to an operating system.

Job entry system
> See JES.

Job stream
> A string of job control statements.

Journal
> A set of one or more data sets to which records are written during a CICS run, usually by CICS but by application programs if necessary. See Journaling.

Journaling
> The recording of information onto any journal.

LAN
> Local area network. A network of connected workstations that share common resources and services.

Language environment/370
> A run-time library that establishes a common execution environment for a number of SAA languages. See also Systems Application Architecture (SAA).

Link-edit
> To use a linkage editor.

Linkage editor
> A computer program used to create one load module from one or more independently-translated object modules or load modules by resolving cross references among the modules. All CICS application programs need to be processed by the linkage editor (link-edited) before execution.

Load library
> A library containing load modules.

Load module
> In MVS, a program in a form suitable for loading into main storage for execution. A load module is the output of the linkage editor.

Local
> In a multisystem environment, the system on which an application program is executing. A local application can process data from databases located on either the same (local) system or another (remote) system. Contrast with remote system. In relation to terminals, a remote terminal is one that is connected through a channel rather than a communications controller.

Local area network
> See LAN.

Lock
> To gain exclusive access to, or use of, a system resource, preventing others from gaining access.

Logging
> The recording (by CICS) of recovery information onto the system log, for use during emergency restart.

Logical unit
> See LU.

Logical unit of work (LUW)
> See LUW.

Logon
> The act of establishing a session with VTAM. Contrast with sign on.

LU (can be LU0 to LU6.2)
> A logical unit of one of the kinds defined for SNA. In effect, a logical unit is a port through which a user gains access to the services of a network. Different kinds of logical unit provide different levels of support, thereby allowing communication with different device types.

LUW
> A sequence of processing actions (database changes, for example) that must be completed before any of the individual actions can be regarded as committed.

Macro
> An instruction that expands when assembled, to produce many source program language statements.

Macro-level
> An obsolescent programming interface for CICS.

Macro resource definition
> The original method of defining to CICS what resources it has to work with.

Map
> The definition of a display screen's layout and attributes that tells BMS how to perform mapping.

Map definition
> Definition of the size, shape, position, potential content and properties of BMS map sets, maps and fields within maps, by means of macros.

Mapping
> In BMS, the process of transforming field data to and from its displayable form.

Massively parallel
> In connection with computer systems: having many identical processors, capable of running programs simultaneously, cooperating to handle a computing work-load.

Master terminal
> In CICS, the terminal at which a designated operator is signed on.

Master terminal operator

Any CICS operator authorized to use the master-terminal functions transaction (CEMT).

Migration

The process of moving programs and their users from one release of software to a later release.

Modification

A minor release of a product such as CICS. Usually, a modification release provides minimal additional function, such as additional support for devices or other programs.

Monitor

This can have several meanings: CICS itself is sometimes called a 'transaction monitor'. Some of the performance-monitoring programs are called monitors. Finally, a display screen is often referred to as a monitor.

Monitoring

The regular assessment of a running CICS system to check that it is operating correctly.

Monitoring package

A program, or suite of programs, that gathers performance and operational information about CICS. Such packages often provide reports, and some can intervene to prevent problems.

MRO

Communication between CICS systems in the same processor without the use of SNA network facilities. This allows several CICS systems in different regions to communicate with each other, and to share resources such as files, terminals, temporary storage and so on. Contrast with intersystem communication.

Multiple Virtual Storage/Enterprise Systems Architecture (MVS/ESA)

The latest version of IBM's MVS operating system. MVS/ESA exploits the high-end System/370 and System/390 hardware for performance and capacity.

Multiregion operation

See MRO.

Multitasking

Concurrent execution of application programs within a CICS region.

Multithreading

Use, by several transactions, of a single copy of an application program.

MVS

An IBM operating system for the mainframe systems of large enterprises.

MVS image

A single copy of the MVS operating system. Note that a single-machine environment can support more than one MVS image.

MVS/370

An IBM operating system for the System/370 family of processors.

MVS/390

> An IBM operating system for the System/390 family of processors.

MVS/DFP

> IBM's MVS/Data Facility Product, a major element of MVS, including data-access methods and data-administration utilities.

MVS/ESA

> The version of IBM's MVS operating system for ESA/390 systems.

MVS/XA

> The version of IBM's MVS operating system for System/370 computers using the IBM System/370 extended architecture. Superseded by MVS/ESA.

NetBios

> A set of protocols used in local area networks.

NetView

> IBM's network management product that can provide automated operations and rapid notification of events.

Network

> An interconnected group of data-processing components—systems, terminals, printers, communication controllers and so on.

Object code

> The output of a compiler or assembler. Before execution, most object modules, including all CICS programs, must be processed by the linkage editor to produce a load module.

Object module

> A program module consisting of a block of object code.

OCO

> The policy of providing system programs, such as CICS modules, in object-code form only with no source code being provided.

Online

> The state of being connected to a computer system.

Online resource definition

> See RDO.

Open system

> A system that implements specified standards common across different computer vendors. Implementing open-systems standards for communications allows computers from different vendors to communicate with each other.

Open System Interconnection

> See OSI.

Open Software Foundation

> See OSF.

Operating system

> A program that provides the most fundamental control and services within a computer. It shields all other programs from the complexities of the computer's hardware and microcode.

Operating System/Virtual Storage
> See OS/VS.

Operating-system console
> See Console.

Operation
> The task of operating the system. After initialization, the system can continue to run, but not necessarily without human intervention from time to time. Operation can encompass a wide range of tasks from routine startup, through monitoring, tuning, and routine administration, to shutdown.

Operations
> The activities involved in keeping large systems running reliably. Often also used to refer to the department or group within an organization responsible for those activities.

Operator
> A term with many possible meanings, and therefore needing qualification. Can be used to refer to a person who operates the entire system—the console operator; anyone entitled to use CEMT—the master-terminal operator; anyone who uses a CICS terminal as an end-user.

OS/2
> IBM's operating system for its PS/2 family of computers.

OS/360
> Precursor of OS/370, which went through evolutionary forms: PCP, MFT, MVT.

OS/370
> Precursor of MVS/370, which went through evolutionary forms: SVS, VS1, MVS, MVS/XA, MVS/ESA.

OS/400
> IBM's operating system for its AS/400 family of computers.

OS/VS
> A generic name for the Operating System/Virtual Storage precursors of IBM's MVS systems. See OS/360 and OS/370.

OSF
> Open Software Foundation. A consortium of leading computer and software manufacturers dedicated to open systems.

OSI
> Open System Interconnection. A communication architecture developed as an international, vendor-independent, standard.

Outage
> A failure of the CICS system, or planned downtime for maintenance or upgrade.

Packages
> Ready-made suites of programs, available as products, ready for immediate use.

Palmtop
> A very compact portable computer—little bigger than a calculator.

Partition

    A fixed-size subdivision of main storage, allocated to a system task.

PC

    Personal computer.

PCRadio

    IBM's portable personal computer that contains a radio for wireless communication.

PD/MVS

    See CICS PD/MVS.

Peer-to-peer

    A form of distributed processing, in which the front-end and back-end of a conversation switch control between themselves. It is communication between equals.

Performance analyser

    A program for analysing performance data.

Peripheral

    Anything attached to a computer—a terminal, printer, and so on.

PL/I

    A programming language designed for use in a wide range of commercial and scientific applications.

Platform

    A hardware and software combination that supports a system. CICS runs on several different platforms, including OS/2 and OS/400.

Point of sale

    Pertaining to terminals and services used in face-to-face contact with retail customers.

Portable

    Capable of execution on more than one platform.

Portability

    The degree to which a program is portable.

POSIX

    An open-system standard.

PR/SM

    Processor Resource/System Manager. A feature of some IBM 3090 processors that makes it possible to treat them as several separate System/390 machines.

Presentation manager

    A graphical presentation interface that runs on OS/2.

Priority

    A rank assigned to a task that determines its precedence in receiving system resources.

Problem determination

>   Starting with a set of symptoms of a problem with a CICS system and tracking
>   them back to their cause.

Processor

>   The part of a computer that interprets and executes program instructions.

Processor cycle

>   The shortest time for a processor to complete execution of one of its instructions.

Production

>   The state (of a program) of being in business use rather than under development
>   or test.

Program generator

>   A program designed to increase programmer productivity. It allows programmers
>   to work at a higher level, concentrating on functional design rather than coding
>   considerations. Programmers use the generator to build programs from ready-
>   made blocks of code.

Programmable terminal

>   A user terminal that has processing capability.

Programmable workstation

>   A personal computer or terminal with some local processing capabilities.

PS/2

>   IBM's personal system that runs the powerful multitasking operating system
>   OS/2. PS/2 computers can also run the DOS operating system.

Pseudoconversational

>   A type of CICS application design that appears to the user as a continuous
>   conversation, but that consists of multiple internal CICS tasks.

Quasi-reentrant

>   The attribute of a CICS application program by which it can be reused when an
>   existing user's task is suspended.

Queue

>   A line or list formed by items in a system waiting for service; for example tasks to
>   be performed, or messages to be transmitted in a message-switching system. In
>   CICS, the transient data and temporary storage facilities store data in queues.

RACF

>   IBM's Resource Access Control Facility. An IBM security manager program that
>   is commonly used with CICS.

RDM

>   Resource Definition (Macro). A method of defining resources to CICS by coding
>   and assembling macros.

RDO

>   Resource Definition (Online). The method of defining resources to CICS inter-
>   actively with the CEDA transaction, or as a batch process by using the
>   DFHCSDUP program.

Real storage
The part of processor storage in a virtual-storage computer system that really exists. Contrast with virtual storage, which is an overflow area on magnetic (or other available medium) storage that simulates a much larger, imaginary computer. Program code and data are moved from relatively static disk storage to real storage when they are needed during program execution.

Real-time
Pertaining to operations or processes that permit human interaction. The operations or processes seem to proceed at the pace of the human world.

Recoverability
The ability of a system to continue processing without loss of data when an unplanned interruption occurs.

Recoverable resource
A resource whose definition specifies that CICS is to take measures to ensure the resource's integrity.

Recovery
The process of returning the system to a state from which operation can be resumed. The restoration of resources following an error.

Reentrant
The attribute of a program or routine that allows the same copy of the program or routine to be used concurrently by two or more tasks.

Region
In MVS, a subdivision of virtual storage allocated to a system task. CICS/ESA runs in an MVS/ESA region.

Relational database
A database that is organized and accessed according to the relationships between the data items it contains.

Reliability
A measurement of the ability of a system to continue processing without failure.

Remote
In data communication, pertaining to terminals that are connected to a data-processing system through a data link. Synonym of link-attached. Contrast with local.

Remote procedure call
See RPC.

Remote resource
In CICS intercommunication, a resource that is owned by a remote system.

Remote system
In CICS intercommunication, a system that the local CICS system accesses via intersystem communication or multiregion operation. Contrast with Local system.

Report controller
A feature of CICS/DOS/VS and CICS/VSE that enables users to manage printed output and other system jobs.

Resource

Any facility or component of a CICS system that is needed by a job or task.

Resource Access Control Facility

See RACF.

Resource definition macro

See RDM.

Resource definition online

See RDO.

Resource manager

A non-CICS program that manages system resources, for example a database manager such as DB2.

Resource-manager interface (RMI)

See TRUE.

Resource table

One of the many CICS tables used to hold details of the resources it has at its disposal.

Response time

The elapsed time between entering an enquiry or request and receiving a response.

Restart

Resumption of operation after recovery. Ability to restart requires knowledge of where to start and ability to start at that point.

RMI

See TRUE.

Rollback

A programmed return to a prior point of synchronization. In CICS, the cancellation by an application program of the changes it has made to all recoverable resources during the current logical unit of work.

Roll your own

See RYO.

RPC

Remote-procedure call. A programming technique that helps to achieve distributed cooperative processing.

RPGII

A programming language.

RYO

Roll your own. A system or application program written by your own staff.

SAA

IBM's Systems Application Architecture. A set of common standards and procedures for working with IBM systems and data. SAA enables different software, hardware and network environments to coexist. It provides bases for designing and developing application programs that are consistent across different systems.

SAM

IBM's Sequential Access Method. A data-access method. CICS uses its BSAM and QSAM forms.

Schedule

To select jobs or tasks that are to be run by a system.

Screen Definition Facility II (SDF II)

IBM's interactive tool used to define and maintain maps, map sets and partition sets for CICS and BMS applications.

Security

Prevention of access to, or use of, data or programs without authorization.

Security administrator

A member of the system-support team responsible for security-system programs such as RACF.

Security level

In RACF, a means of classifying resources to indicate how securely they must be kept.

Sequential Access Method

See SAM.

Service Level Reporter

See SLR.

Shell

An AS/400 concept.

Shutdown

The process of stopping the CICS job that is running under control of the operating system.

Sign on

In CICS, to perform user identification and verification. The CICS user signs on to CICS using a CICS-supplied transaction, CESN. Contrast with logon, which means to establish a session with VTAM.

Single threading

The execution of a program to completion. Processing of one transaction is completed before another transaction is started. Compare with multithreading.

Single-user system

A computer that can be used by only one person at a time.

SIPO

System Installability Productivity Option. A software package that combines a number of IBM products for ease of installation on VSE systems. Now superseded by VSE/SP.

SLR

IBM's Service Level Reporter. A program product that produces reports on CICS performance and service levels.

SMP/E

A program for installing software and service on MVS systems. CICS users use SMP/E.

SNA

IBM's communications architecture that defines structures, formats, protocols and operational sequences for transmitting information through, and controlling, networks.

Snapshot

Information about a system, or part of a system, at a particular instant.

Software

Programs, procedures, rules and any associated documentation pertaining to the operation of a computer system.

Source program

See Compiler.

SQL

Structured Query Language. A language used for processing relational databases.

SQL/DS

IBM's relational database system for the VSE and VM environments.

Startup

The operation of starting up CICS by the system operator.

Startup job stream

A set of job-control statements used to initialize CICS.

Statistics

The data gathered by CICS to enable analysis of system usage.

Storage dump

See Transaction dump and System dump.

Storage overlay

The overwriting of data in part of storage. Sometimes this is done deliberately. If unintended, it is called storage violation.

Storage protection

An optional facility in CICS/ESA 3.3 that enables users to protect CICS code and control blocks from being overwritten inadvertently by application programs.

Storage violation

An error caused by a program overwriting storage.

Storyboard

A film-production technique by which directors sketch out entire sequences of events to help visualize the setting and action.

Structured Query Language

A language used for processing relational databases.

Subroutine
>   A sequenced set of instructions that can be used in one or more programs and at one or more points in each program.

Subsystem
>   A secondary or subordinate system of the main system; for example CICS, which is a subsystem of MVS.

Subsystem storage protection
>   A feature of MVS/ESA that provides a degree of storage protection for CICS/ESA systems.

Subtasking
>   The practice of CICS of performing certain functions as separate subtasks of the operating system.

Synchronization
>   In CICS, a coordinated commitment-control process between communicating transactions that ensures that all logically-related updates to recoverable resources are completed or that all are backed out.

Synchronous
>   In CICS, pertaining to events or processes that interact over a period.

Syncpoint
>   A point in a CICS program at which all changes so far can be made permanent. This requires agreement from other programs or subsystems. After a syncpoint, any other changes can be viewed logically as part of a new transaction. See also Logical unit of work.

SYSPLEX
>   In an MVS/ESA SP 4.1 environment, a set of one or more MVS systems, where a system is a collection of data-processing services under the control of a single control program.

System dump
>   A copy of the contents of a computer's system storage at a particular instant. Often used to solve complex system problems.

System initialization
>   The process of starting a CICS system.

System/360
>   The IBM mainframe architecture that emerged in the 1960s.

System/370
>   The IBM mainframe architecture that superseded the System/360.

System/390
>   The IBM mainframe architecture for the 1990s, which superseded System/370.

Systems Application Architecture
>   See SAA.

Systems Network Architecture
>   See SNA.

Table

See Resource table.

Task

In CICS, a single instance of the execution of a transaction. Contrast with Transaction.

Task-related user exit

See TRUE.

TCAM

IBM's communications access method that supports terminals.

TCP/IP

A de facto open standard for intercommunication.

Telecommunications Access Method

See TCAM.

Teletype

An early kind of terminal in which output was sent to a typewriter-style printer rather than a display.

Teller

A bank cashier or an automatic cash dispenser.

Temporary storage

A special kind of storage available to CICS transaction programs.

Terminal

In CICS, a device, often equipped with a keyboard and some kind of display, capable of sending and receiving information over a communication channel. Can also mean a point in a system or communication network at which data can either enter or leave.

Terminal operator

The user of a terminal.

Terminal-owning region

See TOR.

TM

Transaction Manager. A feature of IMS that handles transaction-processing applications.

Token ring

A form of network in which terminals are connected to form a continuous ring.

Topology

A description of the way a network is laid out.

TOR

Terminal-owning region. A CICS system in a multiregion operation or intersystem communication environment. It specializes in handling terminals, where a DOR or AOR specializes in data communications or program loading and execution.

TP

> See Transaction processing.

TP monitor

> A program purpose-built for handling transaction-processing requests.

Trace

> A CICS facility that keeps a record of the processing that has occurred. It is a useful diagnostic aid, as it records all significant events in a program's life. The data it gathers for faulty programs can show unexpected behaviour and thereby point to the faults.

Transaction

> A business exchange. In CICS, the exchange is between an end-user and a business program, and usually involves an enquiry about, or a change to, some data.

Transaction backout

> The total cancellation of a partially-completed CICS transaction because of a failure in a program or the system.

Transaction deadlock

> A situation in which two or more transactions cannot be completed because of a conflict over use of resources, often data.

Transaction dump

> The collection of data that is the result of saving the storage being used by a particular CICS task. A transaction dump is very useful in debugging CICS programs.

Transaction identifier

> The name that identifies the transaction that an end-user wishes to perform.

Transaction processing

> A kind of data processing characterized by its unplanned, usually short-lived, nature. It usually involves brief enquiries or simple updates. This is the kind of work at which CICS excels.

Transaction processor

> A program purpose-built for handling transaction-processing requests.

Transaction routing

> A CICS facility that allows one CICS system to process a transaction on behalf of another one. The routing is achieved without any changes to programs, and is transparent to the end-user of the transaction.

Transaction work area

> A piece of storage, outside a CICS transaction program, that is associated with a task that is using the program. Any task using the program can have its own transaction work area, allowing the same copy of the program to handle many tasks simultaneously, without confusing their data.

Transarc

> The organization that developed the Encina toolkit, a suite of programs that form a transaction-processing layer for the Open Software Foundation's distributed computing environment. CICS/AIX has been built to use Encina's services.

Transient data

A CICS facility that allows transaction programs to save data temporarily. The data is stored sequentially, forming 'queues' that can later be processed, again sequentially, by the same or other programs.

Translator

A program that turns EXEC CICS commands, and other CICS-specific pieces of program code, into code that can be compiled or assembled for execution.

TRUE

Task-related user exit. One of a number of places within CICS at which non-CICS programs can participate in an event related to a single task. TRUEs use the TRUE interface, otherwise known as the resource-manager interface (RMI) because it is often used by resource managers such as database managers.

Tuning

The process of adjusting system values to optimize the CICS system's performance. CICS configurations, program profiles, workloads and requirements vary so much that each installation will have a different definition of optimum.

Uncommitted action

An action that can later be reversed. See Committed action.

Unit of work

See LUW.

Unit test

A test of a program in isolation from other influences. Such testing follows shortly after code is completed, but before the program is tested alongside other programs.

UNIX

An open-standard operating system. IBM's implementation of UNIX is called AIX.

Update

To modify a file or data set with current information.

Upgrade

To replace older equipment, hardware or software, with a newer equivalent.

Upward compatibility

The ability of a later release of a product to run a program written for an earlier release.

User exit

One of a number of places within CICS at which non-CICS programs can participate in CICS system processing (rather than transaction programming). There are global user exits and task-related user exits. The former can help most users to tailor their systems to their needs. The latter are for use by other systems that need to communicate with CICS tasks.

User-replaceable program

A CICS-supplied program that users can replace with programs of their own. The supplied programs usually perform vital processing in an unsophisticated or generalized way. By making them replaceable, CICS designers permit individual installations to meet very specific local needs.

Utilities

A CICS utility is a program for carrying out routine processing, usually offline from the real-time CICS task.

Utility companies

Companies that supply public services such as gas, electricity, water or telephone.

VDU

Visual display unit. A terminal with a television-style screen.

Vendor

A company that sells data-processing products. In connection with CICS, a vendor is any company that produces complementary or supplementary products.

Version

A product release that is so different from its predecessor that it becomes a different product. CICS Version 3 differs significantly from Version 2, so is a different product, even though they have a great deal in common.

Virtual address

The address of a place within virtual storage.

Virtual machine

A simulation by an operating system of a whole computer, with its operating system.

Virtual Machine/System Product

See VM.

Virtual storage

The computer storage accessible to programs running in a system. It is limited by the addressing capacity of the computer hardware, but can be larger than the physical storage installed in the computer.

Virtual Storage Access Method

See VSAM.

Virtual storage constraint

The effect of reaching the limits of a system's addressing scheme.

Virtual Storage Extended

See VSE.

Virtual Telecommunications Access Method

See VTAM.

VM

An IBM operating system that supplies a virtual machine to each of its users.

VSAM

One of IBM's data-access methods for files.

VSE

An IBM operating system that is an extension of DOS/VS, consisting of VSE/

Advanced Functions, the minimum operating system support, and other IBM-supplied program products.

VSE/VSAM

A version of IBM's VSAM for the VSE environment.

VTAM

IBM's Virtual Telecommunications Access Method: a program that manages data communications, using SNA protocols and, most recently, APPN protocols.

Bibliography

Annual Report (1991). GUIDE International Corporation.

Application Design Guide for LAN transaction systems, GC33-0999-00, IBM Corporation.

CallPath General Information Manual (1989). SC53-0001-00, IBM Corporation.

CICS Communicating from CICS/400 (1993). SC33-0828-00, IBM Corporation.

CICS Communicating from CICS/6000 (1993). SC33-0827-00, IBM Corporation.

CICS Communicating from CICS/ESA and CICS/VSE (1993). SC33-0825-00, IBM Corporation.

CICS/ESA Front End Programming Interface General Information (1992). GC33-0803-00, IBM Corporation.

CICS Communicating from CICS OS/2 (1993). SC33-0826-00, IBM Corporation.

CICS/OS/VS Facilities and Planning Guide (1985). SC33-0202-00, IBM Corporation.

CICS/ESA System Definition Guide (1991). SC33-0664-01, IBM Corporation.

CICS Family: API Structure SC33-1007-00, IBM Corporation.

CICS General Information (1990). GC33-0768-00, IBM Corporation.

CICS Inter-product Communication (1992). SC33-0824, IBM Corporation.

Conference Agenda (1992). Australasian SHARE/GUIDE ASG 27.

Cypser, R. J. (1978). *Communications Architecture for Distributed Systems*, Addison-Wesley.

Cypser, R. J. (1991). *Communications for Cooperating Systems*, Addison-Wesley.

Dictionary of Computing (1987). SC20-1699-07, IBM Corporation.

Dynamic Transaction Routing in a CICSPlex, SC33-1012-00, IBM Corporation.

Member's Handbook (April 1992). GUIDE.

Mounce, D. C. (1989). *CICS: A Light Hearted Chronicle*.

Newsletter 47 (1992). Australasian SHARE/GUIDE.

Person to Person/2 Planning Guide, GC33-0927-00, IBM Corporation.

Piggott, S. (1989). *CICS: A Practical Guide to System Fine Tuning*, McGraw-Hill.

Reference Manual and Membership Directory (1991). SHARE.

Reference Manual (1992/3). GUIDE International Corporation.

Transaction Processing Concepts and Products (1990). GC33-0754-00, IBM Corporation.

Yelavich, B. M. (1985). Customer Information System—An evolving system facility, *IBM Systems Journal*, vol. 24, nos. 3/4, 1985.

Index